MW00476260

Remembering Our Intimacies

Indigenous Americas

Robert Warrior, Series Editor

(continued on page 211)

Remembering Our Intimacies

Mo'olelo, Aloha 'Āina, and Ea

Jamaica Heolimeleikalani Osorio

UNIVERSITY OF MINNESOTA PRESS

MINNEAPOLIS

LONDON

Portions of *Rise Like a Mighty Wave* are adapted from "On the Frontlines of Maunakea," *FLUX Magazine* 37 (2019).

The excerpt in the dedication is from Haunani-Kay Trask's poem "Sons," originally published in *Light in the Crevice Never Seen* (Corvallis, Ore.: Calyx Books, 1994), 55–56.

Copyright 2021 by the Regents of the University of Minnesota

All rights reserved. No part of this publication may be reproduced, stored in a retrieval system, or transmitted, in any form or by any means, electronic, mechanical, photocopying, recording, or otherwise, without the prior written permission of the publisher.

Published by the University of Minnesota Press
111 Third Avenue South, Suite 290
Minneapolis, MN 55401-2520
http://www.upress.umn.edu

ISBN 978-1-5179-1029-7 (hc)
ISBN 978-1-5179-1030-3 (pb)
Library of Congress record available at https://lccn.loc.gov/2021022892.

Printed on acid-free paper

The University of Minnesota is an equal-opportunity educator and employer

UMP KEP

For Eliza Kamakawiwoʻole, Haunani-Kay Trask, Teresia Teaiwa, and all the other ʻŌiwi Wāhine who wove "fine baskets of resilience to carry our daughters in."

Contents

He Mele no Hōpoe

I saw you dancing in the distance
Pulling my glance with the diction of your stance
Gliding over the land like water
over itself
Rolling in the flowered mist

With a name that speaks of your magic
Nānāhuki,
Too heavy for the diphthong of my tongue
Instead, let me call you Hōpoe
I have seen you gathering parts of yourself in the form of yellow lehua
    there
I have been with you from the beginning
I only wait for the pahu to sound for our haʻa to begin

You created of this stranger in me
A lover
Let me cover your body in the sacred skin of this nahele
Let me plant you a fortress of rumbling lehua trees
each blossom a promise to return   my love
to move your rhythm again
for your ea to find home in my mele

Can you see those strange men
Watching from beyond the page
see the way they have drawn us naked and grown
they miss your skin feathered with lehua
writing us into stillness   into silence
how it seems through them,
we have been forgotten

I wonder how it is they cannot see
I wonder
what has made them so blind

Nā Mahalo: Acknowledgments

I must acknowledge first that this book would not be possible if it were not for my kūpuna who fought, survived, and thrived in order for me to be writing this moʻolelo today. These ancestors taught me the great value of memory and the good fortune of grace. They are my first and most important archive and the original caretakers of this ʻupena of pilina. As I write this book, I am thinking particularly of the kūpuna who so intimately shaped the narrative of this moʻolelo. To my kūpuna Eliza Leialoha Kamakawiwoʻole, Clara Kuʻulei Kay Osorio, and Leonetta Keolaokalani Kinard, I am overwhelmed by the aloha and gratitude I have for you.

Many hearts and minds have shaped this work. Among them are some of my earliest kumu at Ke Kula Kaiapuni o Ānuenue who nurtured my thirst for moʻolelo and my appetite for justice. It was under their malu that I first came to know and practice my fierce and unapologetic leo. From their guidance came my enduring appreciation for the political imperative of education and aloha ʻāina. I am immensely grateful to each of you and each and every other kumu I have had the gift of learning from.

I would not be telling this particular story if it were not also for the mana wāhine who first cultivated and nurtured my pilina with Hiʻiaka. Among these wāhine are Kumu Lilikalā Kameʻeleihiwa, Noenoe Silva, kuʻualoha hoʻomanawanui, Kahikina de Silva, and Lehua Yim. Following them came my brilliantly supportive dissertation committee, who each offered a great service to the foundation of this work. I am especially grateful to Craig Howes and Noenoe Silva, who read and offered invaluable feedback across countless versions and drafts of this manuscript. I cannot overstate their contribution to the book you find before you today. Mahalo piha iā ʻoukou.

Then there are those kumu who have taught me far beyond the bounds of any classroom. They have been my confidantes, my compass, and my comrades of aloha ʻāina, justice, and decolonial praxis. They have been some of my greatest inspirers, advisors, and mentors, some of whom I am even lucky enough to call my hoa. They include Aunty Haunani-Kay Trask, Aunty Teresia Teaiwa, Uncle Kanalu Young, Aunty Maxine Kahāʻulelio, Aunty Loretta and Uncle Walter Ritte, Aunty Teri Kekoʻolani, Charles Lawrence, Mari Matsuda, Noelani Goodyear-Kaʻōpua, Presley Keʻalaanuhea Ah Mook Sang, ʻIlima Long, Joy Enomoto, Noʻukahauʻoli Revilla, Elizabeth Soto, Noʻeau Peralto, Haley Kailiehu, Hāwane Rios, Mehana Kīhoi, Māhealani Ahia, and Kahala Johnson. I have also been intimately affected by the passion of my students at the University of Hawaiʻi at Mānoa. This work is molded by the many ways they have held me accountable to my beliefs and vision.

Most recently this work has been transformed by my time living in the malu of Mauna a Wākea. I must acknowledge the Mauna and her wāhine kapu: Poliʻahu, Līlīnoe, and Moʻoinanea, who further shaped me in the image of our ʻāina. My writing and thinking have also been inspired and supported by every kiaʻi who has given their time and aloha toward the protection of our ʻāina. But especially to my beloved Malia Hulleman and Nā Puʻuwai Haokila, our kūpuna of the Ala Hulu Kupuna, and the hundreds of wāhine, kāne, and māhū who put their bodies on the line in the early days of the Puʻuhonua o Puʻuhuluhulu. Your sacrifices changed everything about my understanding of aloha ʻāina and governance. Therefore, to each and every Kanaka Maoli who continues to struggle, fight, and build in and beyond the university, I see you, I thank you, I aloha you. Mahalo for your ʻike, your stories, your sweat, your testimony, your vision, your poems, your songs, your wai, your loʻi, your māla, and your aloha.

I would be remiss to not mention my father, Jonathan Kay Kamakawiwoʻole Osorio, who raised and invested in an entire generation of Kānaka Maoli aloha ʻāina for me to stand beside. Dad, you are my first kumu, my favorite mele, and my most beloved moʻolelo. You are the kalo to my ʻohā. It is an honor to serve this lāhui and ʻohana beside you.

And finally, to my beloved Hōpoe, who called me deep into this moʻolelo, who taught me to read closely and dig furiously. Who taught me to listen and see beyond the page. Who led me back to my body, who offered me so many beautiful visions of aloha, and who urged me to find and mend my ʻupena. Mahalo to you and to everyone else bound in this beautiful ʻupena of pilina with me, who planted seeds for this ulu lehua to grow. Without you all, none of this would be possible.

A Note about Language Use

To maintain the integrity of cited materials from the nūpepa (Hawaiian-language newspapers), diacriticals will not be added to cited materials, and instead passages will be reproduced in the exact form of their original publication. When terms are pulled directly from the source material into figures for further analysis, I will treat them as quoted material and refrain again from adding diacriticals. However, in my own writing, analysis, and paraphrasing, diacriticals will be used in the common spelling of Hawaiian words, including proper nouns where spelling has become standardized. When using less common words and names where spelling has not been standardized, orthography will not be added. This is particularly the case with the names of places and akua that do not appear in existing Hawaiian reference materials such as *Place Names of Hawaiʻi* (by Pukui, Elbert, and Mookini) and have been preserved only in these moʻolelo. In an effort not to transform or limit the meaning of these names, I will not attempt to reduce them through contemporary spelling conventions and instead will leave those names open to further inquiry and interpretation.

Although ʻōlelo Hawaiʻi appears frequently throughout the course of this book, this book does not include a glossary. The terms I will be using have many meanings and to reduce them to a single English gloss would be counterproductive to the ultimate function of this book. Wehewehe.org is an appropriate source for the reader to consult for definitions of Hawaiian terms across multiple dictionaries. Any English translations that may appear throughout this text are my own, unless otherwise indicated.

The word *mana* will be used repeatedly throughout this book without continual clarification. Mana can mean divine power, authority, and privilege, or it can mean a version of a story. I will be speaking frequently about our mana as power, and the many mana of our moʻolelo, leaving it to the reader, now advised, to determine the appropriate or pleasing associations that this important word and idea has in specific circumstances.

Finally, throughout this book I will frequently address the occupying settler state in Hawaiʻi. For the sake of brevity, I will often refer to it as the "State of Hawaiʻi." The reader should be aware that my desire to avoid being frequently tongue tied is meant in no way to suggest the occupying settler state of Hawaiʻi is legitimate in any way.

'Ōlelo Mua

Beginning to (Re)member

'O Maalolaninui ke kāne 'o Lonokaumakahiki ka wahine
Noho pū lāua a hānau 'ia 'o Imaikalani he kāne

'O Imaikalani ke kāne 'o Kekookalani ka wahine
Noho pū lāua a hānau 'ia 'o Paaluhi Kahinuonalani he kāne

'O Paaluhi Kahinuonalani ke kāne 'o Piipii Kealiiwaiwaiole ka wahine
Noho pū lāua a hānau 'ia 'o Charles Moses Kamakawiwooleokamehameha
    he kāne

'O Hainaloa ke kāne 'o Niau ka wahine
Noho pū lāua a hānau 'ia 'o Kaluaihonolulu he wahine

'O Kaluaihonolulu ka wahine 'o Nakooka ke kāne
Noho pū lāua a hānau 'ia 'o Kapahu he wahine

'O Kapahu ka wahine 'o Kua ke kāne
Noho pū lāua a hānau 'ia 'o Daisy Kealiiaiawaawa he wahine

'O Charles Moses Kamakawiwooleokamehameha ke kāne 'o Daisy
    Kealiiaiawaawa ka wahine
Noho pū lāua a hānau 'ia 'o Eliza Leialoha Kamakawiwo'ole he wahine

'O Eliza Leialoha Kamakawiwo'ole ka wahine 'o Emil Montero Osorio
ke kāne
Noho pū lāua a hānau 'ia 'o Elroy Thomas Leialoha Osorio he kāne

'O Manuawai ke kāne 'o Keao ka wahine
Noho pū lāua a hānau 'ia 'o Sarah Piikea Papanui he wahine

'O Sarah Piikea Papanui ka wahine 'o Kam Sheong Akiona ke kāne
Noho pū lāua a ma Kona Hema hānau 'ia 'o Nani Kaluahine Kimoe
Akiona he wahine

'O Nani Kaluahine Kimoe Akiona ka wahine 'o Leroy Adam Anthony
Kay ke kāne
Noho pū lāua a hānau 'ia 'o Clara Ku'ulei Kay he wahine

'O Elroy Thomas Leialoha Osorio ke kāne 'o Clara Ku'ulei Kay ka
wahine
Noho pū lāua ma Hilo a hānau 'ia 'o Jonathan Kay Kamakawiwo'ole
Osorio he kāne

'O Edward Lawrence Dunn ke kāne 'o Genevieve Catherine Offer ka
wahine
Noho pū lāua a hānau 'ia 'o Mary Carol Dunn he wahine

'O Jonathan Kay Kamakawiwo'ole Osorio ke kāne 'o Mary Carol Dunn
ka wahine
Noho pū lāua a hānau 'ia 'o Jamaica Heolimeleikalani Osorio he
wahine.

NOVEMBER 1959, KĪLAUEA IKI

When my father was eight years old, he took a trip with his older brother,
Tom, and their paternal grandparents to witness the eruption at Kīlauea
Iki. The four Osorio kāne piled into the car with my great-grandmother
Eliza Kamakawiwo'ole and made the long drive from Hilo into Volcano.
As they were driving, they could see Kīlauea Iki spitting her magma up

into the atmosphere. My father recalls how they could see the fountain eruption from inside the car. At its highest, it soared up more than eleven hundred feet.

They parked along the side of the road, then walked the lehua- and 'ōhelo-lined path, now known as Devastation Trail. I imagine that when they arrived at the lookout, the two boys were struck by the awe only known to someone who has witnessed some kind of birthing—here, their one hānau expanded before them.

They had only been at the edge of Kīlauea Iki for a moment when my father, the youngest traveler, and too young to have fully internalized what stories are meant to be quiet, or to know which names can be said out loud, leaned over to his very Christian grandmother and asked, "Ma, is that Pele?"

As silently and quickly as Pele's path can change, as swiftly as she can target new prey and swallow new 'ili, my great-grandmother turned her back to the Luahine and walked along the trail, back to the car. She climbed in and shut the door.

Annoyed with his brother's naiveté, Tom snapped, "Why'd you have to go and ask that for?" He had known what my father did not. Tom knew not to speak of Pele—that fierce and powerful akua who had stood starkly in opposition to the teachings the boys had received in their Sunday school classes from their grandmother. Through his elder sibling wisdom, Tom had learned which stories were meant for casual conversation and which were to be left as whispers—caught in the back of the throat, not to be freed casually, if ever.

As the three Osorio kāne took the long trail back to the car, my father absorbed this devastating lesson as well. And I imagine how that punishing silence, closing like a steel car door against a boy's curiosity about how an island can give birth from nothing if she too is not a God, had itself developed through long force of habit.

This story tells me a few things about this beautiful, strong, and resolute woman, my great-grandmother Eliza Leialoha Kamakawiwoʻole Osorio. It tells me that she loved Hawaiʻi. Eliza must have loved Hawaiʻi—she sang about Hawaiʻi, wrote about Hawaiʻi, and must have also believed in the mana of Hawaiʻi if she so clearly wanted to take that drive to bear witness to her one hānau growing.

The story also tells me that she loved her 'ohana. Eliza didn't venture to Kīlauea Iki alone. She chose to take her mo'opuna, to share with these boys that moment of pure awe that comes from observing this birthing. Because to love our 'ohana is to share intimacy with them, to create memories that will become mo'olelo for future generations. From what I've heard, Eliza was full of this kind of aloha.

But most of all, this mo'olelo tells me that my great-grandmother was not only a God-fearing but a Pele-fearing woman. When my father uttered Pele's name, it was her power, not Jesus's, that forced my great-grandmother to look away and retreat from the burning crater. In two syllables, his preeminence had been challenged. My father had realized what Tom did not say, and what Eliza already must have known—that a wahine who births land out of darkness is, was, and will always be a god.

Once spoken, it was Pele's mana that would not allow my kupuna to witness it any longer, because it challenged the mo'olelo Eliza had been taught in her father's sanctuary. In this moment, my great-grandmother was confronted and torn in half by two distinctly different mo'olelo— one that celebrated the mana in everything around and inside her and another that gave her virtue, structure, and a path not to devastation but to paradise.

This is the mo'olelo I think about when I wonder how traditions and memory come to be dismembered over time. How fear turns to shame, and finally hardens to silence. How a 'ohana born from Kīlauea's fiery belly, comes to deny their kupuna and akua's first name, Pelehonuamea. How a young boy and later a whole 'ohana are urged to forget, or like Tom at least remain silent, about their first home in Pele's poli.

AUGUST 1996, PĀLOLO VALLEY

My first major assignment at Ke Kula Kaiapuni 'o Ānuenue, my Hawaiian-language immersion school, was to compile my mo'okū'auhau (genealogies). Over and over again, we were told about the kuleana we carried in our names, and how as Kānaka Maoli we ourselves would come to carry the kuleana of these names with us everywhere we go. 'Ōlelo no'eau filled in the gaps between lesson and practice. "Ua maika'i ke kalo i ka 'ohā"— by knowing and reciting our genealogies, we were engaging in an ancient

family's tree?

practice of accountability and pilina. Our mo'okū'auhau was at the center of this lesson.

The official two-page worksheet laid out a formula for what 'ohana should look like. Two parents, children, a single marriage, kāne, and wāhine were all essential pieces of the complete puzzle. We were taught to treat these mo'okū'auhau as prized possessions, passed down from one generation to the next, and perhaps the medicine to cure this colonial sickness. In many ways, my mo'okū'auhau was the first mo'olelo I was ever told— the first I memorized, and the first I was taught to value.

I've learned since then that mo'okū'auhau are not just important because they place us within a particular, and sometimes even constricting, familial context. They are also important because they are place-based records, evidence, and narrative. They are important as both history and story, past and present, personal and political. But to a storyteller, mo'okū'auhau are also incomplete mana of a larger narrative. And while mo'okū'auhau are effective at telling certain stories, I have come to realize that they are not the only archive I should cherish.

Like 'ohana, mo'okū'auhau can seem fragmented and imperfect. But they are a beginning. My mo'okū'auhau is certainly my beginning. These days I come to my mo'okū'auhau ready to read along its margins, to fill in what lives beyond the genre of this practice. Today I come to my mo'okū'auhau asking what parts of my 'upena of intimacies are intact and what parts have been lost, erased, or forgotten. I ask what this mo'olelo, the mo'olelo of my 'ohana, can tell me about pilina (intimacy). As a child in a 'ohana of storytellers, I find these questions natural and necessary.

It is no surprise, then, that I have chosen to research and write a book about relationships. Many people seem to think of relationships as ecosystems existing between two people at a time. I prefer to think of them in a Kanaka Maoli context, as 'upena or fishing nets of intimacies, a concept I will elaborate throughout the course of this book. With our 'upena, we begin by taking intimacy seriously, then over time work to understand the many ways we can articulate pilina and intimacy with each other and our 'āina. We can learn that being bound and accountable to each other means that I am also bound and accountable to your intimacies and accountabilities. This exponentially expands the possibilities of pleasure and responsibility in our lives.

pilina = intimacies (ʻupena = web)

If relationships are about intimacies, then this book is also about considering the many forms intimacy can take, and how certain relationships and intimacies are pursued and practiced. Some intimacies are realized through sex, some through experiencing together a sunrise or a cold rain, some through the simple yet important act of sharing names. Especially in the face of a settler colonial project that has worked toward punishing, mocking, or eliminating certain forms and practices of intimacy, it is important that this project take intimacy seriously, in its many shape-shifting forms.

ʻUPENA OF INTIMACIES

In the next chapter, I outline some of the valuable tools Indigenous queer theory provides for naming and mapping the violences directed at our practices of intimacy and kinship. A significant contribution of this book, however, will be a theory for Kanaka Maoli intimacy that not only offers a rationale for a place-based analysis and a means for explaining with greater nuanced readings of specific moments in our moʻolelo. I also suggest language for articulating our opposition to these violences in our history, and for revealing the value of our moʻolelo for our practices of (re)membering today. I therefore imagine and cast ʻupena of intimacies over Indigenous practices of desire and kinship.

ʻUpena are materially relevant for discussing pilina (intimacies) because like our pilina, our ʻupena are made out of and reflect our ʻāina and environment. The aho (cordage) that bind our many hīpuʻu (knots) together come from our land, shaped and spun by our own hands. ʻUpena, like pilina, require great and constant care to maintain their good condition. Keeping in mind our ʻupena also encourages us to articulate clearly and strongly how our intimacies are connected and accountable to each other.

ʻUpena can also come with a set of negative connotations. Not always are ʻupena used to catch fish; sometimes we become caught and caged in ʻupena. I honor the metaphor of the ʻupena for our pilina by also being attentive to what our pilina can become if not tended to. As our lives push us to reckon with the violence we have endured and inflicted on each other through our relationships, let us always remember that ʻupena can both cradle and strangle. When we keep this in mind while studying the many attacks on Kanaka Maoli, our practices, and our ʻāina, we

(in)humanity of queers — we remues

ʻupena can both cradle & strangle

kuleana = responsibility

can certainly trace the wear and damage on our beloved 'upena, and know where to begin repairs.

In this book, I offer some suggestions and initial attempts at mending these 'upena we share with each other. I walk through the task of making the aho—the woven or braided cord—that when knotted (hīpu'u) brings us together. In doing so, I think about all the cordage we have already braided as a lāhui—tying together our kūpuna, Haunani-Kay Trask, Imaikalani Kalahele, Noelani Goodyear-Ka'ōpua, Bryan Kamaoli Kuwada, and many others here unnamed. I think about how all this aho helps us in mending the 'upena we have the kuleana to carry.[1]

Ultimately it is both what makes our 'upena and what that 'upena holds that is most important. Our mo'olelo teach us that our 'upena are as diverse as our people, but what all these 'upena share is what they carry for us: possibility. In the face of all we have endured, and all the ways our intimacy between each other has been straightened and damaged, possibility and our many practices of aloha are revolutionary.

Continuing the actions of our haku 'upena, in this book I will display a constellation of intimacies that articulate our distinct ways of relating to one another as Kānaka as learned from our mo'olelo of Hi'iakaikapoliopele. I will acknowledge the trauma our 'upena has suffered—where the lines have been cut, tangled, or displaced. I will also trace the aho that lead us to our bodies, to each other, and to our 'āina.

By beginning with my own mo'okū'auhau, I am saying that my 'upena of intimacies is relevant and necessary to this project. Kanaka Maoli epistemologies are not just handy frameworks but instead are intimate and essential practices of research. To discuss pilina in mo'olelo as an 'upena without unfolding a bit of my own 'upena before you would be a disservice to these mo'olelo and all they have to teach us.

Because this book is about pilina, mo'olelo, and mo'okū'auhau, the work of this prologue must be to haku an 'upena that reveals the important hīpu'u or intersections of scholarship, research, and mo'olelo that have insisted on this work's becoming.

(RE)MEMBERING

This book is above all a (re)membering. In 2002 my father published his first book, *Dismembering Lāhui*. Like those of his university kumu and his contemporaries, his intellectual contribution was a detailed study of the devastation inflicted on our Hawaiian Kingdom, communities, and families by colonialism and the American invasion and occupation of our country. Like Haunani-Kay Trask's earth-shattering speech that called Hawaiians to recognize, now and forever, that "We are NOT Americans," *Dismembering Lāhui* dug deeply into the latter half of Hawai'i's kingdom period to empower our lāhui to understand how haole businessmen and their U.S. allies were able to usurp and exercise enough power to overthrow and eventually stage manage what they would call an annexation of our aupuni. His book became an essential text of Hawaiian scholarship.

Because of my father, his kumu and hoa hana—Kekuni Blaisdell, Haunani-Kay Trask, Lilikalā Kame'eleihiwa, Kanalu Young, Noenoe Silva, and Davianna McGregor—and all their haumāna who have come before me, it is no longer necessary to prove that this tragedy happened. Kānaka Maoli growing up and studying today know, and know how, our lāhui was dismembered. For those coming to this book unaware of our history of dispossession, it would be wise to turn to those scholars named here before diving into this book. It was the brilliant theorizing of my intellectual kūpuna that built the foundation that made this manuscript possible. This earlier intellectual commitment, rigor, and sacrifice to honor our mo'olelo have granted Kanaka Maoli intellectuals of today the opportunity to survey that dismembering, and to think about how we will (re)member and heal ourselves, our communities, and our 'āina.

With this in mind, I present to the scholarly community, and offer to my lāhui, *Remembering Our Intimacies: Mo'olelo, Aloha 'Āina, and Ea.* The labor of my intellectual ancestors has made it possible. It represents, however, my own practice of recalling and piecing together the different mana of mo'olelo I have had the honor to carry—a practice of taking stock and taking action. It examines mo'okū'auhau and the pilina between 'ohana. It also considers how our stories are dismembered and (re)membered again.

Chapter 1 begins with an evaluation of the impact that reading and taking seriously the pilina created through practicing aloha 'āina has had, and can continue to have on our lāhui and 'āina. Chapter 1 also offers a review of Indigenous queer theory and mo'olelo literary criticism—two of the major points of intersection and inspiration from which my work emerges. Chapter 2 explains my Kanaka Maoli methodologies of research, writing, and translation, and describes the interventions our expansive 'ōlelo Hawai'i archive helps me make into established practices of handling and representing 'ike. Chapters 3 and 4 cast our 'upena of intimacies across the Hi'iaka archive. Here I offer close investigations of pilina, intimacy, and 'āina.

In the final two chapters, I bring our mo'olelo to analyze and offer insights into what it means to strive for Kanaka Maoli futures in the settler and occupying State of Hawai'i. In chapter 5, I narrow the focus, moving from suggesting the expansiveness of our 'upena of intimacies to articulating a specific set of relationships that can help us see how the ongoing dislocations, disintegration, and disembodiment of our Kanaka Maoli relationships continue to obstruct our ability to challenge and offer alternatives to settler colonialism. Chapter 5 also offers some proposed actions for contemporary Kānaka Maoli to practice a political and cultural (re)membering.

In chapter 6, I bring this mo'olelo aloha 'āina to Mauna a Wākea and our growing and blossoming movements to protect and honor our 'āina. In this final chapter, I dive into the pilina and 'Ōiwi institutions holding the Pu'uhonua o Pu'uhuluhulu together, and through a political analysis of Indigenous governance and order making, I offer some preliminary understandings of what mo'olelo o Hi'iaka and others teach Kānaka Maoli and our allies about alternatives to nation-state models of governance.

Gathering Our Stories
of Belonging

Mana = energy?

In Moʻolelo Hawaiʻi, time is not a line. Sometimes that makes it hard to pinpoint a beginning. I wish the reader to know that the beginning I am about to lay out before you is just one of many. This mana begins with a childhood marked by my Hawaiian identity. My early years were spent with my father at just about every meaningful gathering of our community. We attended numerous demonstrations, marches, university events, and community meetings all for the singular purpose of advocating and imagining a better and more just Hawaiʻi. At the time, the word we used to describe our ultimate aim was *sovereignty,* and while it isn't uncommon to hear that word thrown around in our communities these days, aloha ʻāina is now the more appropriate terminology for who we are and what we Kānaka Maoli are fighting for.

As I was reared, I came to know aloha ʻāina as love for the land, love for one's country, and patriotism. Our full understanding of its meaning, emerges from a vast collection of moʻolelo, mele, political commentary, and petitions, much of which significantly precedes nineteenth-century literacy in Hawaiʻi. But even so, I grew up with a very specific notion of governance and the nation because of our aligning of aloha ʻāina as patriotism, and in doing so I internalized a whole host of ideas about my relationship to my lāhui and whether I was included in its vision of sovereignty because of my "queerness."

If aloha ʻāina was in fact patriotism, what we are saying is that our vision for Hawaiʻi, for our people and our land, is not so distinct from that of

1

our American oppressors. What we are saying is that we wish to relate to each other through capitalism, through patriarchy and its violences. We are saying that we can only imagine land as something to own, exploit, or conquer. Patriotism calls for the homogenizing of our communities, for our sexualities, desires, and intimacies to be reduced to toxic heteronormative monogamy, leaving very little room for the wahine I was, and still am, becoming. As a child, I was far too wild, too uncontrollable, too queer to fit into the mold of Hawaiian womanhood cast before me.

But my mother, bless her heart, raised a defiant wahine. So, instead of complying, I desecrated womanhood in my outrageous performance of gender. Later I would continue this trend of desecration in my insistence of fiercely loving wahine, after wahine, after wahine with no room in my imagination for heteronormative visions of love. I didn't yearn for love; I sought aloha. Because of this reducing of our vision for a Hawaiian future (i.e., aloha ʻāina as patriotism), everywhere I found aloha, I found myself wondering if I was desecrating my Hawaiianness as well. This is a scar that I am still learning to heal.

And it is true that the defining of aloha ʻāina as patriotism conforms to some of the ways our kūpuna defined it for themselves in the nineteenth century, but in recent years as our communities have come to unpack the meanings of patriotism and all its imports, we have begun to take important strides toward disassembling some of the imported and imposed colonial assumptions, such as the alignment of Hawaiian nationhood and patriarchy.[1] Such critiques warn us to be careful when trying to make meaning of aloha ʻāina, so that we do not perpetuate the very colonial sicknesses that hinder its practice today. I will unpack many of these critiques and challenges in the coming pages.

But for now, it is significant to this moʻolelo that even in my rearing as a child of a Hawaiian activist and being raised in our Hawaiian-language revival movement, this disappointing fact remained true: even the moʻolelo I was told in schools about our past and future failed to articulate an aloha ʻāina that would require me and my lāhui to take seriously the significant relationship between Hawaiian intimacy and our lāhui building. Which is to say, I did not grow up understanding that aloha ʻāina, building a lāhui, and governance had anything at all to do with the intricate nature of aloha and the way that I loved.

mana, Version?,
So grand on
aikane, lover?

So it turns out that I needed a new story. I needed a new vision. And what I've learned from almost a decade of research into our moʻolelo is that our old stories have preserved for us an abundance of "new" visions. Therefore, for the remainder of this story that I am telling, I want to turn to one of my favorite ancient epics, *Ka Moʻolelo o Hiʻiakaikapoliopele.*

It is my hope that those who come to this book without a pilina to this important moʻolelo will ultimately be inspired to experience it for themselves by reading one of the many published versions in ʻōlelo Hawaiʻi or English. In fact, I hope those who read this book will understand that reading one version of this moʻolelo will never fully satiate the appetite, and instead will devour as many mana (versions) of the moʻolelo as they can get their hands on. But in the unfortunate case that beginning your pilina with this moʻolelo is obstructed, I will offer a summary of sorts for those of you who are joining us from beyond the Hiʻiaka universe. Let it be known that this summary will be wholly insufficient in unfolding all the mana this moʻolelo has to offer, but perhaps it will allow you to follow along with the analysis and theory offered through this book and, therefore, end with your being called to experience the moʻolelo for yourself.

Ka Moʻolelo o Hiʻiakaikapoliopele is the moʻolelo of the Pele ʻohana as they travel from Kahiki to find a new home in Hawaiʻi. On their journey, led by their hānau mua (highest-ranking sibling), Pele, the fire and volcano deity, they transform Hawaiʻi and give birth to many lua (craters), puʻu (hills), and shorelines. Depending on the version of the moʻolelo, anywhere from eight to forty Hiʻiaka sisters travel with Pele and their brothers, including their navigator, Kamohoaliʻi. In every version of the moʻolelo, Hiʻiakaikapoliopele is the youngest, the muli loa, and the punahele (favorite) of Pele.

Shortly after they've made themselves at home, Hiʻiaka ventures down into Puna, where she sees Hōpoe dancing in the distance over the water. Hiʻiaka travels down the cliff to her and shares with her an oli. Hiʻiaka is so enchanted by Hōpoe's movement that Hōpoe teaches Hiʻiaka how to hula and in return Hiʻiaka creates a forest of lehua for Hōpoe to dwell in. The two aikāne spend the afternoon surfing, eating seafood, and sharing in all the beauties of Keaʻau.

While Hiʻiaka is enjoying the company of her aikāne, Pele calls for her, then tells her that she is going to take a deep sleep and that no one is to disturb her. As Pele sleeps, her spirit hears the beating of drums and the sound of voices intoning chants of the hula. Her spirit rises from her body in search of the source. On her journey, Pele eventually finds Lohi'au in Kaua'i and they spend three nights together. At the end of their three days, she tells him that she must return home and will send someone to fetch him and bring him back to her.

When Pele finally awakes from her slumber, she turns one by one to her Hi'iaka sisters, asking, "Who of you will go and fetch our kāne, Lohi'au?" When each Hi'iaka replies with some reason to avoid the treacherous trip, the youngest, Hi'iakakaikapoliopele, offers up herself for this task. Pele makes the task clear. She insists that when Hi'iaka brings Lohi'au home to her, he will remain hers for five days, and after the end of the five days Hi'iaka may have him for herself. Before then she is not to engage sexually or romantically with him, or the two of them shall be put to death upon their return. In exchange, Hi'iaka requires that Pele not harm her aikāne Hōpoe and that she bestows the proper mana upon Hi'iaka to help her complete this journey. Pele agrees to these conditions.

The rest of the mo'olelo is the story of Hi'iaka and her traveling companion Pā'ūopala'ā and aikāne Wahine'ōma'o defeating every obstacle thrown their way and eventually reaching Lohi'au in Ha'ena, Kaua'i.[2] Unfortunately, by the time they arrive to Kaua'i, they learn that Lohi'au has killed himself in despair over Pele's departure. Hi'iaka revives him and they all begin their trip back to Hawai'i. In doing so, Hi'iaka has upheld the agreement between herself and her elder sister. But Pele decides the trip has taken far too long, and in a fit of rage she sends her fire to Hōpoe's lehua grove, killing her and breaking the kauoha (agreement) between the two sisters. However, in bringing Lohi'au back from the dead, Hi'iaka has come into her own as an akua with the mana to properly challenge Pele. When the travelers return to Kīlauea, an epic battle ensues between these two powerful sisters, and what remains is a story of how the Pele lāhui/'ohana must navigate and make pono (balance/right) Pele's clear breach of leadership and mismanagement of power along with the rising power of their beloved pōki'i, Hi'akaikapoliopele.

This story is far more than a typical "love" story. I first heard this story as a young queer girl in my Hawaiian immersion classroom. Our introduction to the mo'olelo was meant not just as a cautionary tale of the dangers and ugliness of jealousy but also as a way to explain the incredible geological features we were blessed to witness every day in Hawai'i. The mo'olelo gave us a greater understanding of our environment and our relationship to it. Strangely, it wasn't until I returned to the mo'olelo as an adult that I began to learn about the other relationships that were so essential to the telling of this mo'olelo.

Following the advice of one of my childhood heroes, Lilikalā Kame'eleihiwa, I returned to Hi'iaka with a specific focus on the pilina between Hi'iaka and her beloved aikāne, Hōpoe.[3] Before this meeting, I had never heard of Hōpoe or the word *aikāne*, and it was from that humble beginning that my entire life and trajectory as a Kanaka Maoli scholar had transformed.

Storytelling is about sharing truth, so here's a truth about this story. Hi'iakaikapoliopele is a mo'olelo that has been shared throughout generations. In fact, it would be difficult to find a Hawaiian or long-term Hawai'i resident who was not at least somewhat familiar with the names of the main figures of this story. But it wasn't until very recently that I came to understand just how much this has to teach me and everyone in my lāhui. This mo'olelo is not just about the mapping of our 'āina, or about Hawaiian values of justice and leadership. This mo'olelo in itself is a pu'uhonua (a place of refuge), a gathering for Indigenous queers like myself to see ourselves unapologetically represented in our literatures and histories. There are so many lessons waiting for us in these stories. But they are not lessons I learned as a child. In fact, they are lessons that were strategically withheld from my parents, grandparents, and great-grandparents because these are lessons that would have greatly assisted in the maintenance of our autonomy and the creation of an alternative present from what we now endure.

This mo'olelo and the call to remember our intimacies is about so much more than what others have tried to take from us. This book is about what possibilities lay before us as we remember all that has been strategically dismembered. It is about the world we create and live in as we gather our stories of belonging. Therefore, a part of this mo'olelo is a kāhea (call) for the necessity of creating and protecting queer Indigenous pu'uhonua. I am thinking here specifically of spaces that 'Ōiwi wāhine and māhū have carved out within our larger movements for liberation.

The Hale Mana Wāhine and Hale Mana Māhū created and protected by Kahala Johnson, Māhealani Ahia, Kalani Young, and others at the Puʻuhonua o Puʻuhuluhulu is a key example.[4] Their work reminds me that the way our peoples have been ostracized from our own stories, origins, and practices of pleasure makes it critical that these puʻuhonua be created, named, and fiercely guarded.

Some may raise their eyebrows at the use of the word *queer* in a book that promises to recenter our ʻŌiwi practices of intimacy. Therefore, it is important for readers to know that I use the word *queer* throughout this text as a gloss for all our peoples and practices that do not fit into the heteronormative standards cast before us. While *queer* will appear throughout the text, it is essential for readers to understand that I am not identifying myself or my kūpuna as "queer." Rather, I am calling attention to the fact that the need to mark myself as queer today is a direct result of the way I have been erased systematically from my own history. For fellow Kānaka, it is our resistance and refusal of heteropaternalism and heteronormativity that is essential to what makes us ʻŌiwi. When we embody our beautiful, complex, and overflowing expressions of aloha that desecrate heteropatriarchy, we step into the footprints of our ancestors.

And while this text is certainly a labor of aloha for my lāhui, this book is also a kāhea to other Indigenous and peoples of color and our expanding networks of relations. Therefore, for the purpose of calling out to all our comrades and to make this moʻolelo legible to our ʻohana who also desecrate patriarchy, womanhood, manhood, and all the other heteropaternal expectations, I deploy *queer* as language that might make this puʻuhonua intelligible to those who may need it most.

It is in returning to the refuge of these moʻolelo that I see myself not only as a part of Hiʻiaka, Hōpoe, and Pele but also as an intimate part of this ʻāina. I, and other "queer" Kānaka Maoli, unsettle white settler logics of belonging and occupation when we insist on celebrating and practicing our pleasures and intimacies. We not only "bring sexy back," as Chris Finley has encouraged us to do; we also bring ourselves back into belonging.[5] We heal and (re)member our full communities. We do the work of nation building.

In light of the many ways our ʻāina and bodies are under threat, it is important we continue to create puʻuhonua for queer Indigenous folks to gather. But it is also important that we make space to return to those pu'uhonua that already exist—to reclaim and reoccupy them. We must show and practice our ancient genealogies of aloha and intimacy that laugh in the face of cis white heteropatriarchy. Hi'iaka is just one of those gathering places. And I hope that when you come to her, you are filled with the same excitement and aloha for her and yourself that I feel. But more than that, I hope you go out and find the gathering places of your own peoples so that someday we can meet he alo a he alo (face-to-face) and tell the stories of our kūpuna as the stories of ourselves, just as we were always intended to.

CHAPTER ONE

Aloha ʻĀina as Pilina

◆

Whether the actual term *aloha ʻāina* is used or not, nearly every contemporary Kanaka Maoli scholar has necessarily engaged with its ethics and practice. Aloha ʻāina is central to any moʻolelo of Hawaiʻi because our specific connection and relationship to land informs all Kanaka Maoli ontology and epistemology. It is the central and orienting framework for any attempt to understand what it means to be Kanaka Maoli. And understanding who we are—intimately, personally, and politically, in the face of continued removal—becomes more and more important, as Kānaka Maoli continue to struggle to regain and sustain any kind of personal and political self-determination in Hawaiʻi.

Aloha ʻāina has been translated by scholars in many ways, including love for the land, love for one's country, and patriotism. Our full understanding of its meaning, however, emerges from a vast collection of moʻolelo, mele, political commentary, and petitions, much of which significantly precedes nineteenth-century written literacy in Hawaiʻi. While defining aloha ʻāina as patriotism conforms to some of the ways our kūpuna defined it for themselves in the nineteenth century, critiques of this particular understanding have made important gestures toward disassembling some of the imported and imposed colonial assumptions, such as the alignment of nationhood and patriarchy. Such critiques warn us to be careful when trying to make meaning of aloha ʻāina, so that we do not perpetuate the very colonial sicknesses that hinder its practice today. Noenoe K. Silva's direct challenge of the use of patriotism as a definition of aloha ʻāina is significant here: "where nationalism and patriotism tend to exalt the virtues of a people or a race, aloha ʻāina exalts the land."[1] It is "a complex concept that includes recognizing that we are an integral part of the ʻāina and the ʻāina is an integral part of us."[2]

Silva's definition of aloha ʻāina brings us back to our archive, so that we remember the critical difference Davida Malo draws between moku and ʻāina in his *Ka Moʻolelo Hawaiʻi*: the living of Kānaka on a moku is what transforms it into ʻāina.[3] In this way, we are encouraged to remember the reciprocal pilina between our ʻāina and our Kānaka—which both have the mana to transform and feed each other. It is this recognition of a reciprocal and genealogical relationship that distinguishes aloha ʻāina from other forms of nationhood and nationalism. Patriotism, for example, commonly compels the heterosexual male's duty to the Western imperial war machine as a form of service to his forefathers. Whereas state-centric nationalism therefore depends upon the deployment of patriarchy to maintain itself, aloha ʻāina understands and values the relationship between the self and ʻāina through a complex moʻokūʻauhau of pilina—a model for which patriarchy is neither required nor useful. To celebrate the ʻāina, and one's personal and intimate relationship with her, offers a counterepistemology to Western nationalism—a countergender and counterrelational matrix I have called an ʻupena of pilina.[4]

In the coming chapters, I will describe how Kanaka Maoli articulations and practices of pilina and intimacy with each other are profoundly intertwined with our pilina and intimacy with ʻāina. Our moʻolelo continually show us this correlation, also impressing upon us how aloha ʻāina informs our articulation of aloha to each other. Any unraveling of our complex ʻupena of pilina and intimacy therefore also disembodies our practices of governance and nationalism. In addition to the obvious religious and moral agendas being imposed, bringing patriarchy into Kanaka Maoli relationships through the advocacy of the nuclear household also served the nineteenth-century missionaries' wish to replace aloha ʻāina practices with Western notions of nationalism and patriotism.[5] Because of this history of dispossession, interpersonal intimacy—how we practice pilina—must be restored as a central component of Kanaka Maoli nation building.

Understanding and practicing aloha is the necessary first step. Without reembodying our vibrant and diverse practices of aloha as a people, there can be no aloha 'āina. It will not be enough to deoccupy Hawai'i now, while assuming that we will deal with issues of gender, pilina, and "sexuality" later. Rather, our specific and diverse articulations of gender, relationality, and pilina must lead us into and through a nation-building movement that truly honors our values and distinct needs as a people. Silva's valuable concept of "mo'okū'auhau consciousness" focuses attention on how Kānaka Maoli orient themselves within that web of relations described in our mo'olelo—an 'upena that among other functions determines one's kuleana to the collective (lāhui) and to 'āina.[6] What I am offering here is a look at the intimacy practiced within the mo'okū'auhau, and an argument for the vital importance of understanding this intimacy, if we truly wish to understand the orientating frameworks that aloha 'āina and mo'okū'auhau supply.

Whether I fully realized it or not, aloha 'āina has always played a pivotal role in my analysis of Kanaka Maoli mo'olelo. As an enthusiast, I have paid the closest attention to those moments when mo'olelo and aloha 'āina mutually inform each other, offering an enhanced perspective on a particular Kanaka Maoli epistemology or practice. Nor am I alone in being attracted to such moments. Some of the most insistent proponents of grounding Kanaka Maoli scholarship and practice, and particularly our reading of mo'olelo, in aloha 'āina are wāhine. Haunani-Kay Trask, Noenoe Silva, ku'ualoha ho'omanawanui, Brandy Nālani McDougall, Noelani Goodyear-Ka'ōpua, and Māhealani Dudoit have all contributed significantly to our growing understanding that aloha 'āina is not just an important Kanaka Maoli political ideology but the essential and foundational epistemology from which our mo'olelo and practices emerge.[7] As Silva explains, "All genres of Hawaiian literature, with the exception of translated works from other languages, reflect our people's close relationship to and deep love for the 'āina."[8]

For Silva, and for many other Kanaka Maoli wāhine, aloha 'āina is not simply manifest in our literature but actually practiced through the proliferation of our literatures. These wāhine scholars constantly confirm Trask's claim that "the whole Hawaiian movement is poetic. *Aloha aina* (love for the land) is poetic."[9] Rather than focusing on defining, these wāhine work toward *articulating* aloha 'āina through example— an approach I am following and taking forward here. As Kanaka Maoli scholars, we constantly recognize that it is "impossible to convey all of the cultural coding that English strips away, and equally impossible to avoid the western cultural coding that English adds."[10]

Recognizing these problems and dangers as a necessary consequence of translation, I will therefore practice a politics of refusal, invoking and articulating instances of aloha ʻāina in the moʻolelo and moʻokūʻauhau without succumbing to the pressure to reduce them to a supposed English equivalent.[11] If successful, my method should allow aloha ʻāina not only to suffice but to resonate accurately and fully because it escapes translation. Because of my politics of refusal and my practice of rigorous paraphrase, which I will describe more fully in the following chapter, there are many words in ʻōlelo Hawaiʻi strung throughout my own writing without translation. Wehewehe.org is a useful resource to survey definitions of ʻōlelo Hawaiʻi terms.

We can best guard against mistranslation and misrepresentation by returning to one of our most important waihona of ʻike, our published moʻolelo, and examining carefully how our kūpuna manifested aloha ʻāina in our literature and lives. Our moʻolelo not only offer valuable instruction in the meaning and practice of aloha ʻāina but actually anticipate our need as contemporary Kānaka for this ʻike. Because the nūpepa have served as the primary archive for this book, I turn to them now to offer some examples of how their vivid discussions of aloha ʻāina have informed my own analysis of the ʻupena of pilina in our moʻolelo.

In the late nineteenth century, Joseph Nāwahī, aloha ʻāina and founder and editor of the nūpepa *Ke Aloha Aina,* wrote a series of pieces about aloha ʻāina that offered as an analogy the properties of a magnet.[12] On the penultimate page of the nūpepa's first issue, in an article titled "Ke Aloha Aina, Heaha ia?" [What is aloha ʻāina?], he wrote,

O ke Aloha Aina, oia ka ume Mageneti iloko o ka puuwai o ka Lahui, e kaohi ana i ka noho Kuokoa Lanakila ana o kona one hanau ponoi . . . ina i hookokoke ia na kui hao Mageneti i kahi hookahi, alaila, he mea maopopo loa me ke kanalua ole o ka manao ua ume like no lakou a pau loa kekahi i kekahi.[13]

In the editorial, the author describes the power of aloha ʻāina by comparing it to the mana of a magnet. In this description, we learn how aloha ʻāina articulates a magnetic force that not only draws the individual Kanaka to our 'āina but also creates and maintains a pilina between all Kānaka and 'āina. Further, the author is making a direct connection between aloha 'āina and one's desire and struggle for independence. On the same page, an article titled "Ka Mana o ka Mageneti" explicitly relates the properties of magnets to the pilina between those of the lāhui:

Pela no na kanaka i piha i ke aloha no ko lakou Aina hanau no hoi. Ua hiki ia lakou ke hoolauna mai i na kanaka a me na keiki, a me na ohana o lakou; a ike mai ia lakou iloko o ka ume mageneti o ke Aloha Aina.[14]

In this editorial, the author articulates the way aloha 'āina also results in a pilina between Kānaka, in that aloha 'āina are able to recognize the aloha 'āina in each other and are bound in intimacy together because of our shared intimacy and connection to our land.

This account of aloha 'āina offers a peek into the intimacy of aloha. Rather than a political imperative that draws people together through reason, self-interest, and propaganda, aloha 'āina is an internal love for place and community so strong that it cannot be overcome. Aloha 'āina is also a natural and imbedded Kanaka Maoli practice of relating to one's home. Aloha 'āina is that pull to place, that internal compass orienting Kānaka Maoli toward intimacy and self-governance simultaneously.

The effective practice of aloha 'āina creates and maintains two relationships: to the land itself, to that which feeds; and, through that 'upena of pilina, to one's community. These relationships are themselves inseparable, relying upon each other for survival. Because of the unending series of attacks upon our Kanaka Maoli land base, which forces Kānaka to assert constantly our kuleana to manage and govern our own lands, many contemporary scholars have focused on the political imperative of aloha 'āina—that felt need to recognize, articulate, and live one's pilina to the 'āina. I argue, however, that our engagement with aloha 'āina as that diverse and vibrant collection of multibodied relationships between Kānaka Maoli, our ancestors, peers, descendants, and the environment— the powerful unifying alignment and attraction that Nāwahī likened to magnetism—has been neglected.

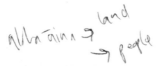

Through careful analysis and evaluation of moʻolelo o Hiʻiaka, this book will show that just as Hiʻiaka is held in the poli of her elder sister Pele, all pilina is carried in the poli (bosom) of our ʻāina. Further, with pilina as its living structure, aloha ʻāina is an embodied counternarrative not only to colonialism and occupation but to heteropatriarchy and hetero-paternalism as well.[15]

Wading into the difficult questions posed by pilina, I look to the moʻolelo of Hiʻiakaikapoliopele and ask what it means physically, emotionally, and spiritually to aloha our ʻāina. What will emerge if we follow aloha beyond plastic consumerism, biblical imagination, and legal definitions, and engage in aloha as transformative kinship beyond anything recently articulated? If we can begin to answer these questions, to understand and remember how we are pili to each other and to our ʻāina, all things linked in a diverse ʻupena of pilina, we can start to understand the potential benefits of disrupting current norms of relations that police our intima-cies and desires, and on the national scale our pilina as a nation. This book therefore seeks to reground the political theory of aloha ʻāina within the personal intimacy of one's relationship to ʻāina and lāhui.

WHY MOʻOLELO MATTER

This project is also about moʻolelo, a diverse collection of stories, histo-ries, prophecies, songs, poems, chants, and genealogies that are written, spoken, sung, chanted, and felt. Just as studying pilina requires over-coming an intricate set of assumptions about relationships and intimacy embedded in us through patriarchy, studying moʻolelo requires chal-lenging established notions about history and literature. Moʻolelo eludes these categories, offering access into a world where ideas about facts and single authoritative truths become complicated and nuanced in produc-tive ways. For this book, fully engaging with the possibilities of moʻolelo also reveals the need for dismantling the borders between the academic and the creative. Studying moʻolelo demands a rigorous creativity; writ-ing about moʻolelo challenges language and, specifically, the English lan-guage in which this book is written.

Above all, exploring moʻolelo requires recognizing and often shed-ding many imported Western assumptions about what literature is and isn't. Specifically, moʻolelo refuse to align themselves within a fiction and nonfiction binary. We must also embrace some further undeniable truths. Moʻolelo is not folklore or legend. Moʻolelo is not fantasy. Moʻolelo is not always written down—an important point, because Western knowledges prioritize the written word. In these cases, moʻolelo must also resist logocentric arguments "that naively assume that writing is somehow unchangeable or incorruptible" and therefore closer to historical fact.[16] Instead of being frozen in time and ink, moʻolelo move and shape-shift. Like our akua, moʻolelo have many kino. Within the context of occupation, when often only one truth, one version of history and justice can be allowed to survive, moʻolelo offers many truths and many versions, refusing to be reduced to a single authoritative fact or mana. Taking moʻolelo seriously allows for a more nuanced reading and understanding of history. By being many bodied, as a genre, moʻolelo are inherently counterhegemonic, regardless of content, and consequently uniquely positioned to challenge white historiography and its occupying grip on Hawaiʻi.

Moʻolelo such as the moʻolelo o Hiʻiakaikapoliopele offer an additional resistance to hegemony. As hoʻomanawanui explains, "The Pele and Moʻolelo o Hiʻiaka published between 1860 and 1928 were an alternative story to Amer-European colonialism."[17] In the ensuing analysis, hoʻomanawanui focuses on how "the hulihia discourse embodied in the Pele and moʻolelo o Hiʻiaka expresses Indigenous literary nationalism, presenting and asserting an alternative moʻolelo of Kānaka Maoli and our ʻāina, a counternarrative to settler colonial religion (Christianity), western science (like geography and geology), and politics."[18] In addition to this hulihia discourse, prevalent throughout every Kanaka Maoli recorded mana of Hiʻiaka, many other sites of resistance to Western hegemony are discernible within this moʻolelo. This book focuses on how the complex nature of relationships displayed in these moʻolelo challenged, and continue to challenge, Western notions of relationality and responsibility.

In brief, Kanaka Maoli writing about pilina and aloha ʻāina necessarily explores the intrinsic and pervasive nature of reciprocity and accountability between Kānaka and ʻāina not always easily found in Western literatures. As Brandy Nālani McDougall explains, Hiʻiaka and other "moʻolelo and moʻokūʻauhau are pedagogical sites offering not only protocols for how the ʻāina and we as Kānaka Maoli should be treated and governed, but also models for various means of warranted resistance in the face of unjust rule."[19] In other words, these moʻolelo represent alternative ways Kānaka could, and should, live, love, and govern.

For this and other reasons, moʻolelo is a practice of kūʻē (resistance) and kūkulu (building).[20] Not only do these moʻolelo challenge those haole narratives that depicted Hawaiians as lazy, illiterate savages; they also offer alternatives to stubbornly enduring structures of violence and occupation, such as patriarchy. Ultimately, these practices of kūʻē and kūkulu are also generative sites of healing. We therefore turn to these moʻolelo, knowing that there is creation in destruction. Our existence and literary production are not reactive but generative. Like Pele, who carefully and fully devours entire ʻili when necessary, we are birthing land for Kānaka to move upon and cause to flourish once more.

I should add that I believe deeply in this intimate and intense practice of reading, analysis, and interpretation. I believe in this method so sincerely that I hope to take this practice into the reading and analysis of additional moʻolelo and archives throughout my life as a scholar. However, for the time being and for the integrity of this particular study, I will rely almost exclusively on the inclusion and analysis of moʻolelo of Hiʻiakaikapoliopele. It is of significance to note that as other scholars take on this particular method of reading and analysis, our manaʻo on pilina and intimacy may grow and transform beyond the immediate scope of this book. That is one of the many beautiful gifts offered to us as Kānaka who are privileged to work from such a brilliant place of abundance.

INDIGENOUS INTERVENTIONS INTO FEMINIST & QUEER THEORIES

Indigenous and women of color feminists and queer theorists have been speaking back to and critiquing "carceral feminism" and Indigenous studies since at least the 1980s.[21] One result of this labor has been a sustained effort to reimagine Indigenous nationhood and the very nature of what it means to be a feminist. To articulate where my research enters into the fields of Indigenous feminism and queer theory, I kāhea (call out to) the Indigenous queers and feminists before me whose work laid the foundation for my theorizing of Kanaka Maoli pilina.

I am thinking here of women and wāhine such as Paula Gunn Allen, Annette Jaimes, Teresia Teaiwa, Haunani-Kay Trask, Maile Arvin, Eve

Tuck, Angie Morrill, Noelani Goodyear-Ka'ōpua, and Chris Finley, whose constellation of critical Indigenous theory has challenged feminist theory, queer theory, and Indigenous studies to push the boundaries of our own work and our pilina to each other.[22]

Therefore, as my work begins, we first remember how Allen opened the conversation for us about the importance of recovering our historic roles as Indigenous women in order to truly understand the gendered nature of the violences of colonialism. In *The Sacred Hoop: Recovering the Feminine in American Indian Traditions,* Allen offered language for understanding the "patriarchalization" of colonialism and therefore raised issues about heteropaternalism before our fields ever imagined that term.[23]

I also kāhea to Annette Jaimes, who would later articulate much of the conflict between these communities (feminism and Indigenous nations). For she understood, as we now do, that while this argument for the connection between patriarchy and colonization is deeply compelling and effectively articulated, Indigenous feminists must nevertheless work constantly against a current of "whitestream" feminism that has excluded many Indigenous women from feminist spaces and therefore deterred many Indigenous women from having any interest in participating in the first place. As Jaimes explains,

> One perspective on "feminism" among Native American women is that the emphasis has been on individuality as conceived by early western feminists who wanted more equality with men in the prevailing patriarchal sociopolitical structures in U.S. American society and who premised their struggle on democratic ideals for gender equity.[24]

For Indigenous feminists, one reaction to this particular obstacle has been to articulate the primary issues and concerns of Indigenous women and to identify how whitestream feminism reproduces some of the causes of these challenges. For Kanaka Maoli (and other Indigenous) wāhine, this means that rather than celebrating feminism outright, we must not just distinguish between the needs and desires of Indigenous women and white women but also celebrate the differences between mana wahine and whitestream feminism.

Scholars such as Trask and hoʻomanawanui have published significant work in articulating a politics of mana wahine. In fact, the differences between whitestream feminism and mana wahine is best described by Trask, who reminds us that our wāhine seek "collective self-determination," which necessarily includes achieving pono (balance) with our men.[25] Mana wahine is also distinct from feminism because it is by definition rooted in place and ʻāina. As hoʻomanawanui explains in "Mana Wahine, Education and Nation-Building: Lessons from the Epic of Pele and Hiʻiaka for Kanaka Maoli Today," a relationship with ʻāina and a land base is a strict requirement for the way mana wahine is inspired and manifested.[26] Mana wahine is therefore an embodiment of the power offered to Kanaka Maoli wāhine through our genealogical relationship to ʻāina that works toward pono with all our relations.

Another immediate obstacle faced by Indigenous feminists comes from within our own communities. Patriarchy has not only disrupted our roles and paths to power as wāhine but is structured in a way that further creates and sustains patriarchical power. One very important tool in sustaining patriarchy is through empowering Indigenous men in the process of its reproduction. "Because American culture, like western civilization generally, is patriarchal," Trask writes in *From a Native Daughter: Colonialism and Sovereignty in Hawaiʻi*, "that is, structured and justified by values that emphasize male dominance over women and nature, American institutions reward men and male-dominated behavior with positions of power."[27] In short, "men are rewarded, including Native men, for collaboration," and Trask states emphatically that our kāne are offered incentives, and even access to institutional power, for reproducing patriarchy.[28] Here we can see the dire need to make Indigenous feminisms relevant to Indigenous peoples of all genders if we wish to achieve decolonization.

By carefully examining the interlocking logics of settler colonialism, heteropatriarchy, and white supremacy, Indigenous feminists of the past decade have offered many paths toward understanding these structures of empire. These movements toward theoretical comprehension have been initiated by Indigenous feminists in response to the lack of discussion in whitestream feminism and traditional Native studies of the critical issues facing Native women. These movements also work to conceptualize the structures of empire, such as settler colonialism, and how these structures operate through the bodies of Indigenous women and men. Engaging with Indigenous visions of feminism can allow a theoretical framework to emerge that has the potential to speak beyond the issue of sexism, and to work toward articulating necessarily new forms of nationhood within an overarching decolonial project.[29]

But what does feminism do for Indigenous peoples seeking sovereignty? How can feminism disrupt settler colonialism? According to Lisa Hall, it was in the women of color (WOC) feminist calls for intersectionality, with their accompanying intersections of race, gender, and class, that the possibilities of Indigenous feminisms were first born.[30] But even when proposed by WOC feminists, intersectionality often failed to address issues of indigeneity and settler colonialism, which Indigenous women have argued are central to dethroning heterosexism. For this reason, Indigenous feminists have argued that in addition to including settler colonialism as one of the many intersections to trace within a feminist critique, a decolonial praxis must become a focal point for understanding how overcoming sexism requires the unsettling of settler colonialism. Within this decolonial praxis, the need for a new vocabulary to theorize the intersections between settler colonialism, colonization, and patriarchy became obvious in the face of the widespread desire to fully articulate the relationship between feminism and sovereignty.

And from this need came new language. Just twenty years after Allen's discussion of patriarchalization, the term *heteropatriarchy* emerged as a way to powerfully engage with intersectionality by describing and outlining how hierarchies are normalized among racialized groups, then taken for granted, in ways that ultimately feed empire and support the continued settler colonial reality that many Indigenous peoples face.

Since these publications, Indigenous women have steadily intervened within women's and feminist studies to describe the many ways patriarchy has come to be taken for granted in (and outside) Indigenous communities as somehow "natural" rather than a part of how Indigenous peoples have been displaced and dismembered. I am thinking here specifically of Dian Million, Leanne Simpson, Mishuana Goeman, Kim TallBear, and others who have been continuing to push the boundaries of what previously seemed unimaginable in both Native studies and feminist theory.[31] Specifically, their works have significantly influenced my thinking around problems with translating aloha ʻāina as "patriotism," since to do so draws us into the same trap of injecting patriarchy into our articulations of governance. One result of this is that a great deal of mainstream nation building in Hawaiʻi has focused primarily on the restoration of the Hawaiian Kingdom without a rigorous critique of the Kingdom's reproduction of partiarchical and statist values. However, the powerful work of Kanaka Maoli wāhine and māhū have continued to call forward the difficult work of envisioning and creating futures beyond the normalizing hierarchies of patriarchy and empire. To continue this important work, we must uncover, recover, and practice ʻŌiwi ways of relating to each other and organizing ourselves.

This movement has continued, with more and more contemporary Native women adding nuance to this complicated moʻolelo of colonialism in our nations. I am thinking here of the work of Maile Arvin, Eve Tuck, and Angie Morrill, who authored "Decolonizing Feminism: Challenging Connections between Settler Colonialism and Heteropatriarchy" in 2013 and mapped the theoretical intersections of patriarchy and its continued violence against not only Native women but also our extended Indigenous communities. In terms of queering Indigenous studies, Chris Finley offered many of us "native queers" a way back to our bodies in her offering "Decolonizing the Queer Native Body (and Recovering the Native Bull-Dyke): Bringing 'Sexy Back' and out of Native Studies' Closet" in 2011. And most recently the work of Kanaka Maoli scholar Stephanie Nohelani Teves, in *Defiant Indigeneity* in 2018, has challenged us all to rethink our analysis of the performance of indigeneity and authenticity in ways that will not continue to foreclose Indigenous futurities. Like our intellectual kūpuna, these scholars are giving us new language and new theory, but, even more important, they are offering us space to be sexy, to feel, and to return to the erotic and the intimacy often stolen from us through our collision with colonialism.

I also kāhea to these scholars for how they have pushed us to challenge our notion of family. By *family*, I mean the coerced Christian and capitalist formation of the household, which has had some of the most detrimental impacts to Kanaka Maoli well-being and intimacy. In their work problematizing how Indigenous peoples have been organized into nuclear families and forced to reduce our pilina to singular expressions of modern sexualities that support the nation-state, Arvin, Tuck, and Morrill argue that this underlying logic of settler colonialism must be revealed and contested.[32] Here we see a direct link between the characterization of heteropaternalism and Allen's discussion of patriarchalization.[33] But Arvin, Tuck, and Morrill further outline the effects of reorganizing Indigenous peoples into nuclear households as part of the larger project to limit Indigenous claims to our ʻāina.[34]

Central to the argument of this book is the understanding of the ways the settler colonial logic of gendering nationhood always includes normalizing the hierarchies informing heterosexism, heteropaternalism, and heteropatriarchy. These interlocking logics integral to settler colonialism create a foundation for normalizing additional hierarchies that inform the construction of colonial nationhood. By damaging and undermining Indigenous forms of kinship (our ʻupena of intimacies) and demanding that many of these relationships be replaced by the "'proper,' modern sexuali[ties]" sanctioned by heteropaternalism, these structures function as the "cornerstone in the production of a citizenry that will support and bolster the 'nation-state' as natural."[35] One need not look any further than the Indian Act of 1876 to see clearly how "the enforcement of 'proper' gender roles is entangled in settler nations' attempts to limit and manage Indigenous peoples' claims to land."[36]

For Kānaka Maoli, the most obvious and crucial example of how heteropaternalism and the gendering involved in colonialism disrupt Native claims to land is the Hawaiian Homes Commission Act (HHCA). In 1921 the HHCA not only legalized insidious blood logics that presumed those with more "blood" were more "Hawaiian" but also adopted principles of nuclear familyhood that allowed only certain Kānaka Maoli with a legally sufficient blood quantum to pass on land—and only to immediate nuclear descendants.[37] Here "modern" sexualities and heteropaternalism combine to mandate that Kanaka Maoli wāhine must pair with Kanaka Maoli kāne, each with the required quantum, to make, protect, or pass on our claims over land.

Hawaiian scholars such as Kameʻeleihiwa, Noelani Arista, Kēhaulani Kauanui, and Jonathan Osorio have written specifically about how the Christianization of the Hawaiian Kingdom resulted in punishing laws around marriage, adultery, and land ownership.[38] It's important to note that many of these laws were informed by an inconceivable population collapse that our people were experiencing at the time due to the introduction of a host of diseases (many of which were transmitted sexually).[39] Noelani Goodyear-Kaʻōpua has shown how meaningful this domestication of Kānaka Maoli was through coverture and other laws. In her article "Domesticating Hawaiians: Kamehameha Schools and the Tender Violence of Marriage," Goodyear-Kaʻōpua takes seriously the way marriage was used to naturalize (white) male control in Hawaiʻi. Through studying this great period of change, it's clear that regardless of intention or stimulus, the fact remains that these changing norms surrounding desire, sexuality, and family making drastically transformed Kanaka Maoli experiences and practices of pilina.

In the field of Indigenous queer theory, queer settler ally Scott Lauria Morgensen responds to such eugenic atrocities by examining the gendered violence of settler colonialism as a "structure" and system that "calls for a sustained denaturalizing critique."[40] Our Native queer theorists, such as Finley, remind us that we must begin with Indigenous queer theory in our decolonial work because "taking sexuality seriously as a logic of colonial power has the potential to further decolonize Native studies."[41] Using much of the same language of Indigenous feminisms, including insisting on an engagement with heteropatriarchy and heteropaternalism, Indigenous queer theorists have begun to demonstrate how "settler sexualities" have variously been imposed on Indigenous peoples to further the project of colonization.[42]

For Kānaka Maoli, taking sexuality and pilina seriously has significant ramifications for how we imagine and materialize our families, homes, communities, and, above all, our nation. When we are attentive to how sexuality comes to define the family, we see how heteropatriarchy is also the backbone of the normalization of the nuclear family. Though presented as a harmless and "natural" phenomenon, the many ways that the state and society only recognize the nuclear family as legitimate commit a significant violence against the very nature of Kanaka Maoli relationships by insisting that they are not isolatable, independent, or "nuclear." Colonialism constantly enlists heteropatriarchy and heteropaternalism to naturalize the very hierarchies that maintain colonial power in Native territories. As Finley explains, "Native interpersonal and community relationships are affected by pressure to conform to the nuclear family and the hierarchies implicit in heteropatriarchy, which in turn, are internalized. The control of sexuality, for Native communities and Native studies, is an extension of internalized colonialism."[43] In Hawaiʻi, the result has been that heteropatriarchy poisons our pilina to each other and our ʻāina.

A significant conclusion to be drawn from Indigenous queer theory is the importance of challenging naturalized notions of "family." Mark Rifkin explains, "Heteronormativity legitimizes the liberal settler state by presenting the political economy of privatization as simply an expression of the natural conditions for human intimacy, reproduction, and resource distribution; thus, the critique of heteronormativity offers a potent means for challenging the ideological process by which settler governance comes to appear (or at least to narrate itself as) self-evident."[44] This book extends this critique into Hawaiʻi by seeking out Kanaka Maoli conditions and embodiments of intimacy beyond privatization.

KANAKA MAOLI INTERVENTIONS INTO
INDIGENOUS FEMINIST & QUEER THEORY

By drawing upon the distinctive perspectives to challenge the status quo in Hawaiʻi, this work also follows the lead of those Kanaka Maoli wāhine who have been instrumental in the blossoming of contemporary Hawaiian scholarship. These wāhine have been vigilantly aware and appreciative of feminism and its powerful critiques but have, for understandable reasons, not fully embraced the principles of feminist and queer theory. Historically, these fields have inflicted an additional violence on our communities by refusing to insist that Kanaka Maoli values and practices to be evaluated from a Kanaka Maoli perspective. Because of this, feminism and her many waves of influences that have inspired and shaped the formation of queer theory have also necessarily been held at arm's length by Kanaka Maoli scholars.

Nonetheless, Kanaka Maoli wāhine have been repeatedly engaging in a kind of Indigenous feminism concerned with the relationship between colonialism, patriarchy, and ʻāina. Many of these activists and theorists are rightfully identified as mana wahine. Kanaka Maoli wāhine writers have also insistently distinguished mana wahine from whitestream feminism. In "Mana Wahine: Feminism and Nationalism in Hawaiian Literature," ho'omanawanui quotes Trask's articulation that "western ideas of feminism react against, resist or seek equality with patriarchy." Trask continues, "Mana Wahine does neither." In the same vein, ho'omanawanui goes on to explain that "Native women's issues differ from haole (white) women's: our struggle is against colonialism as we fight for self-determination as a people, not a gender."[45] These mana wāhine, many of them mentioned in the preceding section, are making arguments that closely parallel how Indigenous feminists have criticized whitestream feminism for failing to address issues faced by Indigenous women seeking self-determination. At its core, mana wahine is invested in pono with our kāne rather than focusing on a power imbalance between kāne and wāhine that results in an injustice. In essence, and above all, we wish to liberate our lāhui.

Mana wahine is also distinct from whitestream feminism in that it is rooted in place and 'āina, and therefore rooted in our 'ōlelo and mo'olelo. Wāhine today draw strength from our contemporaries, ali'i, akua, and from the 'āina, which provides the foundation and life for all inspiration as well as being the canvas upon which to enact and exert mana wahine desires. These desires prioritize aloha 'āina, mo'okū'auhau (genealogy), kuleana, and pono. 'Āina empowers wāhine to exercise leadership in the lāhui and our families. Genealogically related to that which births land, wāhine not only reflect and channel the all-encompassing power of 'āina but are also the servants most prepared to protect her.

In *From a Native Daughter*, Trask discusses how settler colonialism (although not yet named as such) is a structure that oppresses Kānaka Maoli. In part 2 of the collection, she writes frankly about the role of mana wahine and wahine leadership in the Hawaiian sovereignty movement, arguing that Kanaka Maoli wāhine are undeniably our leaders. By turning toward Kanaka Maoli epistemologies that honor wāhine and our responsibility to care for the lāhui as an extension of our kuleana to care for our families, Trask defines Kanaka Maoli leadership in Kanaka Maoli terms that prioritize kuleana and genealogy, thereby revolutionizing the possible imaginings of nationhood.[46]

In addition, Trask's significant work problematizing rights ideologies in an Indigenous context urges Kānaka Maoli to imagine structures built

ea = being of the land + people

pai belg

on our own traditions and language. Here I think of how kuleana and its inherent reciprocal responsibility allow us to reimagine a view of sovereignty rooted in our pilina to each other. This kind of community and nation building is already reflected in moʻolelo, moʻokūʻauhau, and ʻāina. Embodied in our ʻupena of intimacies, these values and principles are guides for how Kānaka must practice pilina and reciprocity.

A part of this significant shift away from the nation-state as our model of governance has come from a return to Hawaiian language. In beginning with our own ʻōlelo, we have been able to articulate futures previously unintelligible. This can most clearly be seen from the way our lāhui has begun to strive for ea rather than sovereignty.

In 2014 Noelani Goodyear-Kaʻōpua, Ikaika Hussey, and Erin Kahunawaikaʻala Wright edited a collection of essays that maps out the work of the Hawaiian sovereignty movement Trask was at the center of in 1993. In addition to celebrating the significant and life-changing work done by Kanaka Maoli activists from the even earlier beginnings of this movement and chronicling how Kānaka Maoli have been actively involved in the making of our histories, *A Nation Rising: Hawaiian Movements for Life, Land, and Sovereignty* also "collectively explores the political philosophy and driving ethic of ea."[47] In doing so, the editors carve out and articulate a Hawaiian political philosophy that offers futurities beyond "sovereignty" and the nation-state.

In Goodyear-Kaʻōpua's introduction, she describes the volume as a gathering of voices that have worked to restore many facets of Kanaka Maoli life for the betterment of all people in Hawaiʻi. Exploring these voices and the movements they emerge from will reveal how ea and other Hawaiian ideologies challenge colonial projections that present themselves as a singular reality. At the root of the collection is ea, which Goodyear-Kaʻōpua defines as being of the land and of the people. Unlike the concept of sovereignty, ea forces us to acknowledge its unbreakable relationship to ʻāina. Furthermore, "like breathing, ea cannot be achieved or possessed; it requires constant action day after day, generation after generation."[48] Here Goodyear-Kaʻōpua articulates the essential nature of ea for Kanaka Maoli survival and demonstrates how Kanaka understandings of self-determination are rooted in interdependence rather than independence.

Healing vs. belg

Like Trask, Goodyear-Kaʻōpua emphasizes the political nature of culture, and therefore how revitalizing culture and language must be at the center of the Hawaiian sovereignty movement. Kānaka Maoli must move our ea through oli, dance, writing, reading, acting, and creating, in order to live "sovereign." I would only make explicit that we must also move our ea through our pilina with each other. Goodyear-Kaʻōpua and Trask remind Kānaka Maoli that our arts and cultures are not just political but the ea and life that sustain us. Goodyear-Kaʻōpuaʻs focus on ea and Traskʻs elaboration of mana, pono, and kuleana, are therefore carrying out the precise work that Indigenous feminist scholars are calling for. By moving beyond the language and desires of the nation-state, and by engaging with ʻōlelo Hawaiʻi, these mana wāhine are imagining futures for Kānaka Maoli rooted in our pilina to our ʻāina and each other.

It is therefore from this junction that my own research into and theorizing of Kanaka Maoli pilina and intimacy depart. Just as the nuclear family, heteropaternalism, heteropatriarchy, and settler colonialism are entwined, pilina and ea are profoundly, though far less destructively, implicated in each other. Indeed, by providing an alternative to the male-oriented and governed nuclear family, pilina and kinship are counter-hegemonic, challenging the single and authoritative claim such a family places on Kanaka understandings of relationality and community. But pilina and kinship offer more than an alternative metaphor for resisting the destructive technology of the settler state. They also represent a whole set of interpersonal accountabilities and possibilities for pleasure at the piko of our relationship to our communities and our ʻāina. A major goal of this book is to articulate more fully and accurately some of these many forms of pilina, thereby allowing us to imagine and realize the possibilities offered by communities freed from the settler state organization of "family." And because i ka wā ma mua i ka wā ma hope,[49] this book proposes to un-"queer" Kanaka Maoli pilina, desires, and pleasures by turning to one of the most common homes for such manaʻo and feelings: our archive of moʻolelo.

While this project undoubtedly seeks to understand and challenge the normalizing logics of heteropatriarchy/paternalism/normativity, it is also important to recognize that queer-identified Native peoples specifically, as they "defy their queered encounters with settler colonialism," are leading

our "peoples in reimagining modes of embodiment, desire, and collectiv-
ity."⁵⁰ At the same time as I am seeking out the aikāne, punalua, poʻolua,
hoapili, kōkoʻolua, and hoʻāo of our kūpuna in our moʻolelo as a method
for understanding the complicated ʻupena of relationships whose aho are
threaded through the entire fabric of Kanaka Maoli society and community, other Native queers are recalling and creating their own languages to
respond to the disruptions and trauma they've experienced as the sev-
enth generation whose sexuality, desires, and genders have been policed
by a foreign settler "authority."⁵¹ This desire to create language to speak to
our current conditions is not only powerful but necessary. These Natives
all remind us to pay attention to the violence of the nuclear family, not
only on other Native queers but on our entire relational orientation as
a lāhui.

In applying the relevant and useful aspects of the theories briefly outlined here to my practice of engaging with a Kanaka Maoli context and
archive, I follow strategies and methods directed toward developing a
theory of pilina from our piko in Hawaiʻi. The first step is insisting on
the mana of moʻolelo as evidence and legitimized ʻike. This project does
not seek to discover or put forth any single definition for any of the terms
central to this project. Rather, by taking moʻolelo seriously as evidence, this
book seeks to become one more mana of the moʻolelo of Kanaka Maoli
pilina emerging from a much older moʻokūʻauhau of desire. Together, these
moʻolelo allow us to be intentional, specific, and grounded when responding to the gendered and sexual violence posed by colonialism. Moʻolelo
can take us beyond the reductive terms of kinship, queer, and sexuality;
moʻolelo ultimately have the mana to offer up a Kanaka Maoli theory of
pilina and desire.

Articulating these manaʻo, and taking pilina and desire seriously, matters greatly to the lāhui. When we begin to recognize and articulate the
many shapes of pilina and relationships within a Kanaka Maoli ethos waiting for us in the archive, we consciously allow ourselves to understand
and create an alternative to existing models of nation statehood. In the
following chapters, I will unfold a section of our ʻupena and examine some
of its hīpuʻu, ultimately to suggest how a greater understanding of pilina
and Kanaka Maoli desire is instrumentally important to our nation building and decolonization.

CHAPTER TWO

Hawaiian Archives, Abundance, and the Problem of Translation

In the introduction, I set forth what aloha ʻāina can contribute to a growing field of Indigenous politics by way of intervening in the intersections of Indigenous feminism and Indigenous queer theory. This intervention centers on a method I call (re)membering ʻupena of intimacies, which reads aloha ʻāina as a pilina that requires contemporary Kānaka to attend to the resurgence of a decolonial intimacy between Kānaka, our ʻāina, and each other. Before we can luʻu (dive deep) into the Hiʻiaka archive to unfold and map our expansive ʻupena of intimacies, however, we must unpack what methods will direct our practice and theorizing in order to enter into our moʻolelo effectively and (re)member our ʻupena.

This project requires that we read and theorize from a place of abundance. To do so honors the richness of our Hawaiian-language archive and insists that "consulting" the archive is not nearly sufficient. When seeking to understand earlier Kanaka Maoli practices of pilina, scholars like myself must luʻu into the Hawaiian-language archive rather than attempt to stand on the shore and merely cast a line or two into its bounty. When working with ʻōlelo Hawaiʻi resources, we must also keep in mind the politics of translation and remain cautious of how our theorizing from Hawaiian-language materials is itself an act of translation. To fully elaborate on this method of theorizing from abundance, I first pose some preliminary questions about the problems of translation, outline my approach of rigorous paraphrase, and offer a mapping of the archive consulted for this project.

After discussing the process of theorizing from abundance, I then suggest how the metaphor of the ʻupena can be applied not only to our understanding of our practices of intimacy but also to our understanding of the pilina between texts in our archive, their authors, and audiences. Paying close attention to the aho between these points supports our practice of theorizing from abundance as well, since such scrutiny requires establishing the context for the pilina between text, the greater archive, and the political histories from which they emerged.

ABUNDANCE

It has been said that "the opposite of violence is not nonviolence, it is creation."[1] When we begin with abundance—with all that has been (re)membered and all that we continue to (re)member today—we do the work of creation. To do so is also to honor our position in this epic moʻokūʻauhau of Kanaka intellectuals, practitioners, and ʻai pōhaku (stone eaters/activists). Where once we had to outline the devastation, survey the fault lines, examine the many ways our kūpuna, we ourselves, and our practices have been and continue to be dismembered, today we are offered the kuleana to honor, celebrate, and theorize from abundance. Where once we had to begin to document the depletion of our resources, the desecration of our sacred places, our collapse of population, and the destruction of our ʻŌiwi institutions, today we practice resurgence, in a collective turn toward creation. This book does both—mourn and heal, grieve and celebrate—but prioritizes the (re)membering from a place of inherited abundance. Thanks to our kūpuna, Kānaka Maoli are blessed with a physical archive to turn to that provides that abundance. Our nūpepa made this book possible.

When I use the term *nūpepa*, I am speaking of an archive of Hawaiian-language newspapers that came into existence in 1834 and continues to expand to this day. This archive is formidable, not only because of the period of time it covers but also because of the number and diversity of the newspapers, editors, authors, and distinct audiences it produced. While a few trickles of this Hawaiian-language newspaper tradition appear from time to time today, the flood of publications entered the archive between 1834 and 1948. During that time, "Hawaiian writers filled 125,000 pages in nearly 100 different newspapers with their writings."[2]

This repository, one of the largest collections of Indigenous writing in any Indigenous language in the world, can certainly be described as "abundant." Previous scholars have discussed with great rigor how and why this archive became inaccessible to most Kānaka today, largely because of the deliberate erasure of Hawaiian-language practices in our communities.[3] As Hawaiian scholarship has developed over the past half century, however, more and more Kanaka Maoli intellectuals have invested in the necessary learning of ʻōlelo Hawaiʻi to benefit from this primary archive of ʻike Hawaiʻi. Because of this dedication, in virtually any field of knowledge relevant to Hawaiʻi, at least one Kanaka or ally is insisting upon the need to consult Hawaiian-language resources to carry out successfully ethical, historically responsible research.

More recently, however, such Kanaka Maoli scholars as Noelani Arista and Noenoe Silva have shown through their theorizing and their research practices that "consultation" of Hawaiian-language resources is not nearly adequate.[4] As a historian, Arista has called on scholars of Hawaiian history to contextualize ʻike garnered from the nūpepa by situating it in its time and location—a practice only possible if one dives deeply into the abundance of nūpepa resources. Silva's most recent publication, *The Power of the Steel-Tipped Pen,* demonstrates this important practice in a clear and decisive fashion. Her deep and intimate study of Joseph Kānepuʻu and Joseph Mokuʻōhai Poepoe sets them within an assembled history of Hawaiian intellectual life. Both wāhine show what is possible when Kanaka Maoli scholars invest decades of attentive consideration and aloha to our Hawaiian-language archives. Neither Arista nor Silva is "consulting" or dipping into Hawaiian-language resources. They are diving deep. Here I attempt to follow their lead, assuring readers that in this book and beyond, I intend to submerge myself repeatedly in this shared, expansive archive, as I progress in my research of the moʻolelo of Hiʻiaka.

PROBLEMS OF TRANSLATION

One reason frequently offered for the necessity of engaging fully with the available Hawaiian-language resources is our increased familiarity with the problems and politics of translation. In *The Scandals of Translation,* American theorist Lawrence Venuti reminds us that "although the history of colonialism varies significantly according to place and period, it does reveal a consistent, no, an inevitable reliance on translation," and many translation theorists and historians have explored how the practice has been deployed as a specific process of colonialism that continues to impact the way we read, interpret, and understand our own pasts.[5] The extensively conducted act of translating Kanaka Maoli culture and practices for outside audiences not only decontextualized and reshaped our traditions but also bestowed on the Western translators the supposed status of unquestioned "experts" on all things Hawaiian. As Cristina Bacchilega observes, additional consequences were that Kānaka Maoli become "informants only" and that the texts selected for translation were often represented as "devoid of political content or strife."[6]

Such colonial translation practices carry out "a discursive strategy of containment or domestication that requires rewriting the other in the dominant language's terms."[7] In Hawai'i, Thomas Thrum, Nathaniel Emerson, William Westervelt, and Martha Beckwith are some of the many haole writers and translators who reorganized or left out large portions of mo'olelo they acquired and appropriated from uncited Native sources. Such intentional acts of colonialism through translation—in this case, the absorption of Hawaiian-language materials into English as the "authoritative" language—result in a great divide, leaving certain languages and people visible and recognizable, and others not.[8]

Nor are historical translations the only ones we must approach attentively when anticipating the problems of the practice. The choice to read contemporary translations, or even to translate ourselves, must be made with a firm understanding that translation is always at best an interpretation, with all the accompanying cultural coding that entails. Such caution is beneficial for ourselves as well as for the audiences of our production. As Bryan Kamaoli Kuwada explains in "To Translate or Not to Translate":

> Contemporary readers outside of the field of translation theory tend to have unrealistic expectations of what translations actually are. Such readers are searching for "literal" translations, as if such a thing could exist—something that successfully makes 1–1 substitutions of language, content, and context. As scholars of Hawaiian language and 'ike Hawai'i we have generally under-theorized the impact of our mo'olelo being reduced to writing.[9]

While the technology of written literacy was instrumental in creating our Hawaiian-language archive, it is also important to be highly attentive to how that technology itself served as more than just the medium for transporting information and moʻolelo.[10] As Laiana Wong explains, "Literacy having been introduced by the missionaries, it is highly unlikely that the writing style of Hawaiian authors developed in the absence of foreign influence and censorship."[11]

In response to these inherent problems of translation, especially in a colonial or heavily coercive context, Subramanian Shankar has argued that we need to develop "now, more than ever, a vigorous culture of translation—a widely disseminated and rich understanding of translation. Important as actual acts of translation are, it is also necessary to popularize a general understanding of translation that foregrounds interpretation rather than fidelity."[12]

In the face of a steadily increasing amount of effort devoted to translating Hawaiian-language materials to provide more access to our community, we must therefore also be developing this recommended "culture of translation" to increase familiarity with how to approach and read translated works appropriately. As we increasingly turn to the nūpepa and other Hawaiian-language archival materials and "consulting" and translating our great works of literature become even more frequent activities, we must recognize that more and more Kānaka will in turn be reading our moʻolelo in translation. Greater access must therefore be coupled with greater educating of readers about what it means to read a text in translation, lest they, and even we, fall into the trap of taking for granted the necessarily inexact and interpretative nature of translated works.

Given these challenges, some Hawaiian-language scholars and advocates for the revival of the Hawaiian language have argued that we should move away from translation entirely. They argue that if people wish to access Hawaiian-language materials, they should learn to ʻōlelo Hawaiʻi.[13] Certainly, there is no downside to more Kānaka investing themselves in learning our ʻōlelo, so although I do not support what would amount to a ban on translation projects, in my own work I try to find ways to encourage Kānaka and scholars interested in ʻike Hawaiʻi to develop our own relationship with ʻōlelo Hawaiʻi, proceeding from the understanding that there is simply no proper substitute for being able to read these texts for ourselves in our 'ōlelo makuahine.

This encouragement extends to another implication of translation theory that deserves more attention when we study Hawaiian materials: how analyzing, critically interpreting, evaluating, or even simply writing about Hawaiian-language materials in English are themselves all acts of translation. Much of the scholarship written about our archive has had to participate in translation to display our work effectively. I am thinking here about how many contemporary scholars provide their readers with the Hawaiian-language source material but also their own translations of this material before conducting their analysis and evaluation. As I have collected, read carefully, evaluated, and then written about these Hawaiian-language materials, I have become increasingly convinced that the problems of translation remain, even when as scholars we draw almost exclusively on those texts written in 'ōlelo Hawai'i. Since neither a total refusal to translate nor the development of a culture of translation fully achieves the goal of accountability to this Hawaiian-language archive, I see a need for new creative and responsible ways of writing about Hawaiian-language materials. Therefore, in this book I am adopting a practice I am calling rigorous paraphrase.

RIGOROUS PARAPHRASE

With the publication of Noenoe Silva's first book, *Aloha Betrayed,* in 2004 came a new standard of how to write thoughtfully and ethically about Hawaiian-language materials in English publications. What we learned was that any and all analysis and translation of Hawaiian-language materials must not just include the original source text but must also grant it visible priority. This allowed Hawaiian-language scholars to read the source and the author's translation side by side before moving on to the analysis, often on the same page. Both the author and the reader were now held accountable to the source text, which could speak for itself. To follow this writing and publication strategy, and to have a major university press agree to this foregrounding, was a revolutionary practice in Hawaiian scholarship that has since been followed by such Hawaiian intellectuals as ku'ualoha ho'omanawanui, Noelani Arista, and Brandy Nālani McDougall. Hawaiian-language scholars reading their work can therefore critically engage with the sources of contemporary scholars' analysis.[14]

Because of the near collapse of our ʻōlelo Hawaiʻi over the past century, however, most readers of contemporary scholarship are not fluent in Hawaiian and thus rely more heavily, if not entirely, on the scholar's translation. Herein lies a problem of translation: because our readers approach our scholarly translations without a knowledge of translation theory and the politics of translation, we reaffirm that long-standing assumption that translations are sufficient substitutes for the source text and therefore facilitate the reader's skipping over the source and relying instead upon our translation and interpretation of the material at issue. Because we earn the trust of the readers by providing the Hawaiian text, our translations are then all too often taken at face value, without nearly enough critical investigation.

Paraphrases, however, are not trusted in the same way that translations are and certainly not accepted as replacements for the source material. In fact, the general public understands that paraphrases are what translations should be understood to be: interpretations and reductions of source materials. By choosing instead to rely greatly on what I am calling rigorous paraphrase within the body of my scholarship, I am therefore attempting to foreground for the readers how I am engaging directly with the Hawaiian-language text without supplying them with the alluring distraction of a full "translation" that pulls them away from the source. What remains is the scholar's critical approach to speaking directly to and with the source text. It should be noted, however, that including the ʻōlelo Hawaiʻi source text is essential to this method of rigorous paraphrase because it still provides Hawaiian-language scholars with the immediate opportunity to engage with that material independently from my provided analysis, while also encouraging nonspeakers to take on the task of language learning to participate more fully in the conversation.

What you will therefore find in this book is an absence of formal translations with the exception of short sentences, and an extensive use of rigorous paraphrase. When Hawaiian-language materials are discussed, you will be offered source texts standing firmly in their own language, because there are ʻike and kaona that develop through the exact unfolding

of the passage that cannot necessarily be reproduced through translation. What will then follow will be a fluid paraphrase, provided simultaneously with the analysis of the Hawaiian-language material. Drawing
from a theory of translation refusal, this practice of rigorous paraphrase
continuously points the reader back to the Hawaiian-language source text
rather than to a supplied translation/interpretation and serves to alert
the non-Hawaiian-language reader such a process is always in operation
with any English-language engagement with a Hawaiian-language text.[15]
While this practice is not meant to alienate, it may leave the reader feeling like they are missing something of importance. This ache of absence
isn't created by the practice of rigorous paraphrase but is intentionally
made visible through this practice of refusal. While translations create
the illusion of capturing the fullness of any given passage, rigorous paraphrase alerts the reader that none of these moʻolelo can be fully understood outside the language, ʻōlelo Hawaiʻi, that they were originally told
and written in. Ultimately, this refusal is an invitation for readers to begin
and continue the difficult work of communing with our kūpuna in our
language.

Although this practice of rigorous paraphrase does not solve all of the
many problems resulting from over a century of our pilina as Kānaka
Maoli to our ʻōlelo Hawaiʻi being damaged or forsaken, it does attempt to
respond to many of the challenges posed by translation. Ultimately, what
I am resisting is that assumption that analyzing Hawaiian-language materials always requires full and formal translations, primarily because the
presence of such translations in practice impedes the process of trying
to understand and learn from these texts within their own logic. Recognizing the contexts, including the linguistic ones, from which Hawaiian-
language materials emerge is ultimately more important. For the sake of
readability, in those cases when substantial passages are cited that have
close or significant parallel passages in other mana of the moʻolelo, those
parallel passages will be noted but are reproduced only when an incon-
sistency or alternate details are the subject of my analysis.

When speaking of intimacy, language must be both precise and nuanced.
When describing the intimacy of Kānaka, language must be able to move
and shape-shift, responding to the vibrant possibilities of all the ways
these intimate pilina can breathe and move. For this reason, language

is arguably the greatest challenge facing this book. I am speaking not only about the differences between ʻōlelo Hawaiʻi and English but also about the difficulties of translating, and making comprehensible, ancient Hawaiian practices of intimacy for our profoundly foreign contemporary context. Multiple acts of translation are taking place at every stage of this project, and the many problems that arise need to be recognized and confronted. And as I have already indicated, this project also situates itself at the intersection of distinct fields of study with their own preferred languages and vocabularies. When necessary and appropriate, this book seeks to speak intelligibly to these fields without losing its primary focus, which is to describe, analyze, and ultimately construct and offer a moʻolelo about Kanaka Maoli pilina that resists as much as possible being lost to colonization and translation.

For example, queer, gay, and lesbian studies resonate with terms such as *sexuality*, but because sexuality often tends to refer to an identity rather than a relationship, the term seems insufficient and inappropriate for discussing how Kānaka related to each other. Terms such as *kinship* similarly draw attention in Native American and Indigenous studies; however, that term's free and ungrounded use in past scholarship not rooted in a Kanaka Maoli archive paradoxically proves to be a limiting factor. Even the term *relationship* itself is so common and familiar, yet so overflowing with specific but often contradictory assumptions and connotations, that it ultimately isn't dexterous enough to capture the conditions of Kanaka Maoli interpersonal relations.

To confront these challenges, I will attempt whenever possible to allow the archive to speak for itself. Rather than attempting to capture some supposed essence of particular relationships through offering a black-and-white definition, I will provide examples that describe certain specific relations materially and metaphorically. Whenever possible, Hawaiian terms will be employed when analyzing Hawaiian manaʻo. For instance, a word such as *aikāne* will not be sharply defined, because to do so would demonstrate a complete misunderstanding of the very nature of Kanaka Maoli aikāne relationships. Instead, pilina such as aikāne, poʻolua, kōkoʻolua, punalua, hoʻāo, and others will be described but also invoked through examples that allow them to dance fully in the book, as they should. Wherever possible, terms such as *sexuality, relationship,* and even *desire* will be subordinated to Hawaiian terms, or avoided entirely. This method is not just corrective but generative, requiring that old language be revived so that new language with the ability to carry and reflect the changing weight of these pilina can emerge.

The challenge of language also arises in any discussion of genre. As previously suggested, Kanaka Maoli genres of writing do not necessarily translate well into English literary forms. For example, canonical English literary texts have conventionally been divided into fiction and nonfiction and then further sorted into existing subgenres—poetry, drama, short stories, novels. Kanaka Maoli "texts" cannot be immediately assigned to fiction and nonfiction categories. This issue of orientation to the text parallels our perceptions of our own ontologies, and in particular our preconceived notions of "fact" and "truth." Like Albert Wendt, I believe Oceania (and Hawaiʻi) deserves "more than an attempt at mundane fact," and therefore when discussing and analyzing the moʻolelo of our kūpuna, unless there is a Hawaiian narrative or aesthetic term for describing a particular mode, these texts will all be analyzed as moʻolelo, and moʻolelo alone.[16]

MAP OF THE ARCHIVE

Because the nūpepa archive includes more than one hundred Hawaiian-language newspapers published between 1834 and our contemporary era, only through significant narrowing can any part of this archive be investigated in any meaningful way. Rather than claiming to luʻu into the entire moana of nūpepa, for this book I have chosen to submerge myself intimately in four mana of the moʻolelo of Hiʻiakaikapoliopele published in serial form: Kapihenui's 1861–62 mana of *He Moolelo no Hiiakaikapoliopele* from *Ka Hoku o ka Pakipika*, John E. Bush and Simeon Paʻaluhi's 1893 mana of *Ka Moolelo o Hiiakaikapoliopele* from *Ka Leo o ka Lahui*, Hoʻoulumāhiehie's 1906 mana of *Ka Moolelo o Hiiakaikapoliopele* from *Ka Naʻi Aupuni*, and Joseph Mokuʻōhai Poepoe's 1908–11 mana of *Ka Moolelo Kaao o Hiiakaikapoliopele* from *Kuokoa Home Rula*.[17] Written by five authors across five different newspapers, these mana of Hiʻiaka represent major contributions to the overall archive of this moʻolelo.

A community of Kanaka Maoli literary scholars agrees that these mana, and the rest of the moʻolelo o Hiʻiaka, were authored and published as part of a larger movement to perpetuate Kanaka Maoli moʻolelo and to serve as counterhegemonic narratives that remain valuable to Kānaka to this day. In turn, these moʻolelo represent a significant component of a larger "Hawaiian literary nationalism" that "provided a counter-narrative to the dominant discourses of settler colonialism, which imagined (constructed) Kanaka Maoli differently from how they imagined themselves."[18] Both McDougall and hoʻomanawanui focus on this lāhui-building function of moʻolelo, which serve as "pedagogical sites offering not only protocols for how the ʻāina and we as Kānaka Maoli should be treated and governed, but also models for various means of warranted resistance in the face of unjust rule."[19] McDougall further asserts that these moʻolelo "articulate a Kanaka Maoli theory of warranted resistance by emphasizing justice, mana wahine, and humor; and that this is precisely why these moʻolelo continue to be so popular, retold again and again within the nineteenth and twentieth centuries and now, in contemporary Kanaka Maoli literature by so many writers."[20] This counterhegemonic and lāhui-constructing function is something that all these mana of Hiʻiaka, to varying degrees, have in common.

As mana of a shared moʻolelo, these texts of Hiʻiaka also share a certain inexhaustibility. Hoʻoulumāhiehie describes Hiʻiaka as a sacred text, and as such Hiʻiaka is not just a narrative but a world-making narrative.[21] Because these authors and audiences were constantly articulating and maintaining the pilina between these mana, each Hiʻiaka mana, while distinct, is also representative of the whole. The authors insist on presenting their mana as complete in themselves but also as contributions to what could be called the larger meta moʻolelo of Hiʻiakaikapoliopele. Because of the frequency and the modes of its reproduction and republication and the analysis offered by the various authors of this moʻolelo regarding the significance of the ʻike found within it, I come to moʻolelo o Hiʻiaka in its entirety as arguably our largest interpretive manual, proving a rich and varied epistemology and hermeneutic for reading other moʻolelo and for understanding nā mea Hawaiʻi.

As part of the obligation to provide context, what follows is a brief account of the newspapers that published these mana of the moʻolelo, the known or presumed authors, and some of what makes each mana distinct.

Kapihenui, *He Moolelo no Hiiakaikapoliopele,* in *Ka Hoku o ka Pakipika,*
December 26, 1861–July 27, 1862

Founded by the ʻahahui hoʻopuka nūpepa and edited by G. W. Mila, *Ka Hoku o ka Pakipika* was the first Hawaiian-language newspaper to be published entirely by Native Hawaiians.[22] Between September 26, 1861, and May 14, 1863, its weekly installments expressed strong Hawaiian nationalistic sentiments.[23] This paper represents a significant moment in Hawaiian history when Kānaka were exercising their intellectual autonomy by publishing their own materials: "*Ka Hoku o ka Pakipika* demonstrated that Kānaka Maoli had mastered the technology of the haole (the printing press and the palapala), and then went further to show off their skills in both traditional literature and modern political writing."[24]

In addition to informing its readers about specific happenings in the Hawaiian Kingdom between 1861 and 1863, *Ka Hoku o ka Pakipika* clearly demonstrates to readers today how seriously our kūpuna believed in the political power of moʻolelo. The publishing of moʻolelo and kaʻao was a major activity of *Ka Hoku o ka Pakipika;* in fact, "Moolelo no Kawelo" fills all six columns of the front page of the very first issue. Through such choices and the general prominence of moʻolelo in this publication, "*Ka Hoku o ka Pakipika* reflected and communicated a specifically Kanaka national identity. This national identity was based in the ancient cosmology and the realm of the sacred that the haole did not share."[25]

It is also clear that neither the editors nor the readers thought these moʻolelo were being published purely as entertainment. In 1862, during the weekly publication of this mana of Hiʻiaka, the paper printed a letter from Kanaka Maoli scholar, writer, and intellectual Joseph Kānepuʻu criticizing *Ka Hoku o ka Pakipika* for shortening and condensing large sections of mele and oli.

Ua ike au, ua hakina ka moolelo o Hiiakaikapoliopele, ua hakina kona mau mele e pili ana i na "huli," a pehea la anei e loaa ai na koena i na hanauna hope o kakou, ke makemake lakou e nana, aole no e loaa, e hele ana kakou i ka nalowale, e hele ana o Kau ka makuahine o M. G. Kapihenui [ka mea kākau i kēia moʻolelo o Hiʻiakaikapoliopele] i ka nalowale. E makemake ana ka hanauna Hawaii o na la A. D. 1870, a me A. D. 1880, a me A. D. 1890, a me A. D. 1990.[26]

In his letter, Kānepuʻu calls the editors to publish the moʻolelo in its entirety. He argues that doing so is necessary because the next generations of kānaka, of the 1870s, 1880s, 1890s, and 1990s, are going to want and need this ʻike. By invoking us, the Kānaka of the future, and our anticipated desire and great need to read these moʻolelo in their entirety, without alteration, Kānepuʻu in this critique of the nūpepa displays what Silva calls "moʻokūʻauhau consciousness."[27] This is the political context that *He Moolelo no Hiiakaikapoliopele* appears within, just three months after the paper's founding, and because this moʻolelo was selected to be published in this first Hawaiian-run newspaper, it is one of the mana selected for further study in this book.

Finished in July 1862, and containing sixty-one thousand words— the equivalent of 112 single-spaced typescript pages—when compared to the twelve other mana of Hiʻiaka published in our nūpepa, Kapihenuiʻs is of medium length.[28] Because this moʻolelo ran for seven consecutive months in a weekly newspaper that appeared for less than two years, Hiʻiakaikapoliopele made up a substantial portion of the nūpepa's overall content.

John E. Bush and Simeon Paʻaluhi, *Ka Moolelo o Hiiakaikapoliopele,* in *Ka Leo o ka Lahui,* January 5, 1893–July 12, 1893

Founded in August 1889 by John E. Bush, *Ka Leo o ka Lahui* was a daily Hawaiian nationalist newspaper in the truest sense of the phrase.[29] Bush and his team of editors were unrelenting in their support of Hawaiian sovereignty and autonomy. *Ka Leo o ka Lahui* demonstrated this through its editorials and its political use of ʻōlelo Hawaiʻi. As haole began to usurp more power in the kingdom, *Ka Leo o ka Lahui* continued to insist on printing only in Hawaiian. Further, "after the overthrow of the Queen, it printed her protest (Caucasian establishment papers did not) and kept her appeals to the U.S. government before the public.[30] When Bush and other editors complained in print of injustices by the Provisional Government and Republic of Hawaiʻi, such as curbing press freedom, they were fined and jailed for 'conspiracy' and 'seditious libel.'"[31]

Ka Moolelo o Hiiakaikapoliopele began appearing in *Ka Leo o ka Lahui* on January 5, 1893, just twelve days before the overthrow of the Hawaiian Kingdom. Bush, the publisher and editor of *Ka Leo o ka Lahui,* and Paʻaluhi continued the daily installments of the moʻolelo until its completion in July 1893. In his introductory remarks ("Olelo Hoakaka") to the first installment, Bush wrote the following:

He nani no hoi a he nanea maoli no na moolelo a me na kaao o ka wa kahiko o ko kakou aina, a he mea no hoi a ka Hawaii e hiipoi ai e like me ka hialaai o kela me keia lahui i na moolelo, na kaao, a me na mele, o ko lakou aina hanau. O keia hauleule ana o na moolelo oia kekahi ouli a na kilo e nana ai me ka naau i piha i na manao hopohopo no ka mau ana o kona lahui maluna o ka aina o kona mau kupuna, no ka mea, e hoike mau ana ka moolelo io maoli o na aina i kakau ia na moʻolelo.[32]

Here Bush described the goodness of relaxing to enjoy the moʻolelo of our past, the moʻolelo that emerged from our ʻāina. To Bush, these moʻolelo were amazing feats of our kūpuna that were meant to be cherished (hiipoi). But these moʻolelo were more significant than pure entertainment. In fact, Bush saw the return to reading these moʻolelo as an important act for those looking to the future with great concern over whether their lāhui would continue to thrive in the lands of their kūpuna. Ultimately, Bush argues that it would be our moʻolelo that would hold and protect the truths of our ʻāina. The next day, Bush continued to contextualize his moʻolelo in another ʻōlelo "hoʻākāka":

Aole he loihi o ka noho ana o ka lahui a nalo aku mai ke ao, ke hoomaloka a hoopoina lakou i ka hiipoi ana me na ohohia nui i na moolelo a me na mele o na ano a pau, a kamailio mau imua o ka poe opio i kumu e mau ai na hooipo a me na liʻa ana o ka naau o ke kanaka i ke aloha aina ma muli o ka hooni ana o na moolelo a me na mele e pili ana i kona one hanau, na wahi pana, a me na hana kaulana a kona mau kupuna.[33]

Here Bush argues that should we lose sight and appreciation for our moʻolelo, it would not be long until we would disappear as a people. Bush knew, as we continue to know to this day, that our moʻolelo would be a foundation and inspiring guide for our people to perpetuate our practices of aloha ʻāina. When this moʻolelo is read closely and these introductions are taken seriously, it is clear that this moʻolelo was being printed with the hopes that it would facilitate a continued aloha and pilina between Kānaka and their aupuni and ʻāina. Thankfully we Kānaka have the opportunity to learn more about our pilina to our ʻāina today by taking seriously the need to luʻu deep into these narratives. This is what has allowed and inspired me to enter into moʻolelo o Hiʻiaka and recognize a pilina to major concerns about land and the lāhui at the time of publication, because these texts were indeed responses to those concerns.

In addition to this contextualizing provided before the first and second installments, the moʻolelo itself begins by declaring itself a narrative about governance and leadership. While other mana of the moʻolelo emphasize Pele's status as an aliʻi, Bush and Paʻaluhi use direct language to tie the Pele ʻohana to ideas of leading and governing. Rather than Pele and her ʻohana setting out on a journey to find Pele's kāne Waiolohia or to escape their elder sister Nāmakaokahaʻi, in Bush and Paʻaluhi's mana of the moʻolelo, the Pele ʻohana are on a "huakai nai aina," a journey to conquer and govern. In fact, in the first installment of the moʻolelo, we see that Pele's coming to Hawaiʻi was not actually welcomed by the kamaʻāina ("ua kuee aku na kamaaina") until after Pele and her ʻohana displayed such strength and virtue that they were eventually respected, and the protesting against them ceased ("hooki pu iho la ke kue o na kamaaina"). Bush and Paʻaluhi offered this moʻolelo in *Ka Leo o ka Lahui* to feed the imagination and pride of the lāhui in the creativity of their own ʻāina hānau.[34]

Like Kapihenui's mana, Bush and Paʻaluhi's Hiʻiaka mana is of medium length. It is the second shortest of the four mana of Hiʻiaka discussed in this book, totaling approximately seventy thousand words.[35] Much of Bush and Paʻaluhi's mana is also closely modeled upon Kapihenui's mana, sharing many distinctly similar passages, phrasings, and episodes not present in the other two mana of the moʻolelo.

Hoʻoulumāhiehie, *Ka Moolelo o Hiiaka-i-ka-poli-o-Pele*, in *Ka Naʻi Aupuni*, December 1, 1905–November 30, 1906

Founded in 1905, *Ka Naʻi Aupuni* was a Hawaiian-run newspaper edited and published by leaders of the Home Rule Party, Charles Kahiliaulani Notley and Joseph Mokuʻōhai Poepoe. This daily paper was created as a companion to the weekly issues published by *Kuokoa Home Rula* and was run by the same editors.[36] Particularly concerned with issues of self-determination for Kānaka Maoli in the face of annexation, the paper published a wide variety of moʻolelo and political editorials as well as national (Hawaiian) and international news. Much like *Ka Hoku o ka Pakipika, Ka Naʻi Aupuni* devoted the entire first page of its first issue to a moʻolelo: *Kamehameha I. Ka Na-i Aupuni o Hawaii.* This moʻolelo obviously served to contextualize and historicize the name choice for the nūpepa while also demonstrating something of the editors' political foundations. *Kamehameha I. Ka Na-i Aupuni o Hawaii* ran continuously from that opening issue until November 16, 1906.

When Poepoe began publishing *Ka Moolelo o Hiiakaikapoliopele* under the pseudonym Hoʻoulumāhiehie on June 1, 1906, both *Kamehameha: Ka Na-i Aupuni o Hawaii* and *Ka Moolelo Hawaii Kahiko* were also under way in *Ka Naʻi Aupuni.* All three moʻolelo have been attributed to either Hoʻoulumāhiehie or Poepoe himself. This particular mana of Hiʻiaka actually began in *Hawaii Aloha* but was reprinted and completed in its entirety in *Ka Naʻi Aupuni.*

> E hoomauia aku ana nohoi ka hoopukaia ana 'ku o na mahele o ka moolelo elike me ia i puka mua mai ai i kinohi ma keia nupepa; a e holo like ana keia mau mahele elua i kela ame keia puka ana o KA NAʻI Aupuni. A o ka poe i loaa ole na mahelehele mua o keia moolelo, elike me ia i puka ai ma ka buke moolelo HAWAII ALOHA, e loaa ana ia mau mahele ia lakou ma keia hoopuka hou ana.
>
>   MEA KAKAU, Moolelo o Hiiaka-i-ka-poli-o-Pele.[37]

In this "Olello [*sic*] Hoakaka" to the first installment, Hoʻoulumāhiehie explains that they will continue with the next *Hawaii Aloha* installment and reprint the previously published installments, so that the entire lehulehu could follow along.

This mana of Hiʻiaka represents an important shift in the way moʻolelo o Hiʻiaka were to be published. When Kapihenui's mana appeared decades earlier in *Ka Hoku o ka Pakipika,* Kānepuʻu raised concerns that mele and oli were being cut and removed for the sake of brevity, asking, "Pehea la anei e loaa ai na koena i na hanauna hope o kākou, ke makemake lakou e nana," How will the remainder be found by those who wish to see it?[38] Years later, the *Naʻi Aupuni* mana of Hiʻiaka seemed determined to answer that question by including all it could of the moʻolelo—from mele, to oli, to long stretches of fantastic narrative. The result was the largest known mana of Hiʻiaka in the nūpepa, totaling nearly 300,000 words.[39]

In addition to increasing the content, Hoʻoulumāhiehie also approaches the composition of this text as a scholar. He cites from and attributes parts of the moʻolelo to different bodies of ʻike. He responds directly to criticism coming from other papers. He even attempts to mediate a conversation about how Hiʻiaka might fit into another popular narrative of the time, the Bible. Time after time, Hoʻoulumāhiehie also speaks directly to his readers, reminding them that this moʻolelo has a far greater purpose than mere entertainment.[40] For example, in the latter half of the series, the great cultural and political relevance of this moʻolelo today is described:

> E ka makamaka heluhelu, ua ike na kilo, na kuhikuhi puuone, na makaula, na kahuna, ka papa huli-honua o kela ame keia mokupuni o Hawaii nei i ka wa kahiko i keia moolelo o Hiiakaikapoliopele, a ua lilo keia moolelo i papa huli honua, i papa wanana a i papa hoola kanaka na ia poe.
>
> A ma ia ano, ua lilo keia moolelo he moolelo kapu loa ma waena o lakou. Aohe e kaoo wale ia keia moolelo aia wale no a ku ka mohai. A iloko hoi o ke kapu e hanaia ai.[41]

Hoʻoulumāhiehie explains how this moʻolelo became an archive of ʻike for prophets, planners, and seers in every part of Hawaiʻi to turn to, that in fact it was a foundation for a great amount of ʻike. Because of the abundance of ʻike shared within the moʻolelo, this story became sacred to our people; it was a moʻolelo that encompassed all of Hawaiʻi, from where our sun rose, to where it set. Hoʻoulumāhiehie was a practicing scholar; he researched and wrote these moʻolelo with at least the same rigor as we research and write academic books today, often offering his readers multiple citations for the information he included in the narrative.

Joseph Mokuʻōhai Poepoe, *Ka Moolelo Kaao o Hiiakaikapoliopele,*
in *Kuokoa Home Rula,* January 10, 1908–January 20, 1911

Founded in 1901, *Kuokoa Home Rula* was a Hawaiian-run weekly newspaper also published and edited by Charles Kahiliaulani Notley and Joseph

Mokuʻōhai Poepoe.[42] The first six years of the paper have been lost to us, so we cannot say for sure what they included; however, we do know that *Kuokoa Home Rula* was a newspaper of the Independent Home Rule Party and therefore distributed information about the party and about Hawaiian politics and Kanaka Maoli rights. Like *Ka Naʻi Aupuni, Kuokoa Home Rula* published many moʻolelo, but it also included more editorials and news.[43]

Ka Moolelo Kaao o Hiiakaikapoliopele first appeared in *Kuokoa Home Rula* in January 1908 and continued in weekly installments until January 1911. It is the second-longest mana of Hiʻiaka, at just under 200,000 words and like the Hoʻoulumāhiehie mana includes well over two hundred chants.[44] In the moʻolelo's first installment, the author wrote:

> Mamuli o ke koiia ana mai o Mr. Charles Kahiliaulani ka Ona a Luna hooponopono nui o keia nūpepa, e na poe he lehulehu loa, e hoopuka hou ia ka Moolelo o Hiiakaikapoli-o-Pele ma keia hoomaka hou ana o ka makou nei pepa makua, KUOKOA HOME RULA, ke hookoia aku nei ia mau leo ikuwa o ko makou poe heluhelu; a, nolaila, ke hoopuka aku nei makou i ka omaka mua o ua moolelo hialaai nui ia nei, ma keia helu o ka makou pepa.[45]

In his introduction, Poepoe explained how this moʻolelo was requested heavily by the readers of that paper and that they were printing it to fulfill that request.

> A ma keia hoomaka hou ana o ka Hiiaka, e ikeia ana he mau aui ana i ko kekahi mau mahelehele i puka mua ai maloko o ka nupepa KA NAʻI AUPUNI ma ka M. H. 1906. O keia mau aui hou e ikeia ana ma keia puka ana mamuli o ka loaa hou ana mai i ko makou mea kakau moolelo, he Hiiaka i kapaia o ko Maui Hiiaka ia. O ka mahele Hiiaka mua i puka ai ma KA NAʻI AUPUNI, a i hoomaka ai nohoi ma keia pepa ma ia manawa no, ua oleloia o ko Hawaii Hiiaka ia. O ka mea i loaa ia makou, oia ka makou e hana aku nei no ka hooko ana i ka makemake o ko makou poe heluhelu.[46]

Poepoe continued by alerting his readers that they would see installments previously published in *Ka Naʻi Aupuni* alongside new materials that he had recently acquired. It is here we learn that these mana come not just from specific authors but also from specific places. Poepoe tells his readers that the mana they will read in *Kuokoa Home Rula* is in fact a mana from Maui, while the previously published Hiʻiaka were mana belonging to Hawaiʻi island.

E hoomaopopoia, eia na poe naauao o kakou iho nei a me ko na aina e, ke apu mai nei i na moolelo kahiko o Hawaii nei, [o ka] kakou poe opio [naauao? naaupo?] hoi, ke hoohemahema nui nei i keia kumu waiwai nui o ka aina oiwi. Aohe huli, aohe imi, aohe no he makemake ia mau mea. Aka, no makou iho, ke hoomau nei makou i keia hana no ka makemake [nui e?] hoouluia [?] a hoomauia aku ka ikeia ana o na moolelo a kaao kahiko o Hawaii nei i hiki ai ke malamaia e kakou, ka lahui.

Me ka mahalo,

JOSEPH M. POEPOE.

Mea Kakau Moolelo Hiiaka[47]

Poepoe finishes by cautioning his readers to be alert to how these moʻolelo have been misprinted and underresearched in the past. He encourages his readers to take seriously this task of perpetuating these moʻolelo together as a lāhui. For Poepoe, the cause of and need for these moʻolelo were paramount, and his kuleana to present the moʻolelo properly was not something to take lightly. As a lāhui, we continue to benefit from his intense sense of kuleana to this task.

MAPPING THE ʻUPENA OUR ARCHIVE CREATES

When closely read and interrogated, each of the four mana of Hiʻiaka outlined here provide an abundance of valuable ʻike relating to ʻāina, pilina, and ea. When we luʻu into these texts individually, we can see up close the hīpuʻu that bind the ʻupena of intimacies within each narrative. Read together as a collection, however, they offer not only a fuller picture of pilina within a wider context of moʻolelo but also an understanding of how these mana themselves, the authors who wrote them, and the Kānaka who read and cherish them are fashioning an ʻupena of pilina themselves. To read these texts is to (re)member the ʻupena of intimacies within the narrative of the text and to (re)member how these texts make

ʻupena of their own that we as readers are also bound into and within. As the authors of these mana of Hiʻiaka talk back to each other, or demonstrate the many aho this moʻolelo creates, or address their audiences directly, an ʻupena joins us, them, and their offered moʻolelo together as well. But for these Kanaka Maoli intellectuals of the nineteenth and twentieth centuries to create ʻupena of pilina, they had to be scholars in their own right. They were deeply familiar with a diversity of mana of Hiʻiaka and often cited them in their compositions. And when Hoʻoulumāhiehie published Hiʻiaka in 1905 and 1906, he celebrated that many mana of these moʻolelo had survived.

> Malia paha, he mahele pololei no keia ma ia kumu o ka moolelo Hiiaka, a o ka ka mea kakau no nae keia i hoike ae la i kana mahele. He mea maikai no ke hoolaha akea ia ae ka moolelo Hiiaka i kulike ole me ka ka mea kakau e hoopuka nei.[48]

To Hoʻoulumāhiehie, the diversity of these mana in their details and narratives was a strength of Kanaka Maoli moʻolelo, and it was a good thing that this paper could make public another mana that was not identical to past publications.

Perhaps this diversity of moʻolelo was important to Hoʻoulumāhiehie because he understood, like Bush and Paʻaluhi, how the fortunes of the moʻolelo over time must certainly have caused some portions of it to change and even to be disfigured:

> E like me ke ano mau o na moolelo o ka wa kahiko i haawi waha ia mai kahi hanauna mai a kekahi hanauna, ua lilo mau ke ano o ka moolelo, a ua hookikepakepa ia iho hoi i kela a me keia manawa o ka poe malama mookuauhau moolelo.[49]

Because Bush and Paʻaluhi recognized the almost certainty of components falling away during the evolution of a specific mana of a moʻolelo through its transition from generation to generation, they knew how necessary it was for all the various mana to be understood in pilina to each other. No single mana is the authoritative "original" from which the others deviate; rather, these narratives and mele are all part of the aho that together create an entire ʻupena to capture the weight of the ʻike this moʻolelo carries. Many passages within the archive that I have examined closely can demonstrate that these authors approached telling and retelling these moʻolelo with this understanding. The following passage, written by Hoʻoulumāhiehie, shows this quite clearly.

Aole ka mea kakau e haakoi ana, eia iaia ka nioniolo loa o ka moolelo o Hiiaka, a he ana-puu a he ana kee aku hoi ka kekaki. Aole pela. Aka, ke hoopuka nei ka mea kakau i keia "Aulani" o Hiiaka, e like me na mea i loaa mai iaia mai kekahi poe kakau moolelo kahiko mai a i paa hoi ka moolelo o Hiiaka, me ka manaolana e loaa ana no na hooponopono ia ana mai e ka poe makaukau maoli i kela moolelo waiwai nui o Hawaii kahiko.[50]

Here Hoʻoulumāhiehie makes it clear that he is not offering his mana of Hiʻiaka as the single true version of this moʻolelo. Instead he positions himself in relation to the other mana, saying this is the mana that he has been offered.

O kela a me keia mea mawaena o ko makou poe heluhelu, e manao ana he mau hoopololei a he mau hooponopono kana i makemake ai ma na wahi o keia moolelo i kulike ole me ka mea i loaa iaia, ua oluolu loa makou e hoouna pololei mai ua makamaka la i kana hooponopono i ka Lunahooponopono o keia Buke Moolelo, a e hoopuka ia aku no ia mau mea maloko o keia buke.

Ke makemake nui nei ka Ahahui Moolelo HAWAII LANI HONUA, e houluulu a e hoakoakoa pono i na moolelo, na mele, na kuauhau a mea ano nui o ke au kahiko o Hawaii nei, no ka pomaikai o ka hanauna opio o "Hawaii Aloha."[51]

In setting forth this mana, Hoʻoulumāhiehie hopes it will encourage those with an intimate pilina to this moʻolelo to correct any errors on his part. Here we learn that authors not only accepted critique and corrections but welcomed them because they understood that it would be through such critique that the moʻolelo would continue to grow and become known to more of the lāhui, which would certainly be for the best for the next generation of Kānaka Maoli.

With these greater intentions in mind, it became critical that Kanaka
Maoli intellectuals of the nineteenth and twentieth centuries did not
undermine each other in their publications. Rather than refute or contradict the work of previous mana, Hoʻoulumāhiehie and Poepoe would
gesture simply to the differences between their moʻolelo and others by
saying "ma kahi mahele o ka moolelo," allowing the reader to follow along
more easily and not be confused by diverging narratives. Such a gesture
did not claim that the other mana were wrong or incomplete. Gracious
in what they were contributing, even though the authors produced very
substantial mana of the moʻolelo, they were not attempting to contain the
entire Hiʻiaka tradition in one mana. The Kānaka who authored mana of
the moʻolelo in the twentieth century knew and indicated very clearly
that they were continuing a tradition and that therefore their work would
draw heavily from the work of previous scholars.

He mahele ano nui keia, a ke minamina nei ka mea kakau i ka loaa ole
ana iaia ona [o na] mahelehele Hiiaka i loaa i kahi poe paanaau, a i ole, e
paa nei paha he mau buke kakaulima o keia moolelo, mai ko lakou mau
kupuna a poe makua mai hoi.

O ka mea i loaa i ka mea kakau i keia wa, mailoko mai no ia o ekolu
mau mahele moolelo Hiiaka i paa i ke kakauia.[52]

It took a certain kind of humility to compose these moʻolelo in the twentieth century—knowing and honoring what ʻike one had yet realizing
that additional ʻike must be found elsewhere. Poepoe spoke directly to
this, recognizing his own shortcoming and even being saddened that
he didn't possess all the ʻike known to those who have memorized the
moʻolelo. But Poepoe acknowledges that he did not learn this moʻolelo
in the way his kūpuna once did, through sharing orally and through
memorization, so he reminds his audience that his latest version of the
moʻolelo was also assembled in part from the three previously published
mana of Hiʻiaka. It is this humility, which Poepoe and the other authors
display in their mana, that allows them not only to coexist but to thrive
in pilina with each other.

It is important, however, to recognize that although difference and even
disagreement could be welcomed, any lack of rigor was discouraged and

publicly exposed. For example, in December 1905, Hoʻoulumāhiehie calls out N. B. Emerson, the translator of Davida Malo's book *Hawaiian Antiquities*, for failing to represent the Hawaiian materials properly, explaining that "ke hoike nei ka mea kakau i keia manao i mea e alakai hewa ole ia ai ka noonoo o na Hawaii opio, ma keia hope aku, i ko lakou heluhelu ana i keia buke moolelo Hawaii a Davida Malo i unuhiia ai ma ka olelo Beretania."[53] Hoʻoulumāhiehie does this to ensure that no readers, and especially young ones, are misled or confused by the translator's erroneous alteration of the moʻolelo.

In the next issue, published on December 12, 1905, Hoʻoulumāhiehie says bluntly that he has no idea who the translator's informant is— "aole i maopopo owai la nei J. K. K. a ua mea unuhi nei e kuhikuhi nei"— perhaps as a way to call out a failure on Emerson's part to reach out to the proper sources. Such a lack of pilina and intimacy to other writers might also point to a lack of authority and accountability in telling these moʻolelo. Here we see how pilina to the literary community and the moʻolelo itself is significant to the overall tradition of this epic. In this case, hoʻopāpā was also an important feature of these moʻolelo, for it can help distinguish between the diversity of ʻike in this tradition and indicate when some folks were simply stepping out of bounds.

BEYOND HIʻIAKA

Moʻolelo o Hiʻiaka were not being retold in a vacuum. In addition to drawing out the aho between Hiʻiaka mana, Kanaka Maoli authors and intellectuals of the nineteenth and twentieth centuries were also recognizing the pilina between Hiʻiaka and other moʻolelo in the literary genealogy. One moʻolelo often cited in Poepoe's and Hoʻoulumāhiehie's mana was *Ka Moolelo o Kuapakaa*, also known as *Ka Ipu Makani o Laamaomao*. The pilina between these two moʻolelo makes sense, given the role makani (winds) play in both narratives, so it is hardly surprising when Hoʻoulumāhiehie points out, "Ua like a ua like ole paha kekahi mau makani me ko ka mea i ikeia ma ka moolelo o Kuapakaa," These makani are perhaps similar to that of the makani in Kuapakaa. As a scholar, Hoʻoulumāhiehie also makes sure to cite books (perhaps unpublished) by J. W. Naihe (Kohala) and D. K. Waialeale as sources of his makani. Hoʻoulumāhiehie includes these makani in his Hiʻiaka specifically because "he mahele hoi keia i ike ole ia ma na moolelo o Hiiaka i hoolahaia mamua aku nei," they have not yet appeared in other mana of this moʻolelo.[54]

It is because these makani and inoa ʻāina have not yet been published in moʻolelo o Hiʻiaka that Hoʻoulumāhiehie asks the patience of his readers as he includes them in this mana. For Hoʻoulumāhiehie this task cannot be avoided—"ʻaole hiki i ka mea kakau ke alo ae"—because he sees it as his kuleana to publish every bit of the moʻolelo he has knowledge of, "no ka pomaikai o ka hanauna hou," for the benefit of the next generation of Kānaka.[55] On April 24, 1908, we learn that the pilina between the moʻolelo of Kūapākaʻa and Hiʻiaka, and the preservation of these makani, are so significant that Poepoe decided to publish these passages in *Kuokoa Home Rula* in almost identical fashion to what was published two years earlier in *Ka Naʻi Aupuni*.[56]

It wasn't just Kūapākaʻa who provided additional material and evidence for the significance of moʻolelo o Hiʻiaka. Poepoe and Hoʻoulumāhiehie were constantly drawing out the aho between moʻolelo o Hiʻiaka and other mele and moʻolelo koʻihonua. In some places, Poepoe relied on mele to demonstrate the validity of a part of his mele or to point out the location of a long-forgotten homeland, Hapakuela. And in others, he effortlessly wove together the moʻokūʻauhau in Hiʻiaka with the mele koʻihonua of famed chiefs. In one passage, Hoʻoulumāhiehie seamlessly substantiates his moʻokūʻauhau of Haumea in Hiʻiakaikapoliopele by following the aho of his ʻupena out in three distinct but important directions. First, Hoʻoulumāhiehie points out that this genealogy of Haumea can be found in the mele koʻihonua of both the Oʻahu chief, Kūaliʻi, and the Kauaʻi chief, Kaumualiʻi.[57] Hoʻoulumāhiehie also uses this as an opportunity to show how his moʻokūʻauhau of Haumea offers an alternative to a famed Hawaiian genealogy, the Kumulipo.[58] It is significant that these moʻolelo could be read in relationship to each other, sometimes because they aligned and sometimes because they differed. This great diversity of ʻike adds to the overall wealth of moʻolelo.

Of the authors studied in this book, Poepoe has the most citations in his mana of Hiʻiaka. Often, he included mele or koʻihonua from beyond the Hiʻiaka archive to substantiate a part of his narrative. For example, when mapping out the many foundations of Kīlauea and describing the final papakū, Loloimehani, Poepoe includes a passage from the mele ko'ihonua "Wela ka Lani, o Owe."[59] In continuing this practice of citing mele and ko'ihonua, Poepoe was strengthening and (re)membering the aho between each of the mo'olelo as well as working to "hooiaio" his own mo'olelo.[60] Poepoe revealed quite clearly in his publication of Hi'iaka that he was not only a scholar but also a skilled aho composer, and his deeply intentional practice of citation has proved to be incredibly meaningful when working toward understanding the relationships among distinct historic mo'olelo today. Ultimately, we also learn a great deal about where 'ike stems from and that our kūpuna understood that mele provided an incredible archive of evidence that should and can be relied upon for historical information.

Breaking the Fourth Wall, or Pilina between Author and Audience

Much of the work described in this chapter was made visible by authors speaking directly to their readers. Authors of Hi'iaka and other mo'olelo broke the "fourth wall" frequently in their narratives—sometimes to provide a citation or evidence for the validity of their particular telling; sometimes to ho'opāpā with another scholar or author; other times to clarify, offer a transition, or even call special attention to a significant moment in the narrative.[61] In *Voices of Fire*, ho'omanawanui calls these moments "authorial asides" and points out how they were employed in mo'olelo o Hi'iaka as "strong storytelling strategies" that pointed back to the literary techniques embedded in Hawaiian literature's long and rich life as an oral tradition.[62] In *The Power of the Steel-Tipped Pen*, Silva argues that these asides also demonstrate "mo'okū'auhau consciousness," in that authors such as Poepoe were persistent in ensuring that current and subsequent generations of Kānaka Maoli would recognize the importance of certain information.[63]

I want to consider this literary technique in terms of its performativity and managing a particular intimacy and pilina between author and readers. In theater, when actors speak directly to their audience, they are breaking that imaginary solid boundary separating the performers and their world from the audience members and theirs. This is much the same for our Kanaka Maoli authors and audiences of the nineteenth and twentieth centuries. When Poepoe, Ho'oulumāhiehie, Bush and Pa'aluhi, and even Kapihenui address the readers directly, often demanding their attention, they are demonstrating how such a boundary between writer and reader is not only unnecessary but also damaging to the writer's overall cause as a haʻi moʻolelo. In this sense, Kanaka use of this technique differs from that of nineteenth-century European authors because our intellectual ancestors were calling attention to an actual pilina and moʻokūʻauhau shared with their readership. This technique also invokes a sense of orality, as breaking the fourth wall in theater and other performance arts actually calls attention to the fact of shared space. By addressing the readers, these authors are not simply offering footnotes of information to follow up on at another time but taking a breath within the overall narrative to share directly and personally ʻike that enriches the understanding of their mana of Hiʻiaka within the larger ʻupena of Kanaka Maoli ʻike and moʻolelo. Finally, such asides call attention to the overall impact of the ʻupena of Kanaka Maoli moʻolelo as well as affirm the great aloha shared between authors and their audiences.

The author often breaks the fourth wall to ensure that readers follow the most significant course in a narrative that offers many different paths. But such moments are more than just aids for readers. Going beyond a rhetorical conceit, the authors' breaking down the fourth wall between themselves, the moʻolelo, and their lāhui is predicated on an actual and sincere intimacy between writer and reader. These readers are more than just an audience. They are hoa, hoa aloha heluhelu, makamaka, and, one day, moʻopuna of the authors themselves. And by addressing readers as hoa, these authors displayed and (re)membered the importance of the role the reader and companion would play in continuing the process of binding and securing these moʻolelo within our ʻupena of literature.[64] Such asides often began with a direct and intimate address—"e kuu makamaka heluhelu," "e ka hoa heluhelu," or "e kuu hoaʻloha"—followed by whatever essential information or citation the author wants to provide. Examples of this technique are found frequently in Poepoe's and Hoʻoulumāhiehie's mana of the moʻolelo, and to a lesser extent within Kapihenui's and Bush and Paʻaluhi's versions.

We learn through these addresses that the audiences are no strangers to the author; in fact, sharing this moʻolelo affirms and maintains a particular intimacy between the writer and the public. Pilina can be affirmed through the great care a writer takes to represent these moʻolelo properly. As we will see, these authors teach us to cherish the pilina displayed between Hiʻiaka and her contemporaries. But direct address compellingly reminds us that we should also pay serious attention to the pilina between nineteenth- and twentieth-century Kānaka as they persevered in collecting, telling, and cherishing their moʻolelo—for themselves, and for future generations.

ʻUPENA AS INTERGENERATIONAL MEMORY

As we look in on these moʻolelo more than a century later, we are not just witnessing their ʻupena as they unfold before us through the authors' composition and from our reading of these texts. In fact, we are the intended and rightful inheritors and kiaʻi of these ʻupena. Our kūpuna created these aho with the hope that they would someday draw us close to our kūpuna—to participate within this literary movement of recovery and (re)membering but, in the process, also to better understand our history and language, which they feared would disappear. We know this because the authors and intellectuals responsible for publishing these moʻolelo wrote explicitly about the purpose of taking on these laborious endeavors, speaking not only directly to their contemporaries but to and about us as well.

At the beginning of this chapter, we encountered Kānepuʻu's address to editors of *Ka Hoku o ka Pakipika*. He insisted that the moʻolelo be published in their entirety because he was dedicated to working intentionally and tirelessly not only for his contemporaries but for the next generation, and for our current generations of Kānaka. As a Kanaka Maoli wahine born in May 1990, it is not at all lost on me that Kānepuʻu's encouragement to his intellectual peers resulted in gifts delivered to the many Kānaka who lived after him, and in fact to me personally. And in offering this gift to us, in this way, he reminds us that we too must take on this work with integrity and aloha, and consider how our pilina to these moʻolelo will ultimately connect us to Kānaka of 2031, 2041, 2051, and 2151. Our moʻopuna will know and build upon our great moʻolelo only if we too recognize that our kūpuna were securing the aho to bind us in pilina to these moʻolelo and to them. Through our pilina, we can recognize and ʻauamo the kuleana of telling these moʻolelo today.

Kānepuʻu was not alone in being invested in passing on the legacy of these moʻolelo into the future. Texts authored by Hoʻoulumāhiehie and Poepoe articulated frequently a deep investment in preserving these moʻolelo properly for the next generation of Kanaka ʻōpio. In Hoʻoulu-māhiehie's moʻolelo, he spoke of the necessity of telling these moʻolelo to ensure the "pomaikai o ka hanauna hou o Hawaii nei ma keia hope aku," the good fortune of the next generation of Kānaka of Hawaiʻi.[65] As a public intellectual, Poepoe was so concerned for the future of Hawaiʻi that he helped found a literary organization, Ahahui Moolelo Hawaii Lani Honua, that would collect and bring together the many moʻolelo, mele, and genealogies for the prosperity of the next generations of Hawaiʻi.[66] According to Hoʻoulumāhiehie, this ʻahahui planned to publish a collection of the many great genealogies of Hawaiʻi, also for the benefit of the next generation of young Kānaka.[67]

Through their tireless dedication, these scholars, authors, and storytellers mapped an ʻupena of their own, one that they hoped we would continue to tend, protect, and cherish, even to this day. Our lives today would perhaps be completely unrecognizable to these ancestors of ours, just as parts of their lives seem often inconceivable to us. And yet our kūpuna prophesized that these moʻolelo would continue to be relevant, would continue to guide us in our understanding of ourselves and of our beloved ʻāina. They believed that if they carefully prepared an ʻupena that could hold our moʻolelo and sustain the pilina between us all, we would be properly cared for. Our kūpuna did the hard work to make this ʻupena possible. To return to this ʻupena, to hold the aho they so intentionally and carefully fashioned, to read their words and hold them close in the language they were raised to think, speak, and dream in, is to (re)member the pilina between ourselves and our kūpuna. It is to practice a kinship so many violences have tried to destroy. It is to do the undoing of dismembering, it is to create, it is to (re)member, and it is a privilege.

As we prepare to engage seriously with the pilina between Hiʻiaka and her intimates, we must honor, give aloha, and care for the pilina between ourselves and our kūpuna, a pilina that they declared time and time again they wished for us to know and maintain.

Mōku

For My Favorite Spring, "Puna" Leonetta Keolaokalani Kinard

This moʻolelo was written during the course of drafting the dissertation from which this book emerged. When it was written, Puna was living among us. However, early in the morning the day after my dissertation defense in May 2018, Puna joined the rest of our kūpuna who have passed into the realm of pō. Out of respect for Puna, and this moʻolelo that was instrumental to my thinking and finishing of the original dissertation, I have chosen to keep the moʻolelo as written. It is my hope that this moʻolelo not only offers greater insight into what these stories have to offer us but also immortalizes Puna in her ninety-two-year-old wisdom, and celebrates the infinite strength she offered me, this project, and therefore our lāhui as well. Ke aloha nō e kuʻu kupuna.

Puna is a *moku* in the southeast corner of Hawaiʻi island and home to at least twenty-seven smaller ahupuaʻa, including Keaʻau, Kapoho, and Keahialaka. Puna is also the home of Pele and Hiʻiaka, where Kīlauea lives and burns. When puna comes from the word *kupuna*, it can serve as an affectionate name for our grandparents and elders. But puna can also be a spring, where water emerges from the ʻāina to feed her people.

In my life, Puna has been all this and more. She is the only living wahine in my ʻohana from my grandparents' hanauna. Puna is ninety-two years young and fierce, but she sometimes forgets things—where she is, how old she is. Sometimes she forgets us: her daughter, grandchildren, nieces, and nephews. But there are a handful of things that Puna always holds safe in the center of her sacred spring.

A few years ago, Puna took a fall at home and ended up in Kuakini Hospital. The doctors tried to ask her a set of standard questions to assess her neurological health. They asked her about the date, their current location, her name, the woman standing next to her (her daughter). She struggled with these questions. But the answers to certain questions she knew like a prayer. If you ask Puna what her nationality is, she will tell you, for herself, that she is Hawaiian. And although most days she struggles to remember that she has lived in Pāoa for the past twenty years, she is always quick to remind us that she is a kamaʻāina of Hilo.

This is a major cause of conflict for Puna. Many times, she struggles with knowing she is not "home." She wants to be back in Hilo, under the ua Kanilehua and in the Moani winds. When I sit alone with Puna in her living room, she will ask me, again and again, "Are we in Hilo?" I say, "No, Aunty, we are in your home in Pāoa." When this upsets her, I consider lying, but instead I comfort her with music. I find an old tape of my father singing "Ua Like nō a Like" and press play. Then, for the next hour, we bounce back and forth the names of all the Hawaiʻi island mele and musicians that we can recall. This is our favorite game. And Puna always wins.

Puna longs so much for an island where she hasn't lived for decades that she often packs a bag when no one is looking, and injures herself trying to carry her belongings to the door. This endless cycle of trying to leave is both devastating and exhausting for our ʻohana, and especially for her daughter Leolinda. But perhaps even worse than our sadness about her physical and emotional pain is the trauma of knowing that Puna is not trying to leave us but trying to return to herself: her ʻāina, her home, her Hilo.

I think about what this means, to feel so displaced from your one hānau, while in a perfectly suitable home that you have filled with your aloha and ʻohana for more than two decades. I think about that primal insistence to return to the sands of our birth. I think about how Nāwahī, the editor of *Ke Aloha Aina*, defined aloha ʻāina as a constant magnetic pull toward one's place that cannot be weakened or deterred. I think about Puna, being pulled, pulled, pulled home, always and every day. I think about how Puna steps outside herself to try to go home, and how much aloha she must have for her ʻāina. And then I think about another kupuna of mine, a kupuna I share with Puna.

Hiʻiakaikapoliopele.

Wahi a ka moʻolelo, during her journey across the Pae ʻĀina, Hiʻiaka comes to Punahoa with her aikāne Wahineʻōmaʻo and attendant Pāʻūopalaʻā. The people of Punahoa are suspicious of these newcomers, so Hiʻiaka lies to the aliʻi, saying that her name is Keahialaka and that she is from Puna. In a sense, Hiʻiaka is saying, I am Puna from Puna. Her tie to place, unlike her name, cannot be severed or cast aside—much like Punaʻs pilina to Hilo cannot be forgotten. What matters most to Hiʻiaka here is to maintain her pilina to her ʻāina kulāiwi, Puna. To do so, she takes on an inoa of her place and wears it like a genealogy. When Hiʻiaka finally gets to Kauaʻi and retrieves Lohiʻau, she then turns right around and fights tirelessly to return to her home, even though home after home is offered to her along the way.

Hiʻiaka survives the trip home and lives out her days in the bosom of Kīlauea, in her home moku of Puna. My Puna will live the rest of her days here on my one hānau, Oʻahu, and I know this will trouble her until the day she is no longer with us on this honua.

But something can be cherished here, something celebrated about our shared pilina and aloha for our place, and for our ʻāina. I know that even after profound trauma of my body and mind, my pilina to my kūpuna, through my ʻāina, will remain. And if someday I find myself forgetting, confused and lost in obscure corners of my memory, I hope I am lucky enough to retain the kind of ʻohana that Puna has cultivated in her poli: a punahele to sing me back home; a moʻopuna to share all the melodies of Hilo and to shower me in the Kanilehua; an ʻohana that will always let me sing, out loud, about what I long for. Home.

When Puna seems lost to herself and to us, we bring out our guitars and play the old Hilo songs. "ʻO ʻoe nō kaʻu i ʻupu ai," she sings, and we know exactly what she means.

CHAPTER THREE

The Ea of Pilina and ʻĀina

◆◆◆

In the past thirty years, Kanaka Maoli scholars have begun to lay the groundwork for unpacking the colonial structures that have plagued Hawaiʻi since 1778. Historians, geographers, political scientists, literary scholars, legal scholars, anthropologists, voyagers, feminist theorists, linguists, and others have all waded into the complicated present and the history of the collision between Hawaiʻi and the West, and its social, political, environmental, and economic effects on Hawaiʻi and Kānaka Maoli. What has resulted from this multidecade movement to ʻimi ʻike is a canon of Kanaka Maoli texts challenging the status quo of largely white historiography that has plagued Hawaiʻi since the landing of James Cook in the eighteenth century.

Kanaka Maoli scholars have demonstrated the excellence of our kūpuna by conducting rigorous research into the civilization that was formed, maintained, and then transformed over many centuries, here in the poli of our moananui ākea. Because of the work of our intellectual kūpuna, Kanaka Maoli scholars today can build our scholarship upon a firm foundation of research on Kanaka Maoli land tenure, legal structures, literature, political engagement, science, and resource management that has developed as part of the ongoing process of sustaining and protecting an ongoing resurgence of cultural practices, and of waging a fight to regain political, economic, intellectual, and social sovereignty. The steady accumulation of original research by Kānaka Maoli has resulted in a thorough theorizing of the historical and ongoing occupation of Hawaiʻi and a highly informed critique of the material effects of settler colonialism. What my intellectual ancestors have given me are the means to honor my pilina to them through this moʻokūʻauhau. My task here and now is to take pilina and relationality seriously, as I seek to join this growing genealogy of Kanaka Maoli intellectuals.

One of the major shaping forces in this resurgence of Kanaka Maoli intellectualism is the essential nature of aloha ʻāina to all things Hawaiian. This book displays its importance by zeroing in on how aloha ʻāina assumes a particular ethic of pilina and relationality. What does it mean, physically and emotionally, to aloha our ʻāina? As I asked in "Gathering Our Stories of Belonging," what would emerge if we took aloha seriously, reaching beyond plastic consumerism, beyond the biblical imagination, beyond imposed legal definitions, to understand how aloha is transformative kinship beyond anything we might currently imagine? In short, what might happen, what might we learn, if we try to understand the ea of pilina?

To begin to construct my own papakū for understanding Kanaka Maoli pilina, I start from the premise that understanding aloha ʻāina requires understanding aloha first. For the purposes of this book, I first consider aloha as verb, as action, as a reciprocal pilina between many bodies. Subsequently, I engage with and further articulate the importance of aloha ʻāina at the nexus of aloha as action within our moʻolelo.

A discussion of aloha is truly a discussion about pilina. When we take aloha seriously, we honor our pilina to each other and all our relations. Often people think of relationships as ecosystems existing between two people at a time. In a Kanaka Maoli context, I have come to understand aloha and the pilina it produces as ʻupena of intimacy. Within many moʻolelo, this idea can be recognized in how siblings, or those in other intimate relationships, take on kāne or wahine lovers as communal.

In Bush and Paʻaluhi's *Ka Moolelo o Hiiakaikapoliopele*, Lohiʻau is often referred to as "kela kane a kakou" (that kāne of ours) and Hōpoe is often referred to as "ko kaua aikane" (our aikāne). When bound and accountable to another, we are therefore also bound and accountable to each other's intimacies and accountabilities. This expands exponentially the possibilities of pleasure and responsibility. Such relationships teach us that reciprocity and accountability matter and that intimacy is many bodied and overflowing. This is the ea of pilina.

If relationships are about intimacies and kuleana, then this book is also about understanding the many forms intimacy can take and how certain relationships and intimacy are pursued, established, practiced, and maintained. Some pilina are pursued through sex, others through sharing a sunrise, and some even through the simple yet important act of sharing names. The abundant forms of Kanaka Maoli pilina stand in direct contrast to the singular presentation of heteronormativity. In the face of a colonial project that works toward the elimination of certain forms of intimacy, it is important that my project take intimacy seriously, in its many varied and shape-shifting forms.

This project must therefore prioritize relationships that stand as alternatives to heteropatriarchal articulations of intimacy. A major strategy of this book is to examine a wide enough range of Kanaka Maoli intimacies to articulate a theory of pilina. By rooting this theorizing within an archive that articulates many nonheteropatriarchal relationships, this project will additionally add nuance to emerging Indigenous queer theories already coming to question any understanding of Kanaka Maoli desire and intimacy organized through straight/queer binaries. Importantly, when Kānaka choose to uphold and share the reciprocal kuleana of a particular pilina, they do so beyond the bounds of a fixed identity. As an example, Hiʻiaka has many wāhine and kāne as intimate companions and lovers, but she cannot be reduced into a contemporary identity within our spectrum of sexualities. Hiʻiaka is many things: an akua, a wahine, a kupuna, a Kanaka Maoli; but she is not queer. And although Hiʻiaka cannot be affixed to a straight or queer identity, that certainly doesn't mean that she cannot be seen and cherished as an affirmative example and place of refuge for contemporary queer Kānaka today. I say this as someone who knows personally how impactful Hiʻiaka has been to my own becoming as a wahine who fiercely loves other wāhine. Hiʻiaka has allowed me to untangle myself from heteropatriarchal expectations and articulations of gender and sexuality. Therefore, throughout this book I would like to challenge us to move beyond the desire to fit Hiʻiaka into our contemporary worldview of relationships and identities and rather to see the many ways Hiʻiaka allows us to fit into her world of pilina and aloha. Hiʻiaka is a site of knowledge and a puʻuhonua for all people who want to understand and practice aloha pleasurably and ethically.

we don't need to fit Hiʻiaka
into our boxes

We must take seriously the ways that Hiʻiaka and her ʻohana are giving us examples of how to practice these pilina with each other and our ʻāina. In doing so, we return home, and in that returning we are empowered to create futures that are not bound to the assumptions and violences of heteropatriarchy. This work is deeply tied to a growing field of Indigenous queer theory that has already begun to mark the connections between the policing and legislation of intimacy and the administration and control of Indigenous land and resources.

In researching and writing about relationships, I have paid special attention to the term *aikāne* because it directs us toward intimacies beyond the heteropatriarchal standard we have been trained to recognize and practice. However, this book is not purely a meditation on aikāne relationships. Instead, aikāne is an opportunity to arrive at and discuss other nonheteropatriarchal and nonmonogamous relationships that lie outside our "civility." Aikāne offers a first step into a world unmolested by toxic monogamy and heteropatriarchy. Beginning with aikāne and gathering from our moʻolelo also allows me to analyze Kanaka Maoli pilina lying perhaps beyond a legalistic imagination but within an elaborate living framework that prioritizes logics of kapu, kuleana, and pleasure. Even a cursory glance into Kanaka Maoli moʻolelo reveals that our kūpuna not only tolerated these modes of intimacy; they also imagined, embodied, and celebrated them. This book is part of my contribution to that continued embodiment and celebration.

MAPPING HIʻIAKA'S ʻUPENA OF PILINA

In the next chapter, I discuss moʻolelo o Hiʻiaka in terms of cartography, unpacking how the moʻolelo itself has an intimate pilina to place, displayed through the mapping of the moʻolelo across our ʻāina. In this chapter, I explore how moʻolelo o Hiʻiaka constitute an archive of intimacy and pilina among Kānaka. Among the qualities that make this archive significant is the publishing of mana of the moʻolelo over time. Extensive and detailed research by such Pele scholars as John Charlot and kuʻualoha hoʻomanawanui reveals that moʻolelo o Hiʻiaka appeared at least thirteen times in serial form within our nūpepa between 1861 and 1928.[1] That these moʻolelo reappeared repeatedly, at great length and with significant overlap and cross-referencing for nearly seventy years represents more than a long-standing appreciation and aloha for this particular narrative. It also suggests that Kānaka found this moʻolelo deeply relevant to a variety of contemporary issues over a substantial period of time.

Scholars such as Brandy Nālani McDougall, kuʻualoha hoʻomanawanui, Noelani Arista, Noenoe Silva, and others have written extensively about how our moʻolelo, mele, and other narratives served as a forum within our nūpepa and other publications for analysis, commentary, and guidance regarding contemporary issues. From the publishing and translating of the *Kumulipo* during the reigns of Kalākaua and Liliʻuokalani as a means for asserting not only their mana to rule but also the mana of the aupuni of Hawaiʻi in the face of great international and internal pressure and encroachment, to the republishing of the moʻolelo o Hiʻiaka in 1893, at the moment of the illegal overthrow and eventual American occupation of our kingdom, my intellectual kuaʻana have shown how moʻolelo such as these have offered counterhegemonic narratives in the face of a multitude of domestic and international challenges.[2] Our kūpuna selected certain moʻolelo deliberately for publication—and the history of moʻolelo o Hiʻiaka is a prime example. Thirteen times over nearly seventy years—this history speaks to the significance and value of this moʻolelo to our kūpuna. And its relevance continues 150 years later, providing lessons and guidance for our lives in contemporary Hawaiʻi.

Among many other things, this archive provides detailed accounts of pilina and their fortunes in the face of multiple waves of foreign influence and transformation in Hawaiʻi. Because moʻolelo o Hiʻiaka are about ʻohana, migration, and aloha among Kānaka, akua, and each other, many distinct kinds of pilina appear throughout its narrative. Throughout my study of this moʻolelo, the following pilina rose to the foreground: aikāne, kāne/wahine, hoʻāo, kōkoʻolua, kaikoʻeke, kaikuaʻana/kaikaina, kupuna/moʻopuna, hoa paio, hoa hoʻopaʻapaʻa, pōkiʻi, haku, akua, hoahānau, and kaikunāne/kaikuahine. While the ʻupena of every one of these pilina connect the Kānaka sharing it to their ʻāina, other terms specifically identify pilina that Kānaka have to land and with others of that place: kamaʻāina, kupa ʻāina, malihini, kiaʻi, aliʻi, and akua. Each of these pilina can be further nuanced by an intentional use of Hawaiian pronouns to signify who and how Kānaka are bound in a particular ʻupena. Through my own research, I have learned that many pilina ordinarily read within a Western framework as exclusively between two people often actually refer to intimacies shared between several siblings, lovers, and companions. The ʻupena of pilina further takes for granted that no matter how seemingly disconnected two or more Kānaka might be, no matter how many hīpuʻu (or degrees of separation) lie between them, no matter how far and wide the ʻupena must be cast to touch them all, when pulled tight in the fist of the lawaiʻa, all these hīpuʻu are drawn and bound close together. As a result, if any hīpuʻu or knot is severed, weakened, or somehow compromised, the entire ʻupena threatens to unravel.

In this chapter, I discuss some of these diverse relational terms and provide examples that show how such relations are distinctly different from their customary English and Western translations, largely because of how Kānaka recognized kuleana and inclusion within these intimacies. An important relational framework that grounds this analysis is the way that possessives in ʻōlelo Hawaiʻi are marked in two specific classes, kinoʻō (o-class) and kinoʻā (a-class). The ways these classes impact our understanding of our relationships to each other and our worlds could take up the subject of whole studies. For the sake of this book, it is important for the reader to know that o-class possessives are one's birthright, or, in other words, relationships and possessions that the subject has no choice in. Meanwhile, a-class possessives are the subject's "achievements"; that is, they require choice on the part of the subject.[3] For the most part, the pilina of ʻohana fall under kinoʻō, and the pilina discussed later relating to romantic collectives are kinoʻā. It is also important to note that there are some exceptions to these rules, but I will leave the analysis of those exceptions and specificities to scholars more equipped in Hawaiian syntax and linguistics.

Through an analysis of these pilina as encountered and enacted in the moʻolelo of Hiʻiaka and in the greater history of our people, I also offer my thoughts on the relevance of these pilina to Kānaka today, as we seek to dismantle such structures of oppression as patriarchy and heterosexism. Finally, by drawing on theory addressing the politics of translation, I offer an additional layer of analysis that addresses how translation often re-creates and reinforces such structures as patriarchy, heterosexism, and white supremacy, and how in turn our moʻolelo can assist us in deconstructing these imposed forces.

Since a primary goal of this research is to disengage from the patriarchy written and translated over our pilina, I will focus on the terms most significantly appropriated by patriarchy—those related to ʻohana (see Figure 1). Because moʻolelo o Hiʻiaka begin with the migration of the Pele ʻohana from Kahiki or Hapakuela to Hawaiʻi i ka wā kahiko, the first pilina we encounter are genealogical. When Pele begins her journey to Hawaiʻi, she leaves behind her makuahine and makuakāne.[4] In some versions, this is because she is driven out of Kahiki by her kaikuaʻana Nāmakaokahaʻi. In others, Pele is on a huakaʻi ʻimi kāne (man-seeking journey) to find her beloved kāne snatched away by her kaikaina, Pelekumukalani.[5] Depending on the mana, Pele, as the hānau mua and hiapo of her ʻohana, is also their aliʻi and travels with various kaikunāne and kaikaina who are subject to her leadership. The one kaikaina who travels to Hawaiʻi in every mana of the moʻolelo is the pōkiʻi punahele, Hiʻiakaikapoliopele. Although anywhere from eight to forty other Hiʻiaka sisters appear in the different mana of Hiʻiaka, as the pōkiʻi, Hiʻiakaikapoliopele is not only the youngest of the Pele ʻohana but also the punahele. While the other Hiʻiaka sisters travel on the waʻa of their kaikunāne, Kamohoaliʻi, to Hawaiʻi, Hiʻiakaikapoliopele is carried in an egg form in the bosom of her aliʻi and kaikuaʻana, Pele. This particularly intimate pilina between Hiʻiaka and Pele accounts for the name Hiʻiakaikapoliopele (Hiʻiaka in the bosom of Pele).

I loko nei no oe o kuu poli i kou wa he wahi opuu wale no, a hookanaka no oe ilaila, a huli, a kolo, a hele a nui no oe i kuu poli nei. A oia no ke kumu i heaia ai kou inoa o Hiiakaikapoliopele. Ua noho kaikuaana a makuahine no hoi au nou. Nolaila, e ae ana anei oe e kii i ke kane a kaua i Kauai?[6]

Here we see that Hiʻiaka is not just the punahele of her kaikuaʻana Pele but is considered to be a child of Pele. Hoʻoulumāhiehie describes how Pele carried Hiʻiaka from her time as a seedling. Pele herself declares that her pilina as kaikuaʻana to her kaikaina resembles—or actually is— the aloha and pilina between mother and daughter. Having shared Pele's bosom, and even "born" of Pele, Hiʻiaka's pilina to her is more entwined than that of "just" siblings. Since Pele has no children spoken of in this

Term	Definition	Examples
haku	n. Lord, master, overseer, employer, owner, possessor, proprietor. A chief was often addressed as ē kuʻu haku, my master. See *Haku-o-Hawaiʻi*. Kona haku, his lord. ʻO Iēhowa ka Haku (Isa. 50.5), the Lord Jehovah. hoʻo haku: To act as haku, dominate; to treat as a haku; to rule others, sometimes without authority; bossy. ʻA ʻole ʻoe e hoʻohaku maluna ona me ka ʻolea . . . you shall not rule over him with rigor.	Hiʻiaka—"Pokii haku" (to her kaikuaʻana) Hiʻiaka—"Haku" (to Pāʻūopalaʻā) Pele—to her kaikaina and kaikunāne
hānau mua	n. First-born child, especially the oldest living member of the senior branch of a family; senior, older brother or sister.	Pele
hoahānau	n. Cousin; brother or sister, as a church member.	All of the Pele clan
kaikaina	n. Younger sibling or cousin of the same sex, as younger brother or male cousin of a male, or younger sister or female cousin of a female; sibling or cousin of the same sex of the junior line, whether older or younger.	Nā Hiʻiaka a pau (to Pele) Hiʻiakaikapoliopele (to her elder Hiʻiaka sisters)
kaikoʻeke	n. Brother-in-law or male cousin-in-law of a male; sister-in-law or female cousin-in-law of a female. Cf. *koʻeke*. Kona kaikoʻeke, his kaikoʻeke. (PPN taʻokete.)	Hiʻiaka and Kahuanui
kaikuaʻana	n. Older sibling or cousin of the same sex; sibling or cousin of the same sex of the senior line, whether older or younger.	Pele (to the Hiʻiaka sisters) Hiʻiaka sisters (to Hiʻiakaikapoliopele)
kaikuahine	n. Sister or female cousin of a male.	Kahuanui (to Lohiʻau) Pele (to her brothers)

kaikunāne	n. Brother or male cousin of a female.	Kamohoaliʻi, Kānehoalani, Lonomakua, etc.
pōkiʻi	n. Younger brother or sister or closely related younger cousin, often spoken affectionately.	Hiʻiaka
punahele	nvs. A favorite or pet; to treat as a favorite (children were often treated as favorites; they might be carried on the grandparents' shoulders, and songs were composed for them); favoritism.	Hiʻiaka

Figure 1. Definitions of ʻohana from Pukui and Elbert, *Hawaiian Dictionary.*

mana, Hiʻiakaikapoliopele is the rightful inheritor of the ʻohana lineage. When Pele's time is passed, whether through death, improper leadership, or some other cause, Hiʻiaka will become the hānau mua of the ʻohana. Other readings suggest that because the two wāhine have shared one body and therefore share mana with each other, Hiʻiakaikapoliopele is another embodiment of Pele herself. This nuanced pilina between Pele and Hiʻiaka is important because of the conflicts that emerge in the moʻolelo regarding governance in the ʻohana and lāhui.

Through the migration and movement of this ʻohana, we learn not only about the shifting dynamics of genealogical pilina but also about leadership, ʻohana, and pono. The primary terms of pilina introduced for ʻohana are kaikuaʻana, kaikaina, hoahānau, kaikunāne, kaikuahine, kupuna, makua, moʻopuna, pōkiʻi, hānau mua, and punahele. All those who travel with Pele to Hawaiʻi are described as being of the same hanauna (generation) as her—kaikaina, kaikūnane, hoahānau, pōkiʻi, and so forth.[7] And here is an issue of translation. While all her traveling companions are frequently labeled "siblings," any of the terms listed here can expand out to embrace any ʻohana of the same generation, regardless of how many times removed. Or as Mary Kawena Pukui explains in the first volume of *Nānā I Ke Kumu,* "you may be 13th or 14th cousins, as we define relationships today, but in Hawaiian terms, if you are of the same generation, you are all brothers and sisters."[8] Furthermore, within a patriarchal society, the eldest brother—Kamohoaliʻi or Lonomakua perhaps—would be the aliʻi of this ʻohana. But as Pukui once more notes, "Genealogy rather than age or sex determined *hānau mua* status."[9] We learn here that Pele's hānau mua status indicates that she is the highest ranking of her hoahānau and not simply the oldest. Recognition of her lofty genealogical roots makes her the aliʻi of her ʻohana, and her siblings are her makaʻāinana.

The next pilina I discuss extends the range of reference beyond the Kanaka Maoli ʻohana. While ʻohana refers to those descended from the same root—that is., those who share a common genealogy—these pilina engage and intersect with the ʻohana and society in many ways.

KĀNE & WAHINE

Hawaiian dictionaries are consistent in their translation of kāne and wahine. Pukui and Elbert, Lorrin Andrews, and Henry Parker all define kāne as both the male sex and man gender and wahine as the female sex and woman gender, importing into the words all the biases inherent to patriarchy and Western gender and sex hierarchies. After defining kāne and wahine as sex and gender in a binary comes the predictable presentation of kāne and wahine as husband and wife.[10] Like all translations, these definitions reduce to a mandated relationship what in actuality can be a far more fluid, shape-shifting, and multibodied pilina than the conventional meaning of "marriage" could ever hold. This substitution introduces and reinforces heteropatriarchy within the intimacy between kāne and wahine by imposing a primary pillar of patriarchy and heterosexism: marriage. In fact, it is not just kāne and wahine that are translated through marriage. Rather, a close analysis of pilina in our Hawaiian dictionaries reveals that nearly all pilina were translated through the institution of marriage. Those that could be reduced and bound to that archaic institution were and those that were too complicated or "queer" were translated as savagery or sin.

When we turn to our moʻolelo, we immediately see how inadequate these translations and definitions are. Many figures are bound as kāne and wahine in the moʻolelo of Hiʻiakaikapoliopele. Some of these figures play significant roles in the overall arc of the moʻolelo; some appear only in passing. Most notably, Lohiʻau is marked as a kāne to Pele, all the Hiʻiaka sisters, and Wahineʻōmaʻo at different points of the moʻolelo. Hiʻiaka is also said to have Kauakahiapaoa, Kaʻanahau, and Makaukiu as kāne, and Pele is known to have Wahieloa and Ulumawao as kāne as well. These pilina do not conflict with or invalidate each other. Rather, figures in the moʻolelo openly discuss how siblings and companions share the pleasure and kuleana that come with having a kāne. Perhaps the most famous example of this can be found in Pele's address to her kaikaina after Pele's spirit returns from Kauaʻi.

E, auhea oukou e oʻu mau pokii? He wahi manao koʻu imua o oukou. He kane ka kakou, aia la i ka moku kaili La o Kamawaelualani, i Kauai Nui moku lehua. O Haena ke Kalana aina; o na Hala o Naue i ke kai, ke awa pae; a o Lohiau ka ipo. O ke kane ka hoi ia, kiiʻna.[11]

In this passage, Pele introduces her kaikaina to their kāne (kane a kakou) and requests that one of her sisters take up the task of fetching him for them. This episode and its assigning of Lohiʻau as a kāne to all the Hiʻiaka sisters is consistent across the archive I have studied. The main condition set in this particular kauoha (command) is that whoever retrieves Lohiʻau will abstain from physical intimacy until after Pele has him and then makes his body noa (free) to them. Lohiʻau is also aware of this agreement. Before Peleʻs spirit returns to her body in Kīlauea (Hawaiʻi), she tells Lohiʻau that she will send for him and that he is to refrain from sexual activity with wāhine until after Pele is able to noa his body.

E hoi au a Hawaii, hana au i ka hale o kaua a maikai, alaila, kii mai ka luna ia oe, i kii mai auanei ka luna ia oe, a he luna kane, mai hele ae oe, aka, i kii mai ka luna a he luna wahine, o ka luna ka hoi ia, hele ae oe i Hawaii, elima po, elima ao, pa i kela kihi o Kilauea, i keia kihi o Kilauea, alaila, noa ko oiwi [sic] kapu iaʻu, alaila, lilo aku oe na ka wahine e.[12]

When Pele is departing from Hāʻena, she tells her kāne that once she has returned to Kīlauea, she will send a wahine to retrieve him and that he is not to sleep with anyone until the two of them have slept together in Kīlauea.

Pele offers a similar kauoha to her kaikaina: "Kipaku aku o Pele, o hele, aohe au aloha ana mai iaʻu, o kii i ke kane a kaua a hiki ia nei, a noa iaʻu, alaila, lilo ke kane nau, na ka wahine maikai."[13] The agreement is clear to all parties. Lohiʻau is a kāne to Pele and all the Hiʻiaka sisters. All Hiʻiaka and her sisters need to do is to wait until Pele first indulges in all the beauties of Hāʻena, and then that pleasure will be allowed to the Hiʻiaka sisters as well.

By understanding the conditions set for these pilina, we can see that it is not only Peleʻs jealousy that throws Pele into a rage after Hiʻiaka seduces Lohiʻau at the edge of Kīlauea but that Hiʻiaka, *like Pele*, has broken a sacred kauoha to mālama the kapu on his body until Pele can hoʻonoa that kapu. It is also important to note that it is not Hiʻiakaʻs being intimate with Lohiʻau that makes them kāne and wahine but Lohiʻauʻs and Hiʻiakaʻs pilina to Pele that initially connects them as kāne and wahine. And for the same reason, once Wahineʻōmaʻo joins her companion Hiʻiaka on their huakaʻi kiʻi kāne, she too becomes a wahine of Lohiʻauʻs and Lohiʻau a kāne of hers.

While the kuleana of and to the kāne is clarified through the intentional use of collective pronouns such as kākou, mākou, or the even more selective kāua, subtle differences exist between the shared pilina of Hiʻiaka, Pele, and Lohiʻau, and the pilina of Wahineʻōmaʻo and Lohiʻau.[14] In the first pilina, Pele and Hiʻiaka both hoʻāo Lohiʻau. The Hawaiian-language dictionaries all agree that hoʻāo refers to a marriage, with Parker saying that hoʻāo is "the ancient Hawaiian marriage custom."[15] This translation poses a few obvious problems, both for our reading of Hiʻiaka and for the greater project of "reading" and interpreting Kanaka Maoli "traditions." The first difficulty is that there was no marriage in Hawaiʻi until after the arrival of missionaries in 1820, and only in the later 1820s did some aliʻi begin to forsake the embrace of multiple intimate partners. Scholars such as Jonathan Osorio have discussed the ways that mid-nineteenth-century laws enabled the conditions and practice of marriage and monogamy to spread.[16] Importantly, however, many aliʻi and makaʻāinana never abandoned the practice of welcoming the embrace of multiple lovers. Pele and Hiʻiaka are figures in a moʻolelo told about Kānaka who lived in ka wā kahiko long before the arrival of missionaries and therefore were not affected by later encroachments of the virtue of monogamy and marriage. Even by Christian Hawaiian readers, Hiʻiaka and Pele could not be expected to practice these recently introduced religious traditions. Therefore, rather than hoʻāo meaning marriage, in this and other moʻolelo, hoʻāo simply means to make daylight with a lover, or to stay with someone until morning.

Much like the restriction of kāne and wahine to the institution of marriage, kaikoʻeke is translated by Pukui and Elbert, Andrews, and Parker as "brother-in-law." Pukui and Elbert add a more gendered dynamic to this pilina, describing it as a term referring to "brother-in-law or male cousin-in-law of a male; [or a] sister-in-law or female cousin-in-law of a female."[17] In the moʻolelo of Hiʻiaka, kaikoʻeke describes the pilina between Hiʻiaka and Kahuanui (Lohiʻau's kaikuahine), Lohiʻau and Nakoa-ola (Kahuanui's kāne), and Lohiʻau and Lonomakua (Pele and Hiʻiaka's kaikunāne).[18]

The term emphasizes a particular hīpuʻu in the ʻupena of pilina in ʻohana. Perhaps because Hiʻiaka, as a wahine, does not have kaikuahine but has kaikuaʻana, and therefore it would be inappropriate to refer to

Kahuanui as "kela kaikuahine a kāua," kaikoʻeke is a term used to show how they are all bound together through the pilina of Lohiʻau and Hiʻiaka. Poepoe and Hoʻoulumāhiehie choose the term *kaikoʻeke* to emphasize the specific bond between these two wāhine, a bond with no relationship to marriage. And here arises another instance where translating pilina into acceptable Christian relations and identities exposes the working relationship between translation and settler colonialism. Transforming these pilina and ancient traditions into tools for affirming Christianity and "settler sexualities" is part of the process of entrenching Western traditions within our own.[19] To write settler sexuality, patriarchy, and the nuclear family into our moʻolelo is to obscure, or even unravel, the complex ʻupena of relations that actually organized our society, thereby furthering the ongoing agenda of settler colonialism by erasing alternatives to the twenty-first-century household and civilization.

Therefore, rather than reduce these pilina to the results of marriage, let us explore what we do know about these kāne and wahine. We know that Pele takes on many kāne in this and other moʻolelo. We know that Hiʻiaka does the same while also taking on multiple aikāne of her own. We know that Lohiʻau is kāne to these two (and other) sisters, and to Wahineʻōmaʻo, and also an aikāne to Kauakahiapaoa. We know as well that these pilina intersect and connect without creating conflict or trauma unless kapu or kauoha are broken. Finally, we ultimately must recognize that none of this looks anything like the relations created and valued by the Western institution of marriage (see Figure 2).

Although using the term *aikāne* and maintaining its practice have declined drastically in the modern era, historically, both were widespread. "Aikāne" appears well over one thousand times within the mana of Hiʻiaka published by Poepoe, Hoʻoulumāhiehie, Kapihenui, and Bush and Paʻaluhi.

When a wider net is thrown into our archive, the term *aikāne* appears in nearly all major Hawaiian-language newspapers through the nineteenth and twentieth centuries, including specifically *Ka Hoku o ka Pakipika, Home Rula Repubalika, Ke Eleele Hawaii, Ka Hae Hawaii, Ka Hoku Loa, Ka Hoku o Hawaii, Ka Lahui Hawaii, Ka Lama Hawaii, Ke Leo o ka Lahui, Ka Lei Rose o Hawaii, Ka Makaainana, Ka Naʻi Aupuni, Ka Nonanona, Ka Nupepa Kuokoa, Ke Kumu Hawaii, Ka Nupepa Kuokoa Home Rula.*

Term	Definition	Source
ai.kāne	nvs. Friend; friendly; to become a friend. Kāna aikāne, his friend. Moe aikāne, to commit Sodomy (*rare*). ho.ʻai.kāne [*sic*], to be a friend, make friends, befriend.	Pukui and Elbert
ai-ka-ne	v. *Ai,* No. 8, and *kane,* male. 1. To cohabit, as male with male, or female with female. 2. To commit sodomy; hence.	Andrews
ai-ka-ne	n. 1. An intimate friend of the same sex; a friend or companion of the same sex. 2. Those who mutually give and receive presents, being of the same sex. 3. Sodomy; dissoluteness of habit.	Andrews
aikane (**āʼi-kāʼ-nĕ**)	n. 1. A sodomite. (Obsolete.) 2. An intimate and trustworthy companion; a friend.	Parker
aikane (**āi-kāʼ-nĕ**)	v. 1. To commit sodomy. (Obsolete.) 2. To exercise a kindly feeling or good will toward another; to act the part of a friend; to become a friend.	Parker

Figure 2. Definitions of aikāne from Pukui and Elbert, *Hawaiian Dictionary;* Andrews, *Dictionary of the Hawaiian Language;* and Parker, *Dictionary of the Hawaiian Language.*

The references to aikāne across these sources range from simple identification of the pilina between two kānaka, to highlighting certain kānaka in moʻolelo, to warnings against sodomy and the uncivilized practices of our past (particularly in those nūpepa run by missionaries).

In particular, aikāne were commonly found in some of our more celebrated and cherished moʻolelo, including S. N. Haleʻole's *Laieikawai* (1862–63), Samuel Mānaiakalani Kamakau's *Ke Aupuni Mōʻī* (1868–69), Hoʻoulumāhiehie's *Kamehameha I: Ka Nai Aupuni o Hawaii* (1905–6), and Stephen L. Desha Sr.'s *He Moolelo Kaao no Kekuhaupio: Ke Koa Kaulana o ke Au o Kamehameha ka Nui, Ka Hoku o Hawaii* (1920–24).[20] More research is needed within these moʻolelo to determine greater nuance and understanding of this important pilina; however, generally what we know of aikāne today is that it is a deeply intimate relationship (although not always romantic or sexual) between two wāhine, kāne, or māhū.

Specifically, within moʻolelo o Hiʻiaka, aikāne describes pilina between wāhine, such as Hiʻiaka, Wahineʻōmaʻo, Hōpoe, Kahuanui, and Pāʻūo-palaʻā, and between kāne, such as Lohiʻau and Kauakahiapaoa. Less frequently, aikāne can refer to the pilina between kāne and wāhine, and sometimes it seems to be equivalent to ipo.[21] Cursory research shows that aikāne also describes pilina of such aliʻi as Kaʻahumanu, Keʻelikōlani, Kiwalaʻō, Kamehameha, Kahekili, Kauikeaouli, Keōua, and Liholiho with others.[22] These relationships directly contradict Pukui and Handy's statement that such relationships would have been "looked upon with contempt by commoners and by the true aliʻi."[23]

If the identification of aikāne pilina in the moʻolelo of Hiʻiaka between beloved aliʻi and akua wasn't enough to confirm that these pilina were respected within Kanaka Maoli society, one need only consider the aloha these late nineteenth- and early twentieth-century authors wrote into the accounts of aikāne pilina. Almost entirely omitted or translated out of our English-language archive of moʻolelo, within the ʻōlelo Hawaiʻi archive the aloha immediately appears. Of all the pilina Hiʻiaka shared with others as a wahine, pōkiʻi, kaikaina, and even haku, none seems so valued, and even transformative, as the pilina with her aikāne, Hōpoe. This pilina quite literally transforms each of these wāhine, their ʻāina, their pilina with others, and the direction and results of the entire moʻolelo. The aloha between Hiʻiaka and Hōpoe ultimately turns the kaikaina against her own kaikuaʻana (and aliʻi) in some versions, and even leads Hiʻiaka to attempt to kill Pele by destroying the crater at Kīlauea. Although I examine other aikāne pilina in this archive, because of its intensity, I begin with Hiʻiaka and Hōpoe.

The pilina of Hiʻiakaikapoliopele offer answers to many questions about such relations' many pleasures and responsibilities. How, for instance, is the pilina between sisters different from that between kāne and wahine, aikāne and other hoapili? How do different pilina intersect, compound, and complicate each other? What does the pilina of Hiʻiaka and Hōpoe

Aloha is always creation

teach us about the nature of aloha? At one moment in the mo'olelo, Hi'iaka discovers that the origin of Nānāhuki's name was her love of gathering lehua at Hōpoe. Upon learning this, Hi'iaka proclaims that Nānāhuki will now forever be known as Hōpoe—that she and the lehua grove at Hōpoe will be one and the same.[24] At this moment, Hōpoe herself becomes the lehua that Hi'iaka carries with her and draws inspiration from throughout her journey and life.

This part of the mo'olelo is often overlooked, but it reminds us that aloha is an active verb; it is tactile. Aloha plants seeds, grows, and transforms the 'āina around us. Aloha is distinct because it cannot be commodified and therefore cannot be bought or sold. Aloha creates—in fact, aloha is always creating. Pele uses lava. Her aloha is both rage and rapture, destruction and creation. For Hi'iaka, aloha can be reforestation. I have learned from this mo'olelo that if it does not transform us, it is not aloha. Further, if it is not marked on the 'āina, it is not aloha, or at least, it is not the aloha our kūpuna were raised with, cultivated, and carefully passed down in our mo'olelo to us.

To better hold and celebrate the aloha and pilina that overflows between aikāne, I have come to this mo'olelo seeking Hi'iaka and Hōpoe in the forest of Kea'au. What I've discovered are six major episodes/themes in their saga of aloha: launa, kauoha, hāli'ali'a, make, na'au'auā, and mākaia. Launa are those māhele that depict the first encounters and meetings between Hi'iaka and Hōpoe. Here we learn most about how aikāne relationships are negotiated; here we learn most about what it means to "ho'aikāne" (to make one an aikāne). If pilina is an 'upena of intimacy, paying attention to launa helps us understand how the aho of aikāne is brought together and tied.

Kauoha are those scenes that depict Hi'iaka's appeal to Pele to protect Hōpoe. Because these kauoha happen as an exchange between the two sisters, they show how kāne/wahine relationships can intersect with aikāne relationships. Hāli'ali'a are the many moments when Hi'iaka looks back fondly on her time with Hōpoe as she continues on her journey to fetch her sister's lover. In both kauoha and hāli'ali'a, we learn about the incredible commitment possible between two aikāne at the same time as we explore some of the great emotional and physical intimacies and pleasures shared between aikāne.

The final three themes are deeply entwined. A major episode in this moʻolelo is the death (make) of Hōpoe, which results in two distinct responses: naʻauʻauā and mākaia. All three speak to the intimacy shared between Hiʻiaka and Hōpoe by representing Hiʻiakaʻs grief at the death of her aikāne, which informs us about the boundless loyalty found in aikāne pilina. Although not every aikāne pilina in the moʻolelo has as many distinct components as Hiʻiakaʻs and Hōpoeʻs, they all display an intense emotional and physical intimacy, a great reciprocal commitment, and that boundless loyalty. Through these qualities, we witness aloha between aikāne.

To analyze aikāne pilina, we must start at their beginning. How do aikāne become aikāne? What does it mean to hoʻāikāne (see Figure 3)?

While Pukui and Elbert did not explicitly, Andrews and Parker define hoʻāikāne as the act of committing "sodomy." To enter into an aikāne pilina

Term	Definition	Source
ho-ai-ka-ne	v. *Ho* for *hoo, ai* and *kane.* See AIKANE. 1. To commit the sin against nature; to commit sodomy; applied to either sex. 2. To be an intimate friend of the same sex, i. e., to give and receive favors from one of the same sex. . . . 3. To act the part of an aikane or intimate friend. 4. To make friends, as two persons about to fight.	Andrews
ho-ai-ka-ne	s. 1. A friend on terms of reciprocity. 2. The house where such friends reside or meet.	Andrews
hoaikane **(hoʻ-aʻi-kā-ne)**	v. Ho for hoo, ai and kane. See aikane. 1. To commit sodomy. 2. To be an intimate friend of the same sex. 3. To be an intimate friend. 4. To make friends with a person of whom one is afraid. . . . 5. To make friends.	Parker

Figure 3. Definitions of hoʻāikāne from Andrews, *Dictionary of the Hawaiian Language*; and Parker, *Dictionary of the Hawaiian Language*.

is to "sin against nature." This is, of course, to be expected when we remember the way all pilina were translated through the institution and
"virtues" of marriage and monogamy. Aikāne were certainly one of those
pilina that were far too "queer" and therefore dangerous to be translated
as anything other than sin and savagery. However, sin and savagery are
definitely not what Hiʻiaka recalls when Wahineʻōmaʻo asks her how she
and Hōpoe became aikāne. Instead, Hiʻiaka offers a touching moʻolelo
about her first encounter with Hōpoe and their acts of hoʻāikāne.

Ia wa ninau aku la au i ua kaikamahine nei i kona inoa. Alaila hoike
mai la oia iaʻu i kona inoa ma ka olelo ana mai: "O koʻu inoa maa mau,
a o ia nohoi koʻu inoa i kaheaia ai au e koʻu mau makua mai koʻu mau
la opiopio mai a nui wale au, e like me kau i ike mai la iaʻu i keia wa, o
Nanahuki no ia. O koʻu inoa keia i kamaaina i na kanaka apau; aka, ua
kahea no nae hoi kekahi poe iaʻu, a he kakaikahi wale no nae ia poe, o
Hopoe koʻu inoa, mamuli o koʻu pii mau i ka ako lehua i kela ulu lehua
e ulu mai la. O ka inoa o kela ulu-lehua, o ia no o Hopoe." Ia wa olelo
aku la au iaia i ka i ana aku: E lawe au ia oe i aikane oe naʻu, a e mau
loa aku hoi kou inoa o Hopoe. Ua ae mai la nohoi kela i kaʻu nonoi ana
aku iaia i aikane oia naʻu; a lawe nohoi oia i ka inoa aʻu i olelo aku ai
iaia, o kona inoa ia. Pela iho la ke ano o ko maua hoaikane ana, a lilo
ai kona hale i hale kipa noʻu.[25]

In this passage, Hiʻiaka describes the two exchanging names at their first
meeting. Hōpoe tells Hiʻiaka that her given name is Nānāhuki but some
(very few) people call her Hōpoe because she is known for ascending to
the grove called Hōpoe to pick lehua. Hiʻiaka responds by asking Hōpoe
if she can take her as an aikāne. To formalize this pilina, Hiʻiaka says that
Nānāhuki will now forever be known as Hōpoe. Through this act of simultaneously confirming her name, her connection to the lehua grove, and
her pilina to Hiʻiaka, the two become aikāne.
    Three important lessons can be drawn from this excerpt. First, the act
of hoʻāikāne is one to be celebrated. Hiʻiaka shares this moʻolelo about
her aikāne with aloha rather than shame of committing some sort of sin.
Second, to hoʻāikāne is to act with nature rather than against it. Hiʻiaka
and Hōpoe's relationship is mediated through ʻāina. Hiʻiaka is the one who

hula le'a *pleasurable dance*

plants lehua groves to flourish after Pele's lava flow, and Hōpoe becomes forever known as that lehua when Hi'iaka insists that Hōpoe become her true name. Third, aikāne are intimate enough to change their inoa—a significant fact, given the importance of naming. That Hi'iaka formally replaces the name Nānāhuki with Hōpoe shows that she is deeply connected to Hōpoe almost immediately. These practices of launa and ho'āikāne continue in other aikāne pilina as well. For Hi'iaka and Wahine'ōma'o, the sharing of names is also a ceremonial part of the process of becoming aikāne.

A nolaila, e ninau aku ana au ia oe,—Owai kou inoa? E hai mai oe i'au [*sic*] i kou inoa, no ka mea, ua makemake au i aikane oe na'u....

["]No ko'u inoa ea, e hai aku no hoi au ia oe, oiai ua hoaikane ae la kaua, o Hiiaka au i ka-poli-o-Pele; a o ko ia nei inoa, o Pa-uopalaa.["][26]

This passage describes the scene of these two wāhine shortly after departing Kīlauea. Hi'iaka comes across Wahine'ōma'o and helps her complete her offering to Pele. When Wahine'ōma'o rejoins Hi'iaka and Pā'ūopala'ā on their huaka'i ki'i kāne, Wahine'ōma'o requests that Hi'iaka offer up her name for the two wāhine to become aikāne. Hi'iaka agrees to share her name specifically because they have decided to ho'āikāne. And echoing the theme that began with Hi'iaka and Hōpoe, later in the mo'olelo, when Hi'iaka mā pass through Hilo, Wahine'ōma'o's home also becomes a hale kipa for Hi'iaka.

In the launa and hāli'ali'a episodes, we also learn about how aikāne share pleasure. For Hi'iaka and Hōpoe, it is through hula and surfing. After they have become aikāne, Hōpoe teaches Hi'iaka how to dance hula. After mastering their hula le'a (the pleasurable dance), they take the dance to the sea.

Ia laua nei i hee mai ai i ka nalu, ua ku ae la o Hiiaka maluna o kona papa, a kani ae la ke oli ma kona waha, oiai nohoi e oni haaheo ana kona kino me ka nani. A na ia nei hoi ka haa iluna o kona papa, oia nohoi ka wa i lewa ae ai ka hope oni o Hopoe i ke kai. O Hiiaka kai luna; a o Hopoe kai lalo, a kaulana ae la na oni ame na lewa elua o Puna, oia hoi ka lewa luna ame ka lewa lalo, hui iho me ke ala o ka polo hinano, aohe mea maikai a koe aku.[27]

Poepoeʻs wording in this episode of the moʻolelo is devoted to sexual and playful kaona. The two young wāhine who have just become acquainted seek pleasure from each other in the ocean. Surfing (heʻe nalu) here provides the language for pleasure, as they dance out their desire on and with each other. The description ranges from playful and tantalizing to specific forms of play between new lovers suggested in the phrase "hui iho me ke ala o ka polo hinano," which will appear in many different variations in the moʻolelo o Hiʻiaka to describe the physical intimacy shared between aikāne; for instance, it appears in the following passage involving many aikāne:

> Ia po nohoi a ao, honi ana o Lohiau-ipo a me Kauakahiapaoa i ke ala
> o ka hinano o ko laua aina; a no ka polo hinano ke ala i honiia, mau
> ana na ihu o ua mau alii nei i na ihu o na wahine a laua, oia o Hiiaka
> ame Wahineomao.[28]   ʻala polo hinano?

Here Hoʻoulumāhiehie describes the kāne inhaling the ʻala polo hinano together, which might lead the reader to assume that these kāne are simply being intimate with their wāhine. From the Hawaiian, however, it suggests that Lohiʻau and Kauakahiapaoa are inhaling the ʻala polo hinano together, as Hiʻiaka and Hōpoe had done earlier. Only after these aikāne kāne share in the hīnano of their ʻāina do they press their noses (honi) to their wāhine. It is also important to note that the kāne do all this together as aikāne. Sharing pleasure with each other and with others is common for Lohiʻau and Kauakahiapaoa; in fact, so significant is this sharing for these aikāne that Kauakahiapaoa laments in moments of pleasure that he indulges without the company of his aikāne.

Toward the end of the Hoʻoulumāhiehie mana of Hiʻiakaikapoliopele, Kauakahiapaoa and Pele come together—first in battle and then in pleasure. After spending several days and nights indulging in the "nani o Puna," he tells her, "Hu mai la ka hoi koʻu aloha i kuu aikane, ka mea nana i o-u mua ka maka o ka wauke i ke kaha o Haena," Love is welling up inside of me for my aikāne, the one who was the first to nip the bud of wauke in Hā'ena. Here we see that 'āina (Hā'ena) participates significantly in the pleasure between Kauakahiapaoa and his aikāne and that the power of their aloha and pleasure is recalled in moments of shared pleasure with others. When Pele asks Kauakahiapaoa why his thoughts are turned to his aikāne, he replies,

> I kuu hoonuu hookahi nohoi paha i ka puni a maua. Nana ka ono e loaa, e kaana pu ana no maua, ina hoi na'u ka ono e loaa, ke hoonuu like ole no maua.
>
> Pela ko maua ano o ka noho ana, a na kona kaawale ana mai ia nei, i ke kiiia ana ae hoi e hele mai i Hawaii nei, no ka hoao ana me oe. Eia ka o kona hele mai no ia a waiho na iwi i ka aina o ka maku koae. O kona hele aina loa aku la no paha ia la?[29]

Kauakahiapaoa is distraught that he has indulged in some of his aikāne's (Lohi'au's) favorite pleasures without him. According to Kauakahiapaoa, in the past should pleasure be offered to one, it would be shared by both. It is therefore not guilt but sadness and grief that trigger Kauakahiapaoa's lamentation about indulging in pleasure without his aikāne. Here with Pele, he realizes for the first time that he may never again share all the delicacies and pleasures life has to offer with his beloved aikāne. This grief turns a moment of great pleasure into one of mourning. The aloha between Lohi'au and Kauakahiapaoa would never allow either of them to forget the many ways they have come together to ai as aikāne.

These aikāne are also unable to forsake the many places that they have moved upon as they loved. This is seen clearly in the aloha and pilina between Hi'iaka and Hōpoe. On the long journey back from Kaua'i, Hi'iaka stops on O'ahu and looks ahead toward Hawai'i island in remembrance of her beloved aikāne. When she does this,

> hu ae-la ke aloha iloko ona no ia aikane ana, no Hopoe.
>
> Ala mai la na hoomanao ana iloko ona no ke kaha one o Aalamanu a laua e holoholo ai, a o ke kai hulei-lua no hoi a laua e auau ai.
>
> Kau mai la kona mau maka i na opihi kau pali a laua e pakuikui ai i wahi kamau no ka la pololi; a hoomanao pu ae la oia i ka wai koo-lihilihi a laua e inu ai.[30]

Hiʻiaka recalls with aloha her affection for her aikāne Hōpoe as well as the seas where they swam together and the cliffs they clung to while gathering ʻopihi.

When read in Hawaiian, the passage states that no desires were left unmet or spared and that ʻāina is part of the pleasure the aikāne indulge in. Hiʻiaka and Hōpoe are sharing their desires and bodies together in acts of pleasure with nature, just as Lohiʻau and Kauakahiapaoa share their kino and ʻāina. When Kauakahiapaoa remembers his most intimate moments with his aikāne, Hāʻena comes to the forefront of his mind. When he shares pleasure with Pele, all of Puna is revealed to him. And when Hiʻiaka reminisces about her time as an aikāne to Hōpoe, she of course recalls ʻAʻalamanu and the kai at Hāʻena (Hawaiʻi). ʻĀina in all these cases is not deployed simply as metaphor to mask pleasure and leʻa from the reader, nor is it setting or backdrop. Pleasure and leʻa come from the ʻāina; it is our pilina to it that we share between us, that makes pleasure possible. This is true for the many different pilina in our moʻolelo, which is discussed further in chapter 4.

When Hiʻiaka and Hōpoe bid farewell, they both feel and understand the weight of this separation. Hiʻiaka has been called to return ma uka, so that her sister Pele can urge Hiʻiakaikapoliopele to take on her huakaʻi kiʻi kāne. As Hiʻiaka is about to depart, she tightly grasps her pāʻū in one hand and turns to Hōpoe to honi her aikāne. As they embrace, both are moved to tears. Hiʻiaka then turns away, to return to Kīlauea.[31] Neither wahine knows for sure that this will be the last time they will share a honi. Neither wahine knows what will come of Hōpoe, her lehua grove, and her hale hoʻokipa. The aikāne only know that the aloha shared between them is grand and painful to leave behind.

Through the launa ʻana o Hiʻiaka and Hōpoe and Hiʻiakaʻs hāliʻaliʻa ʻana for Hōpoe, we learn that these aikāne share names, homes, ai, ʻai, honi, hula, waves, and waimaka. We see that aikāne are invited into the most intimate shared spaces, and their hunger is immediately satisfied. We also see the pain of pulling two aikāne away from each other. We learn that intimacy shared between aikāne is an act shared with ʻāina—an act that cannot be properly described or practiced without ʻāina. When Kauakahiapaoa laments the loss of his aikāne, Lohiʻau, he also laments the distance of their home, Hāʻena. The two, pilina with ʻāina and pilina to others, are deeply intertwined. Hiʻiaka, Hōpoe, and Wahineʻōmaʻo dance in the face of Andrews's definition of hoʻāikāne. They make love that plants lehua, and they share pleasures that tease breaking waves out of a calm bay. To hoʻāikāne in our moʻolelo is to enact all the possibilities of pleasure between our bodies and to learn from how ʻāina grounds that pleasure to be shared and treasured between us.

AIKĀNE: KAUOHA, PROTECTION, AND COMMITMENT

Like the other pilina in this moʻolelo, aikāne is bound not just by pleasure but by kuleana as well. Aikāne are deeply loyal and committed, even when that comes at the greatest price. To begin to understand these kuleana between aikāne, let us turn to the kauoha between the sisters Hiʻiaka and Pele, which display those aspects of intimacy that require us to protect the ones we love. What does kauoha, in this case the command or demand from one sister to another about a loved one, reveal about the intricate and complicated ʻupena of relations? Through the Hiʻiakaikapoliopele epic, kauoha offer us insight into how the Pele ʻohana is governed. In most cases, Pele issues a kauoha to a sister, a brother, or even to her lover, Lohiʻau. The kauoha mutually exchanged between Pele and her youngest sister, Hiʻiakaikapoliopele, however, touch more people, because they are shaped not only by the pilina between these wāhine but also by the pilina with their lovers they are protecting.

When Hiʻiaka returns from Keaʻau, Pele urges her to travel to Kauaʻi to retrieve Lohiʻau, and to do so without breaking the kapu on his body. After Hiʻiaka does this, and after Pele lifts the kapu, he will become a kāne to all the Hiʻiaka sisters, a "kane a kakou." Hiʻiaka's response is relatively consistent across the mana: "E malama pono loa oe i kaʻu mea aloha he aikane oia o Hopoe a hoi hoi au," You must take proper care of my beloved; she is an aikāne to me, Hōpoe, until I return.[32]

While Hiʻiakaikapoliopele's elder Hiʻiaka sisters refused Pele's request to fetch Lohiʻau because they fear the journey, the pōkiʻi is only concerned for the well-being of her aikāne. Hiʻiaka's command also reflects a shared kuleana between the pilina of Hiʻiaka and Hōpoe and that of Pele and Lohiʻau. In fact, Hiʻiaka equates them by saying: "ʻO Lohiau kau ipo aloha, a eia au ke kii nei i kau aloha a loaa i ka loa. O Hopoe hoi kaʻu aloha, e malama oe [Pele] iaia," While Lohiʻau is your beloved and

I am off to retrieve him, Hōpoe is my beloved and you, Pele, shall protect her.[33]

In Poepoe's mana of Hi'iakaikapoliopele, Hi'iaka offers this kauoha to her Hi'iaka kaikua'ana as well, reminding them that she is taking on this journey at great risk to herself: "Eia au ke hele nei i ka makaia a ka haku kaikuaana o kakou," Here I am going on the treacherous journey for our elder sister. In return, she delivers the kauoha that they should not disrupt Hōpoe and her ulu lehua, and they should resist plucking or gathering from Hōpoe's ulu lehua: "Aohe o'u makemake e ako oukou i na lehua o kana ululehua. E kapu ia mau lehua nana." Hi'iaka reminds her kaikua'ana of the abundance of lehua to be found elsewhere in Hawai'i and that they should not trouble or pluck her lehua grove at Hōpoe. Hi'iaka insists that out of respect for her taking on this huaka'i for them, they should heed her kauoha.[34]

These passages show not only Hi'iaka's mana as a pōki'i and punahele of Pele, and therefore someone worthy of issuing a kauoha of her own, but also that aikāne pilina were respected, rather than being queered, as in our modern society. It is telling as well that no significant kauoha are issued in mo'olelo o Hi'iaka outside the pilina between Hi'iaka and Pele, largely because no one else has the mana to kauoha Pele to do much of anything, which also fits within the governing structures, or pilina, of the Pele lāhui.

COMMITMENT AND LOYALTY

Only after Hi'iaka departs from Kīlauea do we begin to learn about what kuleana comes with this particular aikāne pilina. It plays out on the journey, largely between Hi'iaka and her "hoa puku'i i ka ua ame ke koekoe" (embraced companion who endured with me the cold), Wahine'ōma'o. During this huaka'i, Wahine'ōma'o is Hi'iaka's "aikane i ke alo" (physically present aikāne) who will endure with her all the trials and obstacles that come their way.[35] Through this endurance, we learn about the nature of this particular pilina. In contemporary terms, Wahine'ōma'o is quite literally a "ride or die" companion. While a handful of characters join and then depart from Hi'iaka and her huaka'i, only her "aikane i ke alo," Wahine'ōma'o, remains with her until the end.[36] Within the entire Hi'iaka mo'olelo, only twice does Wahine'ōma'o gesture toward departing from her aikāne. When Hiʻiaka mā are in Kailua, Oʻahu, on their way to Kauaʻi to fetch Lohiʻau, Hiʻiaka offers up a chant to Kaʻanahau, her kāne whom she has just slept with. Because of this, Wahineʻōmaʻo becomes quite agitated, and she confronts Hiʻiaka.

"He keu no hoi oe, e aikane! He hana hoohaehae maoli no paha keia au iaʻu, e noke mai nei i ke olioli i ko kane. Mea ae no oe o kuu kane, mea iho no o kuu kane. O kahi aku la nohoi paha ia o ke kane, i noho ia aku la nohoi paha e oe. Ka! Heaha hoi kou ano, e aikane. Ina penei mau oe, e ke aikane, e hana ai, ea, e aho ko kaua kaawale. O koʻu alahele no keia imi ae au i koʻu wahi e pono ai. I lawe mai nei ka oe iaʻu a nei aina malihini, loaa kau kane, a haalele mai oe iaʻu. Ehia ka hoi mea aloha, o nei mau iwi. E waiho paha auanei oʻu mau iwi i ke kula o Kaea, e like me ka olelo a kahiko?"[37]

Wahineʻōmaʻo lashes out at her aikāne for going on and on about her new kāne (Kaʻanahau). A cursory or Western reading might suggest that Wahineʻōmaʻo does this out of jealousy; however, when we read closely, we see that Wahineʻōmaʻo specifically takes issue with Hiʻiaka's description of Kaʻanahau as "Kuu kane" (my kāne). Wahineʻōmaʻo's gesture to leave arises from a fear of being left behind, a fear that Hiʻiaka will not honor the intimate pilina between them. By becoming Hiʻiaka's aikāne, Wahineʻōmaʻo has pledged to go where Hiʻiaka goes. Wherever they both shall die, Wahineʻōmaʻo's bones will rest beside those of her beloved. In this passage, however, she fears her bones will be left behind to dry alone, due to the loss of pono and reciprocity in their pilina. Luckily, Hiʻiaka quickly remedies the situation, putting her aikāne at ease by reassuring her that she has misunderstood.

"Iaʻu i paeaea ae nei i kuu kau i hana ae nei no Ulamawao, a hiki i ka pau ana, ia wa i ano e ae nei kuu mau maka, a ua kuhi au ua ike ae nei oe ia ano e ana ae nei oʻu. O koʻu ike aku nei no ia i ke kaikuaana haku o kaua, ua hele nohoi a kahu ka ena i na onohi maka. Hoomaopopo iho la au, ua huhu ke kaikuaana o kakou iaʻu no kuu hili ana me ke kanaka nana ka ai a kakou i ai mai nei. A oia ke kumu oʻu i

Not love for another that scares
but loss of connection
THE EA OF PILINA AND ʻĀINA

kau ae nei i kela kau au i manao mai nei iaʻu, e ke aikane, he kani‑
aa aloha maoli i ke kane a kaua. Na kaua nohoi paha ia kane, ua loaa
hoi iaʻu.”[38]

Hiʻiaka explains that she offered the chant because she feared Pele was
angry with her for straying from her explicit task to fetch Lohiʻau and for
breaking the kapu on her own body by sleeping with Kaʻanahau. Most
important, she assures Wahineʻōmaʻo that Kaʻanahau is a kāne to them
both, “Na kaua nohoi paha ia kane.” Wahineʻōmaʻo is immediately satisfied
with this explanation, and the two continue along their journey together,
never to speak of this moment again.

The simplicity of this solution may seem strange to us. Hiʻiaka has
just slept with a beautiful man, yet her aikāne is quickly and easily re‑
assured. This is possible because in aikāne pilina, there is no expectation
that commitment and loyalty require monogamy. It is not Hiʻiaka’s aloha
for Kaʻanahau that hurts, angers, and scares Wahineʻōmaʻo but the pos‑
sibility that Hiʻiaka might forsake Wahineʻōmaʻo and cut the cords between
them. When this fear is addressed, and Hiʻiaka assures Wahineʻōmaʻo
that Kaʻanahau is a kāne to them both—another hīpuʻu in their ʻupena
of pilina—pono is restored in their aikāne pilina, and they can continue
their journey together.

The second and final time that Wahineʻōmaʻo considers departing from
her aikāne comes from a fear that she may be contributing to Hiʻiaka’s
troubles. The reciprocal nature of their pilina will not allow Hiʻiaka to
dismiss her aikāne, even if to do so would ease her journey. But when
Wahineʻōmaʻo suggests that her presence is a heavy burden, Hiʻiaka speaks
of the trauma that would occur should their cord be unraveled: “O kou
pili ana mai iaʻu, he mama ia noʻu. O kou kaawale mai aʻu aku, he kaumaha
ia noʻu. Aia kou pilikia a pilikia au. Nolaila, mai haalele mai oe iaʻu,” Your
pilina to me lightens my load; to be separated from you would be a heavy
burden for me. Should you be troubled, so would I. Therefore, do not
leave me.[39] Their ability to overcome burdens together, to struggle for‑
ward on their huakaʻi through many different ʻāina, only strengthens their
pilina as aikāne. This is why Wahineʻōmaʻo can confidently say, “He mau
iwi io no keia ua pili mahope ou,” These bones of mine are indeed bound

my bones are bound to yours

to you.[40] The two know for certain that where one shall go, the other will follow. This is the heavier side of pilina. Deep and intimate pleasure are often shared, but heavy kuleana and arduous undertakings can be required as well.

NAʻAUʻAUĀ

The final three stages in the Hiʻiaka and Hōpoe saga all lie on this darker side: make (death), mākaia, and naʻauʻauā.[41] Because the fates of Lohiʻau and Hōpoe are similar, and because all the pilina in this moʻolelo are interlocked within the ʻupena of intimacies, these stages are also reflected in the pilina between Lohiʻau and Kauakahiapaoa, and between Wahineʻōmaʻo and Hiʻiaka. The death of a loved one links these three cases of naʻauʻauā and mākaia for Hōpoe (Hiʻiaka's aikāne) and Lohiʻau (Hiʻiaka's kāne and Kauakahiapaoa's aikāne). Hōpoe's death arouses within Hiʻiaka a desire to avenge her aikāne. She decides she will uphold the kapu on Lohiʻau's body until she reaches Kīlauea, then defile the kapu before the eyes of her sister.[42] This action not only takes revenge for the death of her beloved at the hands of Pele but also poses a direct threat to her sister's leadership and mana. By breaking her kaikuaʻana's kauoha, Hiʻiaka asserts that Pele is no longer her aliʻi. As previously discussed, here the piko between these two sisters is (severed) mō ʻia. Hiʻiaka's decision to disobey her sister's kauoha is also an act of naʻauʻauā, because she knows that to maintain her position as the aliʻi in her ʻohana, Pele will retaliate with full force against her and Lohiʻau. She does. Lohiʻau is killed, and Hiʻiaka leaves Kīlauea, now mourning for both her aikāne and her kāne.

When word of Lohiʻau's death reaches Kauaʻi, it sets another journey of mākaia and naʻauʻauā into motion. Kauakahiapaoa vows not to wear his malo again until he stands before the eyes of Pele and exacts his revenge.[43] When Kauakahiapaoa arrives in Hawaiʻi, Pele recognizes that he is on a quest for mākaia and also for his own death, so that he may rejoin Lohiʻau. Pele sees this and tells her sister Hiʻiakaikaʻalei:

Ua makemake oia e kupu ae koʻu inaina nona, no na huaolelo ana i hoopuka mai la, a kii aku au e pepehi iaia, a hookahi kona make ana me ke aikane ana. Aka, aole nae oia e make ana iaʻu.

A o kau hana wale no, oia koʻu kena ana aku ia oe, e Hiiakaikaalei, e kii
oe a loaa kela kanaka, a lawe mai ilalo nei i ku ai kana makaia.[44]

Here Pele explains to her kaikaina (Hiʻiakaikaʻaleʻī) that Kauakahiapaoa
is staging a quest for revenge that he knows will end in his death. But
Peleʻs intention is not to kill Kauakahiapaoa, because he has done nothing to earn such a fate. Rather, it was Pele who harmed Kauakahiapaoa
by killing Lohiʻau, and therefore she welcomes Kauakahiapaoaʻs quest for
revenge. It is clear, however, that he still intends to naʻauʻauā in response
to the death of his aikāne, declaring, "Eia au mahope o kuu aikane a moe
pu aku maua i ka ehu a Lono me kuu aikane," Here I am coming for my
aikāne and we shall rest together in the mist of Lono.[45]

CONCLUSION

While each of these mana is a moʻolelo in its own right, differing in
sometimes meaningful ways, a vibrant, strong, and vast ʻupena of pilina
holds the moʻolelo o Hiʻiaka and its waihona together for us. Study of
our moʻolelo teaches us that these pilina are functionally dynamic. They
exist to fulfill particular needs. These pilina are not "identities" but complex relationships. Pilina breathe, move, and shape-shift. Importantly,
these pilina will continue to shape-shift and grow as our analysis of them
expands into more and more of our moʻolelo. That our pilina have survived so many generations of transformation suggests that there might
be something we could learn from them today. Ea is here offered to us,
and what I am breathing in and out from this moʻolelo is that we need our
pilina, in all their shapes and shades, and we need to embrace them with
all their nuances rather than reduce them to Western-supposed equiva-
lents. No substitutes for our vibrant and culturally specific pilina can be
found in the English language or the Western imagination.

It is not just that these specific pilina lack proper English and Western
names but that together these pilina (and others) inform a society whose
understanding of relationality, responsibility, and aloha reaches far beyond
the nuclear household and heteronormativity. Whereas in English, nearly
every meaningful relationship is somehow mediated by marriage, or considered illegitimate, Kanaka Maoli pilina are all legitimate; our many
intimacies are neither contradictory nor reductive. Furthermore, whereas

also kuleana to be Kanak maikaʻi (virtuous)

in Western civilization virtue is the province of those who comply with marriage, monogamy, and heteronormativity, Kānaka Maoli must recognize and carry out our kuleana within our complex matrix of pilina to be a "kanaka maikaʻi" (virtuous).

Unearthing these pilina is but the first and easier step in our decolonization. We must apply this ʻike to our lives to breathe ea back into our pilina with each other. To do so will require that we question our own assumptions about how we take for granted our intimacies. When we do the emotional labor of finding, identifying, and honoring our kōkoʻolua, our kāne and wāhine, our aikāne and kaikoʻeke, our hoa hele and hoa paio, we in turn do the important work of unlearning heteropatriarchy.[46] And in that unlearning, we prepare ourselves for the difficult work of spinning our aho to (re)member and create anew our ʻupena.

CHAPTER FOUR

ʻĀina, the Aho of Our ʻUpena

◆ ◆ ◆ ◆

"In our culture, ancestry is paramount."[1] Our insistence on the primacy of ancestry and the significance of moʻokūʻauhau is one major way that we as Kānaka have continued to sustain pilina to this day. Mana comes from one's great accomplishments and feats of strength and wit but also from one's pilina and kinship within a moʻokūʻauhau.[2] And of course, aloha ʻāina is at the very piko of our moʻokūʻauhau. Our understanding and practice of aloha ʻāina reminds us that we descend from ʻāina; therefore, our valuing of moʻokūʻauhau must be accompanied by an awareness of the role that ʻāina plays within our genealogies and our experience of all things Hawaiian.

The first half of this chapter analyzes how Hiʻiakaikapoliopele moʻolelo are waihona of ʻāina and how ʻāina in Kanaka Maoli moʻolelo in general function not as the "setting" but as active participants in the narrative. I discuss how ʻāina is deployed as record, evidence, character, body, and metaphor throughout narratives, cumulatively representing an aloha ʻāina literary consciousness. The chapter's second half returns to our ʻupena of intimacies as part of a reading strategy for understanding how aloha ʻāina affects and organizes how we practice pilina between each other. What ultimately makes the ʻupena an effective metaphor for pilina and aloha ʻāina is ʻāina's role as the mediating factor between all pilina.

Like the aho in our ʻupena, specific ʻāina often serve to hold the pilina between us together. When asked, What do ʻāina and aloha ʻāina have to do with Kanaka Maoli literature and relationships? this chapter answers emphatically, 'Āina is everything to us, to our mo'olelo and to our pilina. We have seen how these mo'olelo o Hi'iaka function as waihona of pilina, but also as an origin story, not only for Kanaka Maoli ontologies and epistemologies but also for the intimacies with which Kānaka relate to one another through 'āina, which is itself an actor who moves, changes form, and (re)members events. In mo'olelo o Hi'iaka, 'āina grows out of the sea, or as pōhaku flies into the ocean and becomes smaller islands (Mokoli'i, Pōhakuloa), or as lava covers other subjects.'Āina shifts, shakes, and shatters. It also represents multitudes. References to 'āina and place-names far outnumber references to kānaka, kupua, and akua—in Kapihenui, Bush and Pa'aluhi, and Ho'oulumāhiehie, by at least two to one, and in Poepoe's mana by three to one. Clearly, these authors take every opportunity to enrich the mo'olelo by providing specific details about each place the characters occupy or pass through.

When, for instance, Kapihenui introduces us to Pele in 1861, the first thing we learn about her is that she lives "iuka o Kalua" (above the crater).[3] It would not have been surprising for this mo'olelo to begin with a mo'okū'auhau, tracing Pele's lineage, but apparently her 'āina, Kalua (ka lua o Kīlauea), needs to precede genealogy. When Bush and Pa'aluhi take up this mo'olelo in 1893, a combination of genealogy and significant 'āina constitutes the first two substantial paragraphs following the 'ōlelo ho'ākāka in the second installment of the mo'olelo.

> O Kuahailo ke kane, noho ae ia Haumea, ka wahine, hanau mai na kaikamahine, a o Pele ka haku makahiapo o lakou, a mahope mai na pokii kaikaina.... Ma Kahiki kahi i hanau a i hanai ia ai keia ohana kupua, a mailaila lakou i hele mai ai a pae ma na mokupuni liilii o ke komohana, a mailaila i mai hele ai a hiki loa aku ma Hawaii.[4]

According to Bush and Pa'aluhi, Kuahailo and Haumea were the parents of Pele, but she and her siblings, extensively listed in the place marked here by the ellipses, came from Kahiki to Hawai'i. Ho'oulumāhiehie and Poepoe similarly weave genealogical information regarding Pele together with essential information about where she was born and raised (Kahiki or Hapakuela) and how she came to be in Hawai'i. But the description of

Pele's migration to Hawai'i explains not just how Pele's mo'olelo came to
be a Hawaiian mo'olelo but also how Hawai'i came to be Hawai'i. As Pele
and her siblings migrate, 'āina is transformed in their wake, siblings are
left behind as kia'i of wahi pana, craters are dug, and their fires are lit.
From Nīhoa to Hawai'i, Pele thrusts her 'ō'ō to 'eli her way across the
pae 'āina in search of a home. What results from this extended migration
are Halāli'i, Kīlauea (Kaua'i), Moanalua, Lē'ahi, Pūowaena, Ihiihilauakea,
Maunaloa (Moloka'i), Kauhakō, Kalaupapa, Kalanuiohua, Moaulanuika-
naloa, Haleakalā, Pu'uōla'i, Pu'ulena, Ohunui, Kīlauea, and Moku'āweo-
weo. These craters and pu'u are the physical record of Pele's movement,
marking the stages of the mo'olelo and providing for us evidence for the
narrative. In the same way that these wahi pana are Pele's legacy, Mokoli'i
and Mō'ili'ili are the living story of Hi'iaka's travels to Kaua'i. On their
journeys, and even when they stay at home, Pele mā are creating and transforming 'āina, and the 'āina remembers and continues to tell their story.[5]

It is through these moments that we learn that in mo'olelo, 'āina is both
actor and evidence, or, as Bush and Pa'aluhi write, "aole no hoi he aina e
ikea nei i nele i na hoailona o ko lakou noho ana," every land they passed
through and lived in bore their hō'ailona.[6] Just as our mo'okū'auhau orga-
nize how, where, and when we Kānaka lived, our 'āina offers a genealogy for how, where, and when Pele mā lived. Both this mo'olelo and our
genealogies are therefore offering a "Hawaiian concept of time, and they
order space around us," as they also offer a record of the pilina between
Kānaka and 'āina.[7] Because both mo'okū'auhau and 'āina are illuminating
a Hawaiian concept of intimacy, we can investigate how 'āina makes and
organizes its own logics of pilina, and this intimacy includes not just how
'āina came to be but also how certain events are pili to certain 'āina as well.

These mo'olelo share a geography that spans islands and crosses
oceans. We also understand, as explored in chapter 2, that because these
mo'olelo have a genealogy themselves, with each mana written as part of
a larger narrative, the authors are attentive to the mo'olelo that came before
and will follow after and consciously reinvoke or elaborate upon not only
the larger genealogical context but also the 'āina that embodies and en-
acts it. When Poepoe or Ho'oulumāhiehie cite their sources or point to
other mele and mo'olelo, they are expanding the intricate 'upena of these
mo'okū'auhau, but Poepoe in particular teaches us essential lessons about

how these genealogies are deeply pili to 'āina and place. The various mana of mo'olelo o Hi'iaka do not just describe or evoke 'āina but register how they themselves emerge from a particular 'āina. So when Poepoe introduces his mana by providing all the information he thought most relevant for readers to know, he declares that this Hi'iaka is known to be "ko Maui Hiiaka," whereas the previously published mana of Hi'iaka in *Ka Na'i Aupuni* was "ko Hawaii Hiiaka."[8] Later in the mo'olelo, we learn that O'ahu too has its own specific mana of Hi'iaka, although it is unclear through Poepoe's writing if it has ever been published.[9]

Poepoe's introduction informs readers that these mo'olelo are both defining and being defined by place. Furthermore, through the singular possessive pronoun "ko" we learn that mo'olelo *belong* to 'āina. These 'āina are born with these mo'olelo already potentially inhabiting them and inherited by the people of those places—"ka moolelo o ko Hawaii poe."[10] Further, Poepoe often breaks the fourth wall to elaborate when his Maui mana of Hi'iaka differs or diverges from mana born of other 'āina, without trying to establish which mana is "correct." So, for instance, "E ka makamaka heluhelu, ma keia wahi i kaawale hou ai na mana moolelo elua o Hiiaka, ka Hawaii ame ko Maui, a e nana ana kaua ma keia wahi aku i keia kaawale ana."[11] In this way, Poepoe acknowledges these mo'olelo are born not just out of land but from a particular place, always reminding us that, like the pilina between Kānaka and place, the intimacy between mo'olelo and place is specific.

In our mo'olelo, pilina to 'āina can be evoked and described in a multitude of ways. Our beauty and strength can be communicated through 'āina; we can share a specific relationship to 'āina as a kama'āina, malihini, kupu'āina, or kia'i 'āina; or we can represent and come to even embody our 'āina.

BEAUTY

Noenoe Silva and ku'ualoha ho'omanawanui have articulated on multiple occasions how Kanaka Maoli mo'olelo such as Pele offer alternatives to Western beauty standards, in part because wahine strength and beauty are rooted in an appreciation and respect for 'āina.[12] All four of the mana foregrounded in this book demonstrate clear, articulate connections between beauty, strength, and 'āina. In Kapihenui's Hi'iaka, we

[handwritten: beauty intermingled w/ virtue]

see this in how Hi'iaka mā are frequently referred to as "wahine maikai": their physical beauty and virtue are unquestioned and marked by their ability to remain both pili and representative of their 'āina. In the same way that the legend of Hi'iaka's beauty precedes them in their journey, so does their virtue, "aohe wahine maikai e ae ma Hawaii nei."[13]

This trend continues in Bush and Pa'aluhi's mana of the mo'olelo. When she enters any new place, Hi'iaka's beauty and virtue as a wahine maika'i are unquestioned. First, as in Kapihenui's mana, her status as a wahine maika'i is incomparable, "aohe wahine maikai e ae ma Hawaii nei e like me ia nei," and earlier her beauty is described as beyond anything known ("ui launaole").[14] The practice follows for Pele when she arrives at Hā'ena. The people draw upon a popular 'ōlelo no'eau, "pali ke kua, mahina ke alo," to express how Pele's beauty echoes the world around her—in the cliff's edge and the mahina's luster.[15]

In Ho'oulumāhiehie and Poepoe's longer mana of Hi'iaka, these descriptions of beauty and 'āina blossom. Both Poepoe and Ho'oulumāhiehie compare Hi'iaka's backside to the majestic slopes of Maunaloa.

> Eia o Hiiaka ke ku nei, ua kaei ae la no i ka hope nui maikai o Maunaloa (a he u'i hoi tau!), me ka pa-u kalukalu i wiliia me ka mokila a me ka pahapaha o Polihale.
>
> He luaole no hoi ka nani o ua Ui nei o ka Palekoki Uwila o Halemau-mau. Ke alawa iho ma ka aoao, he uhekeheke hoi tau; hoi ae no mahope, e ike ana no oe i ka mea i kaulana ai ka Maunaloa i ke kikala upehupehu, ke hoi mai hoi oe mamua, mai nana oe i na onohi maka o Hiiaka, o kuku auanei oe i na lihilihi o ka eha koni.[16]

[handwritten: To know Hi'iaka B to understand the ng'sh ct volcano]

Poepoe writes of a powerfully stunning wahine, adorned in the kalukalu and pahapaha of Polihale. Hi'iaka's staggering beauty and strength are not just compared to Maunaloa; rather, to know and see Hi'iaka is to understand precisely how majestic Maunaloa is. Here we learn that the magnificence of this woman of the crater, this lightning-skirted beauty of Halema'uma'u, is second to none *because* she resembles and honors her land.

But that is not all. It is also said, "ua like ka nono ula o na papalina o keia wahine me ka wai ula liliko o ka ohelo, a o kona ili, ua like me ka pua hala memele maikai," the red of her cheeks resembled the young sweet nectar of the 'ōhelo, and her skin was fine like the beautiful hala blossom. And "o kona oiwi apau, he ui hooheno e nopu hulili ai ka houpo o ka aoao oolea, a hiki nohoi ke 'lala iho i ka wai' ka olelo ana."[17] Altogether, Hi'iaka's astounding beauty lit and stoked the fires in the houpo (chests) of all who encountered her. To see Hi'iaka was to experience a beauty second to none. Kāne and wāhine alike were dazzled by the earth-arousing beauty of this wahine—a beauty that spoke of Hi'iaka's pilina to 'āina, and aroused the 'āina within her admirers: "'O ka ui keia, aohe kauwila o ka wao laau e ole ke kolo hou o kona mau a a."[18]

Like Hi'iaka, Pele's beauty and mana are described in relation to her 'āina. While the beauty of the Wahine Pō'aimoku (Hi'iaka) can be described through references that cross the entire pae 'āina, the 'āina linked to Pele's mana and beauty are distinctly from Puna and the Kīlauea area. Like her pōki'i, Pele's beauty is unrivaled, "aole i kana mai." But Pele brings with her all the distinctive and enticing scents of Puna: "ke ala o ke Kupaoa, o ke Kupalii, o ka Hala, o ka Lehua, o ka Olapa, ka Maile, ka Hinano, ka Awapuhi, a pela wale aku."[19] Where Hi'iaka's hips conjure mountains out of the sea, Pele carries the fragrance of Puna with her wherever she goes. This chief of the rising of the sun at Ha'eha'e displays every possible shade and scent of attractiveness, and her features are aptly compared to the Māhealani moon.[20] Both Hi'iaka and Pele exhibit a mana and beauty so overwhelming that they are recognized by every new place and person that encounters them.

From their stunning beauty pili to 'āina also comes their strength, for to carry mountains and lightning on our hips, or the power of the mahina in the glow of our faces, is to harness the mana those features embody. This is why Kanaka Maoli articulations of pilina move beyond the rhetorical conceit of a metaphor. When the pilina of our akua and kānaka to 'āina is described, we must understand it as a real material relationship to 'āina rather than simply a comparison through a literary device. In Western literature, metaphor is primarily a rhetorical tool that makes compressed comparisons between two things by presenting them as an identity. In 'ōlelo Hawai'i, we are actually experiencing the already existing mana of pilina.

It is 'āina itself that allows both Hi'iaka and Pele to have their way in this mo'olelo. Pele carries out her deeds with her hot and penetrating 'ā; Hi'iaka's battles are won with the help of her lightning skirt and lima kapu o Kīlauea. Without their compelling pilina to 'āina, these wāhine would not have the mana to complete any of their famous actions or overcome any of the obstacles confronting them in this mo'olelo.

'ĀINA AND INOA KANAKA

Earlier in this chapter, I mentioned that in terms of numbers, there are far more references to different 'āina than kānaka, ali'i, or akua in this mo'olelo. The reason now becomes clear—when our kūpuna shine in the mo'olelo, they do so by being likened to or by embodying 'āina in some way. In our mo'olelo Hawai'i, such comparisons go beyond the rhetorical conceits of metaphor or personification; our authors are articulating an intimacy between these Kānaka and their 'āina. One very common way that Kānaka Maoli are related to 'āina is through the sharing of inoa. Pilina between Kānaka and their 'āina do not merely result from an expression of admiration. Such pilina are reflective, displaying the way Kānaka embody our 'āina. In the mana of the mo'olelo of Hi'iakaikapoliopele, dozens of akua, ali'i, kia'i, and kama'āina are both Kānaka and the 'āina itself. They share personality traits, physical likeness, and identity. When we say aloha 'āina is a significant part of a Kanaka Maoli worldview, we are therefore saying that our aloha for 'āina is so intimate that we aspire to be 'āina, and we draw out and celebrate the pilina of our greatest chiefs and protectors to the 'āina itself, so that both are immortalized in our mo'olelo.

Familiar examples of this in the mo'olelo are Hōpoe being the name of Hi'iaka's aikāne and the ulu lehua she embodies; Punahoa, the beautiful surfing ali'i who rules over the kai at Punahoa; and Ka'ena, the kaikunāne to the Pele 'ohana who is the kia'i of the most western point of O'ahu, Ka'ena. But there are dozens more examples. "Personification," the bestowing of human qualities on nonhuman things, is the exact opposite of what is going on here. Our kūpuna made Kānaka out of these places, to guard, protect, honor, and exalt our 'āina. We also learn from examining these pilina between 'āina and Kānaka that terms we might think of as identities are also intimate relationships. When we say that Punahoa is the ali'i wahine of Punahoa, we are also saying that to be a chief means to be bound to a particular place. Our successes and accomplishments are our 'āina's successes and accomplishments. Everything that we do and achieve is literally in the name of our Kānaka and our 'āina. Leadership (or being an ali'i) is not a position or a distinction. Leadership is a relationship. This connection between 'āina and Kānaka is especially strong for the most significant figures in the mo'olelo. The vast majority of the many epithets given to Hi'iaka, Pele, Lohi'au, and Hōpoe are aho tethering them to their 'āina (see Figure 4).

Inoa	Source
Ai Pohaku o Haumea	Ho'oulumāhiehie, March 13, 1906, 4
Aimoku	Poepoe, March 11, 1909, 4
	Ho'oulumāhiehie, March 20, 1906, 4
Aliiwahine	Bush and Pa'aluhi, January 5, 1893, 1
Awihiokalani	Poepoe, June 26, 1908, 1
Hanaumua	Bush and Pa'aluhi, January 18, 1893, 1
	Bush and Pa'aluhi, January 19, 1893, 1
Haumea Wahine	Poepoe, June 25, 1909, 4
	Poepoe, June 3, 1910, 4
	Ho'oulumāhiehie, April 11, 1906, 4
	Ho'oulumāhiehie, July 10, 1906, 3
	Kapihenui, February 13, 1862, 4
Keiki makahiapo o kai o Puna	Bush and Pa'aluhi, June 16, 1893, 4
Kukuena wahine	Poepoe, June 3, 1910, 4
	Ho'oulumāhiehie, July 10, 1906, 3
Kumu o Kahiki, Ke	Ho'oulumāhiehie, March 13, 1906, 4
Kupuna wahine	Poepoe, June 3, 1909, 4
Lua wahine o ka lani	Bush and Pa'aluhi, March 22, 1893, 4
Moi wahine o Halemaumau, a o ka ahi kanana hoi o Kilauea, Ka	Ho'oulumāhiehie, June 12, 1906, 3
Moi wahine o ke ahi a loa ma Puna, Ka	Ho'oulumāhiehie, June 20, 1906, 4
Moiwahine nei o Mauliola Hale	Poepoe, May 29, 1908, 1
Pele-ai-honua	Poepoe, October 19, 1909, 4
Peleaihonuamea	Ho'oulumāhiehie, August 18, 1906, 4
Pelealiiwahine	Bush and Pa'aluhi, January 6, 1893, 1

Inoa	Source
Pelehonuamea	Poepoe, June 3, 1910, 4
	Hoʻoulumāhiehie, July 10, 1906, 3
	Hoʻoulumāhiehie, April 11, 1906, 4
	Hoʻoulumāhiehie, April 18, 1906, 4
	Hoʻoulumāhiehie, September 5, 1906, 4
	Hoʻoulumāhiehie, September 21, 1906, 4
	Kapihenui, February 13, 1862, 4
	Bush and Paʻaluhi, March 22, 1893, 4
Ua alii wahine nei o ka lua	Hoʻoulumāhiehie, June 8, 1906, 3
Ua moi nei o Halemaumau	Hoʻoulumāhiehie, June 5, 1906, 3
Wahine a Makalii	Poepoe, June 3, 1909, 4
	Bush and Paʻaluhi, March 22, 1893, 4
Wahine ai lehua o Kaimukupuku	Bush and Paʻaluhi, June 16, 1893, 4
	Kapihenui, June 19, 1862, 4
Wahine i Kilauea, Ka	Poepoe, June 3, 1910, 4
	Hoʻoulumāhiehie, July 10, 1906, 3
	Kapihenui, February 13, 1862, 4
	Bush and Paʻaluhi, March 21, 1893, 4
Wahine nei o ka lua	Poepoe, March 6, 1908, 1
Wahine o ka lua, Ka	Poepoe, March 25, 1910, 1
Wahine o ka paia ala o Puna, Ka	Hoʻoulumāhiehie, June 15, 1906, 3
Wahine o ka polohinano o Puna, Ka	Poepoe, April 3, 1908, 1
Wahinekapu	Poepoe, January 28, 1910, 4
	Hoʻoulumāhiehie, March 6, 1906, 4
	Kapihenui, January 9, 1862, 1
	Hoʻoulumāhiehie, June 21, 1906, 3
	Hoʻoulumāhiehie, August 31, 1906, 4
	Kapihenui, July 10, 1862, 4
	Bush and Paʻaluhi, January 5, 1893, 4
	Bush and Paʻaluhi, January 19, 1893, 4
	Bush and Paʻaluhi, February 8, 1893, 4
	Bush and Paʻaluhi, February 9, 1893, 4
	Bush and Paʻaluhi, March 9, 1893, 4
	Bush and Paʻaluhi, April 14, 1893, 4
	Bush and Paʻaluhi, June 20, 1893, 4

Figure 4. Nā Inoa o Pele (The Names of Pele).

He wahine kino lau nō ʻo Pele, Pele is a woman of many forms. And with every form comes a name to honor that form. Like all inoa, Pele's represent her dynamic personality and her many personal qualities. As a wahine both of and from the Lua, she is most often given names that articulate her pilina to Kalua (Kīlauea) and ahi (fire). We learn through these names that Pele is not just like lava, Kīlauea, Puna, or even Haumea; she is that which she has been named. Her pilina to Kīlauea, Puna, Haumea, Kahiki, and her ahi and ʻā make her Pele Ka Wahine Kapu, Pele the sacred woman, because it is from these pilina that her mana emerges. As we can see in Figure 5, Hiʻiaka follows the example of her kaikuaʻana; she too is a wahine of many names—in fact, in these four mana there are more names for Hiʻiaka than Pele. She is the woman of Puna, of the bosom of Pele, and the woman who encircles the islands. Furthermore, Hiʻiaka belongs and is pili to Puna, Ka Hikina, Pele, and Ka Lua—and so are her accomplishments.

The aligning of these magnificent kupua with ʻāina is of course aloha ʻāina. If we are attentive to the pilina between these Kānaka and their ʻāina, we can easily recognize that Pele is not just an akua who lives in Kīlauea.

Notice, for example, the way there is an overwhelming use of the article "o" rather than "i" in the naming and linking of Pele and Hiʻiaka to their ʻāina. This particular article indicates that Pele and Hiʻiaka are both from and made of (o) those places rather than simply residing in (i) them. Therefore, Pele is the lava, the crater, and the kindling fire. And by virtue of their pilina, so too is Hiʻiaka. Hiʻiaka and Pele not only have names that bind them together (Hiʻiakaikapoliopele, Wahine i ka poli o kinolauwahine, ke kaikaina mana o ka wahine o ka lua); they also share names (ka wahine o ka lua, Wahinekapu, aipohaku, keiki makahiapo o kai o Puna). Their inoa tell a moʻolelo about pilina to each other and to ʻāina. These epithets are not literary ties between Kānaka and their ʻāina but acts of assertion toward recognizing that these amazing wāhine, akua, aliʻi, and kiaʻi are their ʻāina.

In the moʻolelo of Hiʻiakaikapoliopele, this truth is told most clearly through the descriptions of Pele and the killing of Hōpoe (see Figure 6).

Like Hiʻiaka and Pele, Hōpoe is a woman of several names and therefore several bodies. We know from the previous chapter that when Hiʻiaka meets Hōpoe, Hiʻiaka learns that Hōpoe's given name is "Nānāhuki," but

Inoa	Source
Akua wahine o Puna	Kapihenui, February 20, 1862, 4
	Bush and Pa'aluhi, March 31, 1893, 4
Alii wahine opio o ka lua o Kilauea	Ho'oulumāhiehie, June 19, 1906, 4
Eueu o ka Palekoki Uwila o Halemaumau, Ka	Poepoe, December 31, 1909, 4
Eueu o Kilauea, Ka	Poepoe, December 11, 1908, 1
Hii i ka iu o Puna	Ho'oulumāhiehie, July 23, 1906, 3
Hii i ka poli a ke aloha	Ho'oulumāhiehie, August 30, 1906, 4
Hii i ka wekiu o na moku	Ho'oulumāhiehie, February 20, 1906, 4
Hii nei i ka iu o na moku	Ho'oulumāhiehie, May 10, 1906, 4
Hii nei i ka poli o Pele	Ho'oulumāhiehie, April 14, 1906, 4
Hii Wahinepoaimoku	Ho'oulumāhiehie, November 30, 1906, 4
Hii-(aka)-i-ka-iu-o-na-moku	Ho'oulumāhiehie, January 19, 1906, 4
Hii-i-ka-iu-o-na-moku	Poepoe, August 5, 1910, 4
	Poepoe, September 3, 1909, 4
Hii-i-ka-poli-o-ko-ipo	Poepoe, December 31, 1909, 4
Hii-i-ka-wekiu	Poepoe, December 10, 1909, 4
Hiiaka au i ka poli o Pele	Poepoe, March 25, 1910, 4
Hiiaka i ka iu o na moku	Ho'oulumāhiehie, April 16, 1906, 4
Hiiaka, ka eueu o ka palekoki uila o Halemaumau	Ho'oulumāhiehie, February 26, 1906, 4
Hiiakaikaiuonamoku	Ho'oulumāhiehie, November 9, 1906, 4
Hiiiakaiuonamoku	Ho'oulumāhiehie, April 25, 1906, 4
	Ho'oulumāhiehie, May 5, 1906, 4
	Ho'oulumāhiehie, May 26, 1906, 4
	Ho'oulumāhiehie, July 20, 1906, 3
	Ho'oulumāhiehie, September 14, 1906, 4
	Ho'oulumāhiehie, September 19, 1906, 4
	Ho'oulumāhiehie, November 9, 1906, 4
	Ho'oulumāhiehie, November 20, 1906, 4

(continued)

Inoa	Source
Kahelehookahi	Poepoe, April 9, 1909, 4
Kaikaina Haku	Kapihenui, January 23, 1862, 1
Kaikaina mana o ka wahine o ka lua, Ke	Hoʻoulumāhiehie, July 23, 1906, 4
Kaikaina Muli Loa	Bush and Paʻaluhi, February 7, 1893, 4
Keahialaka	Hoʻoulumāhiehie, October 1, 1906, 4
Koolauwahine	Poepoe, April 29, 1908, 4
Kuu Pokii i ka poli	Hoʻoulumāhiehie, June 5, 1906, 3
Kuu poli	Hoʻoulumāhiehie, June 30, 1906, 3 Hoʻoulumāhiehie, September 25, 1906, 4
Lala i ka ulu o Wahinekapu, Ka	Bush and Paʻaluhi, March 31, 1893, 4 Bush and Paʻaluhi, April 13, 1893, 4
Lehua o puna, Ka	Poepoe, July 2, 1909, 4
Mea maikai o Puna, Ka	Hoʻoulumāhiehie, July 30, 1906, 4
Palekoki Uwi la o Halemaumau, Ka	Poepoe, April 22, 1910, 4
Ua ui nei o ka palekoki uila o Halemaumau	Hoʻoulumāhiehie, December 25, 1905, 1 Hoʻoulumāhiehie, January 4, 1906, 4 Hoʻoulumāhiehie, January 9, 1906, 4 Hoʻoulumāhiehie, June 19, 1906, 4 Hoʻoulumāhiehie, June 22, 1906, 4
Wahine ai laau o Puna, Ka	Hoʻoulumāhiehie, January 29, 1906, 4 Bush and Paʻaluhi, March 31, 1893, 4 Kapihenui, February 20, 1862, 4
Wahine ai pohaku / ai moku / ai moku lehua	Hoʻoulumāhiehie, August 8, 1906, 3
Wahine hoi o ka hikina a ka la, Ka	Hoʻoulumāhiehie, January 29, 1906, 4
Wahine i ka hikina a ka la, Ka	Hoʻoulumāhiehie, April 16, 1906, 4 Poepoe, July 1, 1910, 4

Inoa	Source
Wahine i ka poli o Kinolauwahine	Hoʻoulumāhiehie, January 2, 1906, 4
Wahine mai ka hikina a ka la ma Haehae, Ka	Hoʻoulumāhiehie, March 30, 1906, 4 Poepoe, April 15, 2010, 4
Wahine o ka palekoki uila o Halemaumau, Ka	Hoʻoulumāhiehie, July 4, 1906, 4
Wahine o Kalua, Ka	Kapihenui, January 23, 1862, 1
Wahinepoai-moku	Poepoe, January 31, 1908, 4 Poepoe, November 13, 1908, 4 Poepoe, November 20, 1908, 1 Poepoe, December 11, 1908, 1 Poepoe, December 25, 1908, 1 Poepoe, January 29, 1909, 4 Poepoe, February 5, 1909, 4 Poepoe, February 26, 1909, 4 Poepoe, April 15, 1910, 4 Hoʻoulumāhiehie, August 8, 1906, 4
Wahinepoaimoku	Hoʻoulumāhiehie, January 2, 1906, 4 Hoʻoulumāhiehie, February 2, 1906, 4 Hoʻoulumāhiehie, February 5, 1906, 4 Hoʻoulumāhiehie, February 8, 1906, 4 Hoʻoulumāhiehie, March 30, 1906, 4 Hoʻoulumāhiehie, April 21, 1906, 4 Hoʻoulumāhiehie, May 14, 1906, 4 Hoʻoulumāhiehie, May 26, 1906, 4 Hoʻoulumāhiehie, July 24, 1906, 4 Hoʻoulumāhiehie, August 6, 1906, 3 Hoʻoulumāhiehie, August 8, 1906, 3 Hoʻoulumāhiehie, October 3, 1906, 3

Figure 5. Nā Inoa o Hiʻiaka (The Names of Hiʻiaka).

ai = eat, conquer, have sex

Inoa	Source
Mokulehua	Kapihenui, February 20, 1862, 4
Uulu o Wahinekapu, Ka	Kapihenui, January 9, 1862, 1
Wahine kui lehua o Hopoe	Ho'oulumāhiehie, August 7, 1906, 3
Wahinekapu	Kapihenui, January 9, 1862, 1

Figure 6. Nā Inoa o Nānāhuki/Hōpoe (The Names of Nānāhuki/Hōpoe).

she is commonly called Hōpoe because of all the time she spends at
the sea of Hōpoe gathering 'ōpihi. When Hi'iaka learns this, she offers
Hōpoe an ulu lehua all her own in Kea'au. Through this exchange, Hōpoe
does not only become Hi'iaka's aikāne, or the wahine kui lehua. She is the
"Mokulehua" itself. This becomes clearer when we read closely the account
of Hi'iaka giving her kauoha to her sisters about not disturbing Hōpoe.
Hi'iaka does not focus exclusively on Hōpoe's human form but warns her
kaikua'ana not to disturb the entire place of Hōpoe, and especially the
ulu lehua.

Kauoha mai hoi o Hiiakaikapoiliopele i ke kaikuaana. Ke kii nei au i ke
kane, a kaua, ke noho nei hoi oe, a i ai hoi oe i kahi nei o kaua, e ai no
oe ma na wahi o kaua a pau, a o kuu moku lehua nei la, mai ai oe
malaila, ae mai la o Pele. Olelo hou aku la no o Hiiakaikapoliopele, i
noho oe a, kuia e ko la inaina, i ai oe ia uka nei, a i iho oe i kai o Puna
e ai ai, ai no oe ma na wahi a pau o Puna, o kuu aikane, mai ai oe, ae
mai la o Pele i na kauoha a pau a ke kaikaina. No ka mea ua maikai ia
mau mea i ko Pele manao, e like hoi me ka Pele kauoha iaia nei.[21]

Hi'iaka is emphatic with her kaikua'ana. While she is off retrieving her
kaikua'ana's beloved, Pele is not to "ai" (eat, conquer, or have sex with)
Hi'iaka's beloved moku lehua. In fact, Hi'iaka's love for Hōpoe is so great
that she permits Pele to send her fires to "ai" anywhere in Puna, her beloved
home, so long as she stays clear of her aikāne and her ulu lehua at Hōpoe.
When Pele breaks this kauoha and Hōpoe is killed, it is not only an act of
betrayal but an act of invasion of that 'āina, as the mo'olelo describes Pele's
lava descending on the ulu lehua rather than upon Hōpoe's human form.

When Wahine'ōma'o asks Hi'iaka for whom she is crying out, Hi'iaka tells her that she is grieving for their aikāne, Hōpoe.[22] When this happens in Bush and Pa'aluhi's mana, Wahine'ōma'o is confused and in disbelief. Wahine'ōma'o questions her aikāne, "Wahahee oe e Hiiakaikapoliopele, owai ka mea nana e ako ka lehua? Hele mai la no oe ka mea nana e ako, aole mea nana e ako hou mahope, a he kanalua au i ka hiki ia Pele ke hana peia."[23] Wahine'ōma'o goes so far as to question Hi'iaka's truthfulness. She cannot believe someone else would ever disturb her beloved lehua.

Dozens of passages throughout every mana of this mo'olelo show Hi'iaka mourning both the death of her aikāne and the burning of the ulu lehua itself.[24] In these passages, the deep and intimate pilina between Hi'iaka and Hōpoe is repeatedly referenced in concert with the pilina between Hōpoe and her ulu lehua. Hōpoe's human and her ulu lehua forms were entirely devoured by Pele when she sent her fires into Hōpoe, and because Hōpoe was also the lehua itself, Hi'iaka mourns both fully.

Lohi'au's many names follow the trend of the other Kānaka in the mo'olelo, in that each inoa deeply ties him to his 'āina of Hā'ena, Kaua'i (see Figure 7). Unlike Pele and Hi'iaka, however, who are made of and making their 'āina, his names use the article "i" to demonstrate that Lohi'au

Inoa	Source
Kamakaokealoha	Kapihenui, July 10, 1862, 4 Bush and Pa'aluhi, July 3, 1893, 4
Lohiau i ka polo hinano i Haena	Ho'oulumāhiehie, May 9, 1906, 4
Lohiau i na hala o Naue i ke kai	Ho'oulumāhiehie, April 17, 1906, 4
Lohiauipo i ka makani Pahelehala o Wainiha, i ke kupaoa o na polo hinano o Naue i ke kai	Ho'oulumāhiehie, November 9, 1906, 4
Lohiauipo i na hala o Naue i ke kai	Poepoe, July 1, 1910, 4 Ho'oulumāhiehie, August 8, 1906, 4 Ho'oulumāhiehie, August 15, 1906, 4 Ho'oulumāhiehie, September 14, 1906, 4 Ho'oulumāhiehie, May 12, 1906, 4
Ua Keiki hula ka laau nei o Kauai	Ho'oulumāhiehie, June 20, 1906, 4

Figure 7. Nā Inoa o Lohi'au (The Names of Lohi'au).

resides "in" or "on" his 'āina. This is not altogether surprising, considering that in this mo'olelo the wāhine make and transform 'āina, then place kāne as kia'i or ali'i of 'āina as they continue their journeys.

NĀNĀ I KE KUMU, 'ĀINA, AND HAWAIIAN INTIMACY

As early chapters have noted, many contemporary Kanaka Maoli scholars have repeatedly written about what it means for Hawaiians to practice aloha 'āina. Much of this work begins with an undeniable truth: Kānaka Maoli have a deep and personal relationship with their 'āina that determines what aloha 'āina means, looks like, and produces. And yet, while important and valuable work has discussed aloha 'āina in terms of politics and society, little has considered aloha 'āina in terms of relatedness and pilina. What does aloha 'āina teach us about intimacy? In the first half of this chapter, I have offered examples from mo'olelo o Hi'iaka of how Kānaka and 'āina are related to each other through the sharing of names, characteristics, places, and even identities. Now I will look at how 'āina influences how we practice, describe, and remember intimacy with others. I argue that 'āina has been and always will be our kumu for understanding and practicing pilina.

As a creation story, Hi'iakaikapoliopele describes the birth of islands, of lehua groves, of volcanoes, and through volcanoes, of 'āina. And because it relates the act of creation, it is also a story filled with pleasure. Throughout the hundreds of pages of these mana of the mo'olelo, we are constantly encountering accounts of Puna's sweet caressing scent of the polohīnano, or of the satisfying taste of the wai ko'olihilihi. Ho'oulumāhiehie's mana is the most descriptive: long, beautiful, and detailed accounts of lovemaking between Kānaka are frequent.

What will not be found, however, are detailed anatomical descriptions. When we read about the nights Pele and Lohi'au shared together after they ho'āo, we are not told about Pele's or Lohi'au's bodies. In fact, very few specific details appear anywhere in this mo'olelo about what Lohi'au looks or feels like. Instead, we are offered elaborate descriptions of the lands that these two ali'i came from. In the first scene of Lohi'au and Pele making love, Ho'oulumāhiehie writes, "Ua ike o Lohiau-ipo i ka nani o Puna—ua honi i ke ala o ka hinano—ua mukiki i ka wai lehua o Panaewa—ua lei ia Hoakalei—ua inu i ka wai koo lihilihi—ua kaa niniau i ka wiliwai—

a ua eha i ka eha lima ole a ke aloha. Aloha wale Puna aina paia ala i ka hala."[25] Ho'oulumāhiehie describes Lohi'au witnessing all the beauties of Puna. In this experience, Lohi'au is overcome by the intense pains of pleasure. In later encounters, Lohi'au is so enticed by Pele that he becomes quite lost (lilo loa) in the beauties of Puna.[26] Through these passages, we learn that for Lohi'au, having sex with Pele means experiencing far more than her assumed human form. It is to enjoy deeply all the beauties of Puna, including the scent of the hīnano and hala, and the sweet taste of the wai lehua of Pana'ewa. Pele's name appears nowhere in this passage, but because we know that Pele is not only her human form but all her wahi, we recognize that what we read is detailing a Pele and Lohi'au affair of aloha.

And we also learn by example that the most intimate thing we can do with another person is to share our 'āina with them. Few if any Kānaka in this mo'olelo are as pili as its namesake, Hi'iakaikapoliopele, and Pele, who held her in her bosom. In fact, these women share not only Pele's poli but the same pilina to Puna. As a result, when Hi'iaka seeks revenge and sleeps with Lohi'au at the climax of the mo'olelo, the passage describing the lovemaking duplicates the earlier account of Pele's having sex with Lohi'au: "Ua ike o Lohi'au-ipo i ka nani o Puna—ua [sic] ua honi i ke ala o ka hinano—ua mukiki i ka wai lehua o Puna—ua lei ia Hoakalei—ua inu i ka wai koolihilihi—ua kaani-ni au i ka wili wai—a ua eha i ka eha lima ole a ke aloha. Aloha wale Puna, aina paia ala i ka hala."[27] That these passages are identical except for one substitution of Puna for Pana'ewa suggests that the author is above all calling attention to the complicated nature of the 'upena of intimacies connecting Pele, Lohi'au, Hi'iaka—and Puna. But for all the overlapping hīpu'u and aho, we are left with a simple truth: to be intimate with Pele or Hi'iaka is to be enticed into Puna, to smell the hīnano, and to drink the waters of the lehua of Pana'ewa and Puna. They are quite literally ali'i of Puna and the surrounding area. But the pilina between Pele, Hi'iaka, and Puna also ensure that Lohi'au's experiences of intimacy with these two formidable wāhine will be very similar.

In fact, many accounts of sex with Hi'iaka foreground references to Puna. Take, for example, the description of her night of pleasure with the beautiful ali'i of Kailua (Ka'anahau), which at times sounds familiar.

Ua ike iho la o Hiʻiaka i ka nani o Kailua—ua hoopapa i ka oopu maka peke o Kawainui—ua ike kumaka i ka ui o Makalei, a ua eha Kaukaopua i ka eha lima ole a ke aloha, ke wili la i ka wili wai a ka makemake. A o Kaanahau hoi, ka ui o Kailua, ua inu oia i ka wai koo-lihilihi o Puna, ua nowelo i ka pua lehua o Panaewa, ua ike i ka nani o Aipo—ua maeele i ke anu o Hauailiki—A pela iho la i hookoia ai na makemake elua i holo like ke kaunu i Waiolohia.[28]

Here Hiʻiaka experiences and is very pleased by all the famed beauties and tributes of Kailua—from the ʻoʻopu of Kawainui to the strong trunk of the Mākālei. In turn, Kaʻanahau is granted the gift of sipping the pleasurable waters of Puna, just as Lohiʻau has with Pele and later will with Hiʻiaka. Nor is it only the affairs between Pele, Hiʻiaka, and their lovers that are described through ʻāina; in fact, it is the only way physical intimacy is portrayed in the moʻolelo. Take, for example, the passage describing the sexual encounter between Kauakahiapaoa and Pele near the close of the moʻolelo.

Ua ike ae la o Kauakahiapaoa i ka nani o Halemaumau, ua inu i ka wai ono hoomalule o ka puna wai koo lihilihi o Puna, ua wela ke kikala o ua keiki nei o ka ua hoopulu hinano o Naue, ua kai-olohia i ka pupu o Puna, ua uo ia ka nani o Kauai, ua kuiia ke aloha i ka iwihilo. Aohe mea nani a koe aku.[29]

Like Lohiʻau, Kauakahiapaoa experiences the beauties of Halemaʻumaʻu and the wai ʻono and koʻo lihilihi of Puna. And again, Pele's name need not be mentioned, because to evoke Halemaʻumaʻu is to evoke the woman of the crater, Pele.

We also find evocations of ʻāina in passages describing the intimacy between aikāne. When Hiʻiaka and Hōpoe's lovemaking is first mentioned in the Bush and Paʻaluhi mana, Hiʻiaka is described as plucking and stringing a lei lehua (e nanea ana i ka ako a i ke kui pua lei lehua). Of course, the verbs "ʻako" (pluck) and "kui" (pierce/penetrate) are for obvious reasons often used to describe both lei making and sex. And because the lehua is of course a kino lau of Hōpoe, when Hiʻiaka strings her lei lehua, we are meant to understand that Hiʻiaka and Hōpoe are being intimate

hula le'a = pleasurable dance

with each other. Immediately following this passage, Hi'iaka offers the following mele:

Ke haa la Puna i ka makani,
Haa ka uluhala i Keaau,
Haa Haena me Hopoe,
Haa ka wahine ami i kai o Nanahuki la
Hula lea wa—le
I kai o Nanahuki—e[30]

In this mele, three wāhine—Puna (Hi'iaka), Hā'ena, and Hōpoe—are all engaging in a "hula lea," a pleasurable dance together in the sea of Nānāhuki. It is only in Bush and Pa'aluhi's mana of this mo'olelo that Hā'ena is revealed to be more than just a place. This often cited and performed mele takes on greater and more pleasurable meaning when read with the understanding that before Hi'iaka was able to ho'āikāne with Hōpoe, Hōpoe was seen dancing hula with Hā'ena at the waters of Nānāhuki, so in fact this is a mele about these wāhine and their 'āina enjoying their hula le'a together.[31]

In the shorter mana of Hi'iaka written by Kapihenui, and by Bush and Pa'aluhi, there is customarily less time devoted to describing sexual encounters, so the most substantial accounts come primarily from the mana of Ho'oulumāhiehie and Poepoe. What we still find, however, is that whenever sexual intimacy appears in the mo'olelo, whenever the author takes the opportunity to ho'omanawanui in the pleasurable moments shared between Kānaka, such encounters are described with and through 'āina. These passages are important for several reasons. First, they offer a significant amount of 'āina based knowledge. When Ka'anahau makes love with Hi'iaka, place-names (Kailua, Kawainui), including names of significant features (Mākālei), are passed on. Other passages preserve the names of winds, rains, and streams. These features of our 'āina are therefore a primary and favored way of thinking about how our Kanaka bodies engage in pleasure.

Following this example, if one of our authors had composed a mo'olelo about a moment of sexual intimacy between me and my wahine of Kahalu'u, it would perhaps read:

Pi'i kōko'olua māua i 'Ioleka'a
A 'ike i ka nani o Kahalu'u
mūkīkī 'ana kāua i ka ua Pō'aihala
a ahe i ka makani Ulumano
'o ka hopena, ua mā'ona nō

A iho lua kāua i ka lua o Ka'au
Inu ā kena i ke kahawai momona o Pālolo
pili ho'i kāua i ka hu'ihu'i o ka nāhele
Pulu pē i ka ua Līlīlehua

'A'ole le'a i koe wale
He nani lua 'ole nō

We climb by two up the ridge of 'Ioleka'a
And all the beauties of Kahalu'u expand before us
We sip together Pō'aihala's dripping kiss
And inhale deeply the sweet breath of Ulumano
We indulge until fully satisfied

And we descend upon Ka'au
Drink our fill from the head of Pālolo's fertile waters
Our bodies held close in the chill of the forest
Drench together in the embrace of Līlīlehua

No pleasure is spared
No beauty can compare

Aside from being a superior way to describe the intense pleasure of being intimate with another Kanaka, these passages are useful because they teach us about the pilina between our intimates and their 'āina. The poem records both my pilina to Pālolo and my wahine's pilina to Kahalu'u while also detailing the specific features of these 'āina: the 'Ioleka'a ridgeline, chilling and misting rains (Pō'aihala and Līlīlehua), and of course the gusting winds. These passages are therefore mnemonic devices that ensure we properly recognize the wealth and beauty of our 'āina and insist on our pilina to her. A careful reading of mo'olelo o Hi'iaka therefore reveals that this is how Kānaka Maoli discuss and celebrate intimacy. These devices are not screens or analogies, employed out of fear of missionary disapproval or out of shame in our own sexuality and desires. Rather, they recognize pilina and admire our 'āina. We know from the rigorous scholarship of Noelani Arista that kaona means far more than just hidden meanings, or "figurative multiplicity." In fact, the mana of kaona is that it moves the audience to think or "conceptualize history—in a kaona conscious way."[32] For McDougall, the use of kaona is also an exercise of aesthetic sovereignty, or what she calls "kaona connectivity," which, "as a practice, requires us to connect with our kūpuna as well as with each other."[33] McDougall's investigation of kaona is well paired with my own because it also focuses on how practicing pilina is an essential part of practicing kaona. Only when we read these mo'olelo carefully and enjoy the pleasure of these encounters do we fully realize that 'āina provide an opportunity for deploying kaona to celebrate pilina and intimacy. Being intimate and pili with our 'āina teaches us how to be intimate and pili to each other. Like Bush and Pa'aluhi, the composer of the famed "Manu 'Ō'ō" does not choose to describe an 'ō'ō sipping the nectar from a lehua blossom because of shame or a desire to conceal the experience of one wahine sipping the wai ko'o lihilihi from another. Rather, it was from watching manu mūkīkī their lovers (i.e., lehua) that we Kānaka learned to care for, cherish, and enjoy our lovers.[34]

When our composers describe Kailua meeting Puna, or Hi'iaka fondling the 'o'opu of Kawainui, they do so because being raised by our 'āina, experiencing its flourishing and loving our 'āina, informs how we practice aloha and pleasure with each other. When we deploy kaona sexually, as when we playfully compare ourselves to manu 'ō'ō and our lovers to lehua, it would be good for us to reflect on the pilina these metaphors are (re)membering for us Kānaka today. They are lessons in love, pleasure, care, and consent.

These passages also reveal an important additional layer to the conversation of pilina and intimacy in Hawaiian society. That Pele and Hi'iaka are both most often described as Puna in their lovemaking shows there is a possible overlap of pilina and also of rule in Puna. And therefore, the sister's shared pilina to Puna reveals an important conversation about the relationship between intimacy, pilina, and power in Hawaiian society. Before leaving on her journey, Hi'iaka tells Pele that all their shared 'āina (including Puna) will be Pele's to rule and devour as she wishes so long as Pele does not disturb Hōpoe.[35] However, after Pele kills Hōpoe, Hi'iaka returns to Kīlauea and embodies a particular kind of rule to Puna in her sleeping with Lohi'au.

Hi'iaka's sleeping with Lohi'au as described previously is not only an act of disobedience to her ali'i/elder sister (Pele); it is also an act of invasion. Because to "ai" is to eat, to engage in sex, and to rule or conquer when Hi'iaka chooses to "ai" with Lohi'au, the two inevitably challenge the existing ali'i of Puna, Pele.[36] Said another way, when Hi'iaka indulges in all the desire of Hā'ena with Lohi'au and offers him all the beauties of Puna, both Hā'ena and Puna are not just drenched in pleasure. They are also devoured, claimed, and ruled by Hi'iaka. In this way, Pele's rule and claim as the sovereign of Puna is challenged.

This reading of Hi'iaka and Lohi'au's lovemaking certainly opens up a greater understanding of the dynamics between Hi'iaka and her ali'i Pele. It also helps us understand how Hi'iaka's breaking of the kapu on her body (and by extension the unnamed kapu on Puna) with Ka'anahau as I described earlier in this chapter results in such a violent response from her sister to kill Hi'iaka's beloved Hōpoe. When read in this way, Hi'iaka's pilina to Puna is destabilizing of her sister's rule, especially as Hi'iaka continues to develop and gather more and more mana and power through her pilina to more and more kānaka, ali'i, and 'āina. When Hi'iaka returns to Puna, carrying all the mana of the 'āina she became pili to on her journey, she does so as a serious threat to Pele's unquestioned rule.

In many ways, Pele anticipates this pilikia (problem). Pele's wish to place a kapu on her punahele while she embarks on this journey and until she returns under her watchful eye has greater depth and meaning. We can begin to read this kapu as a way to mediate and limit the pilina Hi'iaka develops along her huaka'i because Hi'iaka's amassing of those pilina comes with an incredible amount of power. And therefore, this reading allows us to understand these seemingly volatile interactions between sisters as being based in something far more nuanced and complicated than jealousy of the flesh—and rather as a set of complex political moves for rule and mana.

COMMITMENT AND 'ĀINA

Physical intimacy is probably the more le'ale'a (fun and pleasurable) part of our pilina to 'āina to discuss, but 'āina binds the aho between us and those we are pili to in many significant ways. We have discussed how Kānaka are represented by the places they are from, and how Kanaka pilina to their one hānau or the places they choose to noho pa'a. But as we have also seen, mo'olelo o Hi'iaka do more than confirm that the places we come from are important. These mo'olelo also show us how pilina with our intimates is marked by and mapped on the 'āina we cross. Throughout the mo'olelo, Hi'iaka describes her pilina through those places that they have become intimate to together, that remind them of their pilina. When Hi'iaka witnesses the burning of her aikāne from Pōhākea, Hōpoe becomes her "hoa ... i ka wai o Pohakea."[37] This happens not because Hi'iaka and Hōpoe were ever in Pōhākea together but because Hi'iaka carries her pilina and aloha for Hōpoe on this journey, and it is at Pōhākea that she realizes her beloved has been killed. But being together in the same place can also create multiple specific pilina that strengthen the sense of pilina. Through this chant Hi'iaka offers to honor each of her intimates, we learn that Wahine'ōma'o is Hi'iaka's aikāne and hoa of Hā'ena, Kalalau, Ko'olau, Mahinui, and "na wahi a pau" (everywhere).[38] We also learn that Lohi'au is her kāne of Hā'ena, Polihale, 'Ewa, Pu'uloa, Mānā, and Puakukui.[39]

No episode in mo'olelo o Hi'iaka displays this more intensely than the Kapihenui and the Bush and Pa'aluhi mana when they describe Hi'iaka's response to Lohi'au being killed by Pele. After Pele has killed Hōpoe, Lohi'au, and Wahine'ōma'o, Hi'iaka leaves Kīlauea, vowing never to return. This departure frustrates and angers Pele, so she seeks out and revives Wahine'ōma'o, now Hi'iaka's only remaining aikāne, to ask her about the details of the huaka'i to Kaua'i and back. Wahine'ōma'o responds angrily:

Ae, aole no ko kaikaina ka hewa, nou no ka hewa, i ka maua hele ana a Oahu, ma Kailua i kahi o Kanahau [sic], moe maua ilaila a ao ae hele no maua a Kahuku, ike mai mai [sic] no ko kaikaina i ka mokulehua kapu a olua, ua pau i ka ai ia e oe, a ka moana o Kauai, ike no ko kaikaina i ka make o ke aikane ana ia oe o Hopoe me ke kane a laua o Haena, ua ai ia e oe ua make, oia ke kumu o ko kaikaina ho-ao ana i ke kane a olua.

A hiki maua i Kauai, ua make ke kane a olua, hoi mai no oe make no ko make, i haawe no ko aloha ka mua i make ai, lapaau maua ola, o ka pili ana no ia o ke kane me ko kaikaina pili me aʻu pau ka pa ana o ke kane me ia, me aʻu wale no ke kane a hiki wale no makou i Hawaii nei, a no kou malama ole ana i ke kauoha a ko kaikaina, nolaila, lawe mai nei kela i ke kane a olua me ka malama i kau kauoha, me ka malu o ke kino o ke kane a olua, a ike oe.

Alaila, hana kela e like me kona manao, oia la, aole i hewa ko kaikaina, o oe no kai.[40]

For Wahineʻōmaʻo, Pele is wholly to blame—"nou no ka hewa"—for the death of Lohiʻau and for Hiʻiaka leaving Kīlauea. In this passage, Wahineʻōmaʻo provides a detailed timeline of their journey from the time they were leaving Oʻahu on their journey back home to Kīlauea. It was from Kailua and later Kahuku that Hiʻiaka witnessed the death of her aikāne while traveling. This was the act that provoked Hiʻiaka's desire to seek revenge on her sister by sleeping with Lohiʻau.

We learn a great deal about the pilina between Wahineʻōmaʻo and Hiʻiaka from Wahineʻōmaʻo's standing up to Pele in this way. Wahineʻōmaʻo knows, as we do, that to speak back to Pele can easily result in death. But Wahineʻōmaʻo does this eagerly, because it is her kuleana to rest beside her aikāne, making her defiance a "olelo naauauwa no." Because Wahineʻōmaʻo does not believe that Hiʻiaka will be spared by their kai-kuaʻana, she intentionally angers Pele, hoping that this rage will also be cast upon her and allow her to die with her aikāne.[41] Instead of killing Wahineʻōmaʻo, however, Pele gives her a task: "e kii oe i ko aikane, i kii oe a hoi mai kuu kaikaina ia oe ola oe iaʻu, aka, i hoi ole mai kuu kai-kaina ia oe, make oe iaʻu i keia la."[42] Here Pele instructs Wahineʻōmaʻo to retrieve her beloved aikāne, warning her that if she fails to bring Hiʻiaka back to Kīlauea, she and her aikāne will be put to death. Be-cause Wahineʻōmaʻo is determined to spend the rest of her days with her aikāne—in life or death—she wholeheartedly takes on this task and

haku a mele?

leaves Kīlauea immediately with Hi'iaka's kaikunāne, Keowahimakaakaua, to find her beloved Hi'iaka.

Wahine'ōma'o finds Hi'iaka in a full state of mourning for her beloved Hōpoe and Lohi'au. Wahine'ōma'o urges her to return with her, but Hi'iaka refuses.

O hoi, aole au e hoi aku, wahi a Hiiakaikapoliopele, aole au e hoi, eia au mamuli o ke kane a kaua, o ka luhi a kaua i au ai i ke kai makamaka ole, i au ai kaua i ke alanui papawaa, i hele ai kaua i ke kaha makamaka ole, kuleana ole, hookahi no kuleana o ke kane; i hele ai kaua i ka la kulolia wale iho no, ai ole, ia ole o ka la pololi, a maona aku i ka pua o ke aloha, o hoi, eia au mamuli o ke kane a kaua.[43]

Instead, Hi'iaka wails out in mourning for their kāne, Lohi'auipo, and for the long and lonesome journey she and Wahine'ōma'o took, with no kuleana other than the kāne who is now gone. Frustrated by Hi'iaka's refusal, Wahine'ōma'o turns to Keowahimakaakaua and reveals that Hi'iaka will not be returning with them. Keowahimakaakaua then urges Wahine'ōma'o to call out with aloha for her aikāne and to remind her of the places they journeyed to together, the places they were intimate. Keowahimakaakaua insists that this will cause Hi'iaka to return.[44]

While Wahine'ōma'o worries that she cannot haku a mele that will persuade Hi'iaka to return, Keowahimakaakaua is convinced that recalling these places will inspire an effective mele even if she is not a true haku mele.[45] Wahine'ōma'o follows his instructions and composes a series of mele to entice Hi'iaka home with her. The first three mele honor the 'āina and kai of Kaua'i, the land where they together revived then retrieved their kāne Lohi'au (see Figure 8).

Because of this recitation of these places and mo'olelo of their journey together, Hi'iaka begins to recall her own pilina to Wahine'ōma'o through her own mourning for Lohi'au and Hōpoe. Although Hi'iaka continues to insist that she will not return with Wahine'ōma'o, she does give up her na'au'auā for their kāne Lohi'auipo, suggesting that Wahine'ōma'o and Hi'iaka's collective remembering of all their shared troubles and hardships at these places is what encourages Hi'iaka to "hookuu" her na'au'auā for the kāne.[46]

#	Kapihenui	Bush and Pa'aluhi
1	Kuu aikane i ka wai liu o Mana Pahaleolea i Maulua hoolale waa, E holo ka lawakua, E uwe aku oe e ke koolau, Aloha na hoa i makamaka ole, Kuu aikane i ka hale uiki a ka leo e, Auhea oe, hoi mai kaua e. (July 3, 1862, 4)	Kuu kane[a] i ka wai liu o Mana Paha leolea i Maulua hoolale waa E holo ka Lawakua E uwe aku oe e ke Koolau Aloha na hoa i makamaka ole Kuu kane i ka hale uiki a ka leo e Auhea oe hoi mai kaua (June 23, 1893, 4)
2	Kuu aikane i ka wai iliahi ula o Makaweli Hinana ia wai o Luhi Hoa i ke kapa ahoa, Eu hoi kaua he koolau nei, Kuu aikane i ka moana, Ka malama wale no—e, Auhea oe, hoi mai kaua, (July 3, 1862, 4)	Kuu kane i ka wai iliahi ula o Makaweli Hinaha ia wai o Luhi Hoa i ke kapa Ahoa Eu hoi kaua ke Koolau nei Kuu aikane i ka moana Ka malama wale no—e Auhea oe hoi mai kaua (June 23, 1893, 4)
3	Kuu aikane i ka pali o Kalalau Mai ka pali kuukuu kaula o Haena, Kookolu kakou e haele nei, I ha i ka manao e, Auhea oe, hoi mai kaua e (July 10, 1862, 4)	Kuu aikane i ka pali o Kalalau Mai ka pali kuukuu kaula o Haena Kookolu kakou e haele nei I ha i ka manao e Auhea oe hoi mai kaua e (June 26, 1893, 4)

[a] Kāne was often used as an abbreviation in mo'olelo for aikāne. Ho'oulumāhiehie, *Ka Mo'olelo o Hi'iakaikapoliopele*, 80.

Figure 8. Nā Mele o Wahine'ōma'o (Wahine'ōma'o Compositions).

Because Hi'iaka continues to refuse Wahine'ōma'o's request, Wahine-'ōma'o continues to haku mele for her beloved. The next four mele detail their travels back to Hawai'i from Kaua'i (see Figure 9). In these mele, Wahine'ōma'o recalls the dirt of Līhu'e, the ua Pō'aihala of Kahalu'u and Kailua. She calls upon the kuahiwi (Maunaloa) and wai ko'o of Moloka'i, finally returning to Puna, their beloved home. With each mele, Wahine'ōma'o begs her beloved, let us return (hoi mai kaua).

When Hi'iaka continues to refuse, Wahine'ōma'o is distraught. She has followed the instructions of their kaikunāne, to no avail. She has called

4	Kuu aikane i ka hale wai e,	Kuu kane i ka hale wai e
	Hale hau anu o Lihue,	Hale hau anu o Lihue
	Hale kamaa i ka lepo e,	Hale kamaa i ka lepo e
	Hoohoa i ke kukui o Kanehoa,	Hoohoa i ke kukui o Kanehoa
	Auhea oe, hoi mai kaua,	Auhea oe hoi mai kaua
	(July 10, 1862, 4)	(June 26, 1893, 4)

5 Kuu aikane i ka ua poaihala o Kahaluu, Kuu aikane i ka ua poaihala o Kahaluu
  Nihi Mololani a puakea,   Nihi mololani Apuakea
  Kuu aikane i ka ua holio o Koolau,   Kuu aikane i ka ua Holio o Koolau
  Kuu aikane i ka mehana a ka uha e,   Kuu aikane i ka mehana a ka uha e
  Auhea oe, hoi mai kaua,   Auhea oe hoi mai kaua
  (July 10, 1862, 4)   (June 26, 1893, 4)

6 Kuu aikane i ke kaha o Hilia,   Kuu aikane i ke kaha o Hilia,
  Mai ka lai luahine o oa Kamanu,   Mai ka lai luahine o Oakamanu.
  E hoolale mai ana i ka Malako,   E hoolale mai ana i ka Malako
  E ala ua ao kaua e auwe,   E ala ua ao kaua e, auwe
  E uwe aku ana ia Kalae,   E uwe aku ana ia Kalae
  I kuahiwi o Maunaloa   I kuahiwi o Maunaloa
  Ola i ka hale Ohai,   Ola i ka hale Ohai
  Huakai o Hilia la,   Huakai o Hilia la
  Auhea oe hoi mai kaua,   Auhea oe hoi mai kaua
  (July 10, 1862, 4)   (June 26, 1893, 4)

7 Kuu aikane i ka waa koo o Molokai   Kuu aikane i ka waa koo o Molokai
  E koo aku ana i halana Laemakani,   E koo aku ana i hala na Laeamakani [sic]
  Ke palauma wale la no i ka umauma e,   Ke palauma wale no i ka umauma
  Kuu aikane i ke ola a ka hua o ke kai, Kuu aikane i ke ola a ka hua o ke kai
  Auhea oe hoi mai kaua,   Auhea oe hoi mai kaua.
  (July 10, 1862 4)   (June 26, 1893, 4)

8 Kuu aikane i ka uluhala o Puna e,   Kuu aikane i ka uluhala o Puna e
  Kuu aikane i ka ua kanikoo o Hilo e,   Kuu aikane i ka ua kanikoo o Hilo
  Auhea oe, hoi mai kaua   Auhea oe hoi mai kaua
  (July 10, 1862, 4)   (June 27, 1893, 4)

Figure 9. Nā Mele o Wahineʻōmaʻo (Wahineʻōmaʻo Compositions).

out all the places they were intimate together, until none remained ("aole aku wahi i koe").[47] But once more Keowahimakaakaua advises his hoa-hele (Wahine'ōma'o), "Noonoo hou ia aku paha ma na wahi a olua i pili ai me ke kane a olua, i moe pu ai, i hele pu ai i ke anu me ke koekoe," Think again of the places you both were pili to your kāne, the places you three slept together, the places you endured in the blistering cold.[48]

Up until this point, Wahine'ōma'o had focused on recalling her own pilina to Hi'iaka, as her aikāne wale nō. But within our 'upena of intimacies, pilina can compound, as when Hi'iaka and Wahine'ōma'o took on Lohi'au as their kāne. Not only was their pilina as aikāne strengthened, but the pilina and kuleana *between the three of them* was compounded.

In the final mele, Wahine'ōma'o follows the instructions of her hoa hele and recalls the pilina between herself, her aikāne, and their kāne (see Figure 10).

Wahine'ōma'o sings out, recalling the spraying seas, how the three were fed together, the warm embraces that helped them endure the shivering cold. And when she does this, when she composes a mele that (re)members the aho between the three of them and calls out to her aikāne, "hoi mai kaua," Hi'iaka finally and wholeheartedly agrees: "ae, akahi au a hoi me oe." At this moment, Hi'iaka honors the hardships she and her aikāne endured together in all the places that they journeyed, "i au ai i ke kai makamaka ole, i ka pololoi ai," as they hungered in their quest across the lonesome seas.[49]

#	Kapihenui	Bush and Pa'aluhi
9	Kuu aikane i ka la o lalo e,	Kuu aikane i ka la o lalo e
	A po kaena i kehu a ke kai,	A po Kaena i ka ehu a ke kai,
	Kipu ae la i ka lau o ka ai,	Kipu ae la i ka lau o ka ai
	Pala ehu i ka la,	Palaehu i ka la
	Ka lau o ka ulu o Poloa e, po wale hoi,	Ka lau o ka ulu o Poloa, no wale hoi
	E hopo mai ana ka oe ia'u,	E hooipo mai an aka oe ia'u
	I ke hoa o ka ua o ka la,	I ke hoa o ka ua o ka la
	O ke anu o ke koekoe,	O ke anu o ke koekoe
	Auhea oe, hoi mai kaua	Auhea oe, hoi mai kaua
	(July 10, 1862, 4)	(June 27, 1893, 4)

Figure 10. Nā Mele o Wahine'ōma'o (Wahine'ōma'o Compositions).

These episodes are significant because they confirm that just as the pleasure shared between aikāne is marked by 'āina and place, so too is their kuleana to each other. Throughout the Hi'iaka archive, there are countless examples of Hi'iaka honoring her pilina to Wahine'ōma'o by recalling in verse and prose all the places and trials they had journeyed through together. Hi'iaka recalls the cold rains, the turbulent seas, the vicious opponents; and she does this all by name. These obstacles are entirely specific to the 'āina where they encountered them. The relationship to place is so central in their pilina that it is those places and pilikia that Wahine'ōma'o must remind Hi'iaka of to convince her to give up her mourning for Lohi'au and Hōpoe and return home to Kīlauea. We learn here that pilina and kuleana can be recounted and remembered through 'āina. In fact, because Hi'iaka eventually chooses to return to Kīlauea, the recollection of 'āina is what saves both Hi'iaka and Wahine'ōma'o from being killed by Pele. Should that 'āina have been forgotten or forsaken, Hi'iaka and Wahine'ōma'o would have been killed.

As we work to unpack and understand more fully what it means to practice aloha 'āina, these mo'olelo must be taken seriously. What binds Hi'iaka and Wahine'ōma'o so closely together is not just their mutual aloha for each other but their aloha for their shared 'āina. It is the aho that entwines them, tying them to each other and to 'āina aloha.

CONCLUSION

These mana'o I offer should not be surprising. Kanaka Maoli scholars have argued repeatedly that our mo'olelo reflect a deep connection between our Kānaka and our 'āina.[50] This 'ike has been firmly established in our contemporary scholarship. This chapter has therefore been devoted to peering into parts of our archive to see exactly what that "connection" looks like. When we read Hi'iaka closely, it becomes clear that this pilina to 'āina is the standard by which we understand our pilina with each other. Our relationship to our 'āina is our kumu, and every pilina we practice thereafter echoes the pilina learned from our beautiful home.

Eve Tuck and Wayne Yang remind us that "decolonization is not a metaphor," and I assert that neither is aloha 'āina.[51] Aloha 'āina requires practicing and (re)membering our entire 'upena. Aloha 'āina means that we must take useful theories crafted beyond our shores seriously but then place them in rigorous conversation with our archive and our 'ōlelo if they are to take root and become relevant. As Chris Finley writes, we must "historicize our traditions."[52] Our nation building requires us to understand these moʻolelo, and especially in the service of a movement that insists on the primacy of aloha ʻāina. It is not enough to say that Kanaka Maoli are distinct or even exceptional; we must understand and practice what makes our people unique, and one way that can begin is by mending our ʻupena of intimacies. Only by doing this difficult, sometimes uncomfortable but also deeply pleasurable work will we come to understand why we cannot plan to deoccupy Hawaiʻi now, and deal with issues of gender, pilina, "sexuality," and other forms of gendered violence later. Our specific and diverse articulations of gender, relationality, and pilina will lead and guide us into and through a nation-building movement that honors our values and distinct needs as a people. By studying, understanding, and practicing pilina, we will demonstrate that our movement for ea is not one that strives to change who governs but one that labors to transform what governance means.

And at another level of pilina, our archive and our ʻupena of intimacies have lessons to teach our Indigenous, queer, and POC ʻohana as well. Pilina remind us that leadership is not a position but a relationship. Pilina insist on protecting the intimacy of solidarity and taking seriously our intersectional identities and experiences. Our ʻupena of intimacies and moʻolelo provide countless examples of healthy relationships and modes of governance that offer alternatives to the ones we are participating in now. It will be up to us to decide how to apply this ʻike. Will we allow this ea to feed us, or will we allow ourselves and our kūpuna to continue to be buried and erased?

Kānaka Maoli know that something more than Christian and Western relationality exists. We know this in our naʻau, and we practice it in our ʻohana and communities. But we do not speak of our ʻupena of intimacies openly. We don't call out these pilina by name; we do not widely possess the vocabulary or the intimate knowledge of our moʻolelo to deploy them in conversations or use them to affirm ourselves and to fight the patriarchy, homophobia, and bad governance that continue to plague our lives and our home. In the fight to dismantle patriarchy, we must offer an alternate ground to stand upon. Here I offer a small handful of alternatives among the thousands in our archive. These alternatives have the mana to take

you back to your body, to your aloha, and to your 'āina. I know because
they have taken me back to mine. Practicing these alternatives is practicing decolonization.

Therefore, I offer you these ideas, these moʻolelo, in the hopes that they
give you back some ea, some aloha, some alternative to the status quo.
It is my hope that we use this ʻike to question our own assumptions and
the things we take for granted. It is my hope that we find and identify our
kōkoʻolua, our kāne and wahine, our aikāne and kaikoʻeke, our hoa hele
and hoa paio. Use their names, pay attention to the way they transform
us and our world, understand the ea each pilina brings to our lives and
community, and then do the hard work of making the aho, the rope that
will heal and remember our torn 'upena, so that we may all hoʻoulu hou
i kēia lāhui together.

CHAPTER FIVE

Kamaʻāina

◆ ◆ ◆ ◆ ◆

Pilina and Kuleana in a Time of Removal

A DISMEMBERED HOME

We know by now that all pilina is personal, and the disruption and refusal of our pilina are political. To discuss pilina to ʻāina, I must therefore begin here, at my piko, my one hānau: Waikīkī.

When I was a child, my ʻohana spent our weekends rolling in the shore break at Kaimana Beach Park. It might be hard to imagine, but even in the early 1990s, parts of Waikīkī were still ruled by Kanaka Maoli and local families—before the city and county of Honolulu were mining sand from the ocean floor to beef up a shoreline eroding into the sea because of overdevelopment. This was before the metered stalls that ran along Kapiʻolani Park, long before the State of Hawaiʻi was expecting more than ten million visitors a year, and before it imposed a sit-and-lie ban that specifically targeted and criminalized Hawaiʻi's poorest for simply existing, for being an eyesore on that prime commodity, Waikīkī Beach.[1]

Over thirty years, the transformation of Waikīkī has been overwhelming. Its shoreline and those who frequent it are nearly unrecognizable to me. Kanaka Maoli and local families navigating between the hordes of visitors are now the exception rather than the rule. And because we come to this shoreline less and less, it is not just that Kaimana becomes less familiar to us. We become foreign to her.

Kaimana is a place intimately entwined into my relationship—my pilina—with my ʻohana. Here is where I learned to swim in the ocean, securely clinging to my father's broad shoulders. Where I almost drowned when I decided to disobey my mother. Where my brother and I conquered our fear of heights when we jumped off the Natatorium wall and the lifeguard tower together. Where I taught my sisters to bodyboard—unsuccessfully. This is where we celebrate birthdays and adoptions and bid farewell to lifelong friends.

But I do not go to Kaimana much anymore. In fact, I only go there when my mother or father insist on my attendance at a particular family gathering. The beach itself is uncomfortable. The manufactured sand is chalky and clings to the skin in an unnatural way. The shoreline is crowded with American, European, and Japanese tourists, and the parking lots are hostile. So now when I come to Kaimana, I am overcome with the feeling that I do not belong. As a Kanaka Maoli born and raised in the ahupuaʻa of Waikīkī, this is not only saddening but troubling to me. By historical standards, this shoreline was a kuleana given to me by birth—a kuleana I would have to work to uphold but a kuleana that I had every right, and responsibility, to practice. Today, access to aloha ʻāina is obstructed by hotels, parking fees, and massive crowds of malihini. In some ways, these obstructions have also impacted my pilina with my ʻohana and, to a larger extent, to my lāhui. This is a trauma many of us are still desperately trying to heal.

In the previous chapters, I offered an overview of the theoretical fields to which this book responds. Chapter 1 drew upon and evaluated significant scholarship from Indigenous studies, Indigenous feminisms, and Indigenous queer theory to show how some fields of study have begun to draw our attention to the intimate and productive relationships between feminism, queer theory, and ea Hawaiʻi. Indigenous literary critique has been joined with Kanaka Maoli moʻolelo critique to provide vocabularies and methods for approaching Kanaka Maoli moʻolelo in terms of our own standards of excellence.

In chapter 2, I offered an overview of my archive and described my methods when consulting Hawaiian-language and nūpepa resources. I articulated a theory of rigorous paraphrase necessary when analyzing large collections of Hawaiian-language material in English scholarship and insisted on the necessity of approaching this archive from a place of abundance. Chapter 3 identified and evaluated the multitude of Kanaka

Maoli relationships that together form an expansive and dynamic matrix that I have called an 'upena of pilina. And in chapter 4, I discussed the intimate, pervasive role of 'āina in mo'olelo as something more than setting or backdrop, and I offered a series of readings that demonstrate how each and every one of these pilina between Kānaka is informed and mediated by a pilina with 'āina, thereby celebrating the links between the expression of intimacy and place.

In this chapter, I narrow the focus to a specific set of relationships that can help us see how the ongoing dislocation, disintegration, and disembodiment of our Kanaka Maoli relationships have affected, and continue to obstruct, our ability to challenge and offer alternatives to settler colonialism. The pilina at issue are those between kama'āina and malihini, and, more specifically, how the kuleana of such pilina are articulated in mo'olelo. Essential here will be our understanding of these positions within relationships, which contrast sharply with how they are represented and practiced as part of the technologies of settler colonialism in Hawai'i. I conclude with some thoughts on how Kānaka Maoli can initiate the practice of (re)membering these pilina through specific acts of *survivance* and resurgence as kama'āina on our 'āina.[2]

KULEANA

Kuleana, malihini, and kama'āina are words so commonly used in Hawai'i that they seem at times to elude definition. They all gesture toward values that resonate with many, but their complexity and richness of meaning also make them vulnerable to appropriation and commodification. Our insistence on maintaining the mana of these words and their related values are political acts. In this chapter, I describe what our mo'olelo o Hi'iaka teach us about kuleana, malihini, and kama'āina and discuss how these practices and values are inherently political. I also argue that returning as kama'āina to a responsible articulation guided by our mo'olelo will put us on the path toward becoming aloha 'āina, who can effectively challenge the settler state apparatus and its control of our aupuni and 'āina.

When people use the word *kuleana* in Hawai'i, they usually assume it means something like responsibility. But like most translations, this is far too flat a term to capture what kuleana actually is. In the *Hawaiian Dictionary,* Mary Kawena Pukui and Samuel Elbert define kuleana as a "right, privilege, concern, [and] responsibility" but also offer "property," "estate," "title," "claim," and "ownership" as meanings.[3] This cluster of definitions illustrates how the term and the value of kuleana have been appropriated and commodified to assist in creating and maintaining the U.S. occupation and settler colonialism in Hawaiʻi. Even in the most supposedly neutral source of information about meaning, we can watch how through the definition of kuleana, ʻāina is transformed into property, ready for sale and exploitation.

Significantly, Pukui and Elbert provide examples of usage that link kuleana to pilina: "ʻO Hina kō mākou kuleana, ʻaʻole ʻo ke kāne, we are related through Hina, not through the husband."[4] Relation therefore produces kuleana. And yet, while Pukui points to how pilina comes with kuleana, such definitions become buried within such state apparatus terms as *property ownership* and *marriage*. What we are encountering here is the methodical relationship between translation and settler colonialism. If we wish to mediate this problem, and to engage with these terms, values, and relationships for ourselves, we must turn to primary ʻōlelo Hawaiʻi sources and encounter kuleana and pilina in places where institutions such as marriage and capitalism are not entirely naturalized.

In *Lei Momi o ʻEwa*, Sarah Nākoa declares her kuleana that arises from her relationship to a particular place: "Noʻu iho, ua loaʻa he kuleana iaʻu e kamaʻilio aku i kēia pūpū no koʻu ʻike ʻana, koʻu lawaiʻa pū ʻana, a me koʻu ʻai ʻana i ia mea i koʻu wā kamaliʻi."[5] Nākoa explains that her kuleana to these pūpū o ʻEwa comes from bearing witness, from being a practitioner concerned with a resource's sustainability, and from being someone who is literally fed by her pilina to that place. Therefore, for Nākoa, kuleana is something practiced rather than something held or owned as property. ʻEwa is Nākoa's ʻāina because it feeds her, and because of that, she has a kuleana to ʻEwa.[6] This kuleana comes from a lifetime of living in reciprocity with the moku of ʻEwa. Does Nākoa hold title to a parcel of land in ʻEwa? Perhaps—but any land title held by her or her ʻohana would be irrelevant, having no bearing *in itself* on her kuleana to ʻEwa and to the moʻolelo she offers us.

In Kapihenui's mana o Hiʻiakaikapoliopele, Hiʻiaka demonstrates how stepping beyond our kuleana and being mahaʻoi can be incredibly dangerous and result in great hardship. After she returns to Kīlauea and their kāne, Lohiʻau, is killed by Pele, she is distraught and leaves once more. When Pele sends Wahineʻōmaʻo to retrieve Hiʻiaka and convince her to return, Hiʻiaka responds in anger:

Eia au mamuli o ke kane a kaua, o ka luhi a kaua i au ai i ke kai maka-maka ole, i au ai kaua i ke alanui papawaa, i hele ai kaua i ke kaha makamaka ole, kuleana ole, hookahi no kuleana o ke kane.[7]

Hiʻiaka reflects on the arduous task of retrieving their kāne, emphasiz-ing how this task required her to travel as a stranger in unfamiliar lands. For Hiʻiaka, to be in a land as a stranger (malihini), to be without pilina to the land, is to be in a land without kuleana. Hiʻiaka declares here that this was a journey of great personal sacrifice, because to be estranged from land is a hardship in and of itself. She shows us the magnitude of this sacrifice, and her investment in its result, by refusing to return to an ʻāina she has long been bound to, Kīlauea.

In Hoʻoulumāhiehie's mana of Hiʻiakaikapoliopele, Hiʻiaka makes sure to maintain that kuleana to her beloved home, Kīlauea, regardless of her return: "Heaha la auanei hoi! Ua hoi la au mamuli o kau kauoha. Eia nae; aole au e noho ana me oe. O koʻu kuleana noho no nae o ka lua nei o Kilauea a pela a hoea i Lalo o-Mehani me aʻu no ia."[8] Here we learn that kuleana can be maintained by those no longer living in a particu-lar place. Hiʻiaka's pilina to Kīlauea continues, even after her physical displacement. Hiʻiaka's kuleana to Kīlauea allows her to return whenever she pleases but on her own terms. She will not be estranged from her ʻāina. This example has far-reaching consequences because it sheds light on the contemporary issue of diaspora. Our moʻolelo offer us insight that can help us understand how Kānaka in the diaspora can begin to unpack their particular kuleana to place and lāhui.

Hiʻiaka also shows us that pilina can produce kuleana in the form of opportunity and rites of passage. When Papanuioleka asks to join Hiʻiaka and her companions on their journey to retrieve Lohiʻau, Hiʻiaka only agrees because she believes that Papanuioleka's pilina to her is enough to trust that she will uphold her kuleana as a traveling companion: "He pilikana oe no Haumea, a ua pili no hoi oe iaʻu. Nolaila, ina ua make-make loa oe i ka hele, alaila, e hele no."[9] In stating this pilina, Hiʻiaka acknowledges that she and Papanuioleka are pili through their shared relation to Haumea. Hiʻiaka believes that these shared bonds will be enough to inspire Papanuiolekaʻs loyalty. Both Hiʻiaka and Papanuioleka understand kuleana well enough to know that this privilege to join the journey comes with a responsibility. In this case, the kuleana is simple; Papanuioleka agrees that their pilina means that wherever Hiʻiaka shall go, Papanuioleka will follow: "he pili au iloko ou, nolaila, o kau wahi e hele ai, o koʻu wahi no ia e hele aku ai; aohe mea nana e wehe i kaʻu pili me oe."[10]

Here Hoʻoulumāhiehie shows how this pilina and the kuleana to uphold it are powerful enough to meet biblical standards.[11] But Papanuioleka goes back on her word and abandons her kuleana to Hiʻiaka mā. As a result, she quickly falls ill and dies.[12] Moʻolelo o Hiʻiaka therefore push us to recognize the consequences of dishonoring our pilina and the kuleana that comes along with it. Papanuiolekaʻs disrupting, then turning away from the kuleana that comes with being pili to someone, has the most serious personal result possible—death.

For those outside a Hawaiian context predictably struggling to understand kuleana, thinking about positionality might be a good first step. This cultural studies concept offers a framework for beginning to grasp something as dynamic as kuleana because, like positionality, kuleana involves a tremendous amount of personal and community awareness and a well-formed familiarity with systematic power structures such as white supremacy and settler colonialism.[13] Kuleana, however, is a more dynamic, less fixed set of authorities, responsibilities, and privileges that shift within a complex ʻupena of pilina. Kuleana is therefore both positionally and relationally articulated and practiced.

Understanding kuleana in this way also assists in effectively articulating its obligations as opposed to American "rights" discourses. Ponder for a moment Haunani-Kay Traskʻs foundational analysis in *From a Native Daughter*, which describes the links between rights ideologies and the "greatly obscured historical reality of American colonialism."[14] Trask demonstrates how the language of "civil rights" has been deployed to legitimize American control and authority. Such ideological assertions further displace Kānaka Maoli from cultural practices that define who we are. While she doesn't actually use the term *kuleana,* a close reading suggests that she is revealing how replacing *kuleana* with *rights* is a purposeful colonizing measure designed to make Americans out of Hawaiians. Her central assertion is that awarding Native Hawaiians the right to participate in the American democratic process did not liberate Hawaiians but "accelerated the de-Hawaiianization" of our people, lands, and lāhui.[15] Such a discourse presumes that the greatest gift Hawaiians can be offered is an abstract set of rights that somehow replaces kuleana to place.

By making mana and pono essential to her articulation of proper Kanaka Maoli leadership, Trask shows how returning to 'ōlelo Hawai'i is a necessary step in the process of decolonizing the nation-state and creating new forms of governance that honor how Kānaka exercise power. Her criticism of "rights," with its corollary that Kānaka must return to practices that are definitively Hawaiian, is another example of showing how language matters. By replacing equality, power, and rights with pono, mana, and kuleana, with all the attendant elaborations and distinctions, Trask pushes Kānaka Maoli toward a wholly reimagined understanding of sovereignty, one rooted in responsibility and balance entirely reflected in our genealogies and 'āina.

This understanding of our interlocking authority and accountability to each other (kuleana) is an increasingly important lesson to share with ourselves, settlers, and visitors, as we continue the struggle to build solidarities, allyship, and pilina across multiple intersections of oppressions and privilege. Not understanding positionality and relationality in Hawai'i creates huge problems for everyone with regard to kuleana, representation, and decision-making. That governing institutions malihini to our people and run by settlers are making major decisions about development, education, and militarization confirms that there is an urgent need to more fully understand pilina and relationality to the people, places, and histories that surround us.

KAMA'ĀINA, THE ONES WHO (RE)MEMBER

We have seen that Kānaka Maoli recognized an abundance of distinct and dynamic practices that enacted pilina between kānaka, akua, and places in our mo'olelo. From aikāne to kaiko'eke, such relationships are practiced by Kānaka sensitive to the dynamics of that specific pilina. Here we will explore what our moʻolelo can tell us about relationships that have been appropriated and usurped to maintain the tourist settler state in Hawaiʻi. The two relationships are malihini and kamaʻāina, and unpacking and then historicizing the fortunes of these pilina will assist us in finding a path toward reclaiming our intimate pilina to place as well.

In Hawaiian dictionaries, malihini is a term used to designate people who are strangers or foreigners to a particular place or people. Pukui and Elbert define malihini as "nvs. Stranger, foreigner, newcomer, tourist, guest, company; one unfamiliar with a place or custom; new, unfamiliar, unusual, rare, introduced, of foreign origin; for the first time."[16] Andrews adds that to be a malihini is to "be or to live as a stranger."[17] And Parker defines a malihini as "a stranger; a non-resident; a transient person; a person from another place.... One that has not been seen for some time."[18] Although calling someone a malihini seemingly offers an identity to that person, it is crucial to recognize that malihini is not an identity but a relationship. Malihini describes someone without pilina to specific lands, people, and cultures—a stranger to someone, something, or someplace.

Positioned in contrast to malihini is kamaʻāina. According to Pukui and Elbert, kamaʻāina means "native-born, one born in a place, host; native plant; acquainted, familiar, *Lit.*, land child."[19] In the Andrews dictionary, kamaʻāina is defined as "*kama*, child, and *aina*, land.... A child of the land. A native born in any place and continuing to live in that place."[20] Whereas these definitions focus on the role of birth in determining one's relationship to place as kamaʻāina, Parker defines kamaʻāina as "the present residents in a place; a citizen; especially one of long standing."[21] In Hawaiʻi today, Parker's definition comes closest to reflecting how kamaʻāina has been perverted, exploited, and commodified into a consumer reward system offering kamaʻāina—or locals, by this definition—certain rights and privileges. Such appropriations of Kanaka Maoli pilina for commercial purposes do not completely invalidate Parker's interpretation of kamaʻāina as having to do with a relationship to where one currently resides. But the equating of kamaʻāina with residents demands that we be cautious and mindful about how kamaʻāina as a concept is stripped here of its practice of kuleana and pilina in ways that can help maintain a settler state that centers local peoples, thereby erasing the

Def of settler colonialism
Come to places claim it as own → disappr Indeg iboriginal ppls

distinction between settler and Indigenous, and then advocating instead for local claims to Indigenous lands and resources. Such recoding has implications for the meaning of malihini, which has come to be equated with tourist, a specific brand of visitor created by global capitalism and corporate tourism who neither has nor recognizes kuleana to anything other than capital.

This purposeful and insidious translation of malihini and kamaʻāina into an identity void of kuleana erases the specific intimacies that traditionally mark one's pilina, replacing them with capitalism as the defining matrix for one's relationship to place. This is textbook settler colonialism. As Arvin, Tuck, and Morrill explain, settler colonialism is "a persistent social and political formation in which newcomers/colonizers/settlers come to a place, claim it as their own, and do whatever it takes to disappear the Indigenous peoples that are there."[22] Replacing our pilina to ʻāina with commerce and capitalism becomes the justification for settlers physically displacing our Kānaka. Declaring oneself a kamaʻāina, without any understanding of what kuleana that requires culturally, therefore re-enacts the long-practiced strategy of "immigrants (particularly haole from the U.S. continent) to proclaim themselves Hawaiian while asserting our indigenous heritage, including our lands, as their own."[23]

Our moʻolelo o Hiʻiaka teach us that being in, entering into, and maintaining a kamaʻāina pilina are not passive states of happening to be born or existing in a particular place. Because questions of pilina and kuleana immediately arise whenever anyone arrives somewhere new, moʻolelo o Hiʻiaka foreground malihini and kamaʻāina as central concepts, with many substantial sections of the moʻolelo devoted to how various figures question or comment on the malihini relation of Hiʻiaka as she enters each and every ʻili on her journey. As for being kamaʻāina, that is shown to be actively earned and practiced in a variety of distinct ways. On many occasions, characters sustain their pilina to their own one hānau while becoming kamaʻāina in other places through an intimate pilina informed by a particular practice of kuleana.

In moʻolelo o Hiʻiaka, kamaʻāina is not exclusively defined by where one was born but demonstrated by one's ʻike and practice of maintaining it. For example, after following the sounds of Lohiʻau and Kauakahiapaoa's drums and chanting all the way from Kīlauea, Pele arrives on Kauaʻi and is greeted as a malihini. The kamaʻāina of Hāʻena are enchanted by the staggering beauty of this stranger, whose exquisiteness is unmatched on the whole island of Kauaʻi. Before long, Pele is confronted by a moʻo kiaʻi of that place, Kilioe, who is immediately suspicious of Pele's presence and intentions. When Lohiʻau asks Pele to offer up a hula, Kilioe's jealously is aroused. Pele replies, saying that rather than dance she will offer up the wind names from Nīhoa to Kauaʻi. To which Kilioe responds: "ʻE! Hele no hoi apau ua makani o Nihoa mai a ianei alaila, he kamaaina oe no nei mau paemoku, a he malihini makou,'" If you should offer up all the winds from Nīhoa to this place then you would be the kamaʻāina of our island, and we would be the malihini.[24] Kilioe is now doubly jealous— both of Lohiʻau's admiration for Pele and of the pilina Pele has asserted to Kilioe's own ʻāina. It is as if Pele's presence and pilina threaten Kilioe's pilina to her home ʻāina. Pele demonstrates for the reader that in order to earn a pilina to the people of Kauaʻi, and to Lohiʻau in particular, she must show her pilina to Kauaʻi first.

Earlier in the same mana of the moʻolelo, Pele addresses Lohiʻau's distrust of her as a malihini by calling upon all the winds of Kauaʻi: "i mea e hoike aku ai i ka oiaio o koʻu kamaaina mai Kaula mai a hiki i ka mokupuni o Kauai nei, ua paanaau iaʻu na makani apau o keia mau mokupuni."[25] As in the moʻolelo of Kūapākaʻa from *Ipumakani a Laʻamaomao*, ʻike about ʻāina, and in particular about makani, becomes significant evidence for demonstrating one's pilina and kuleana to place.[26]

This is certainly not the only time a member of the Pele ʻohana demonstrates an intimate pilina with a place through their extensive ʻike. ʻIke and pilina become a commonly woven theme in moʻolelo o Hiʻiaka to demonstrate the mana of ʻike, ʻōlelo, and one's own ability to uphold one's kuleana to place. Much later in the moʻolelo, after Hiʻiaka and her aikāne and kōkoʻolua have revived Lohiʻau, they begin to make their trip home to Kīlauea. As Hiʻiaka mā are departing from Kauaʻi, Hiʻiaka's aikāne, Wahineʻōmaʻo, asks Lohiʻau to offer up the name of the places as they pass them. But before Lohiʻau can answer, Hiʻiaka responds: "Auhea oe e aikane, he kamaaina au no Kauai nei. O koʻu aina mua keia o ka noho ana i ko makou holo ana mai a Nihoa, Kaula, Niihau a hoea nohoi ia nei."[27] Hiʻiaka boastfully claims that she is a kamaʻāina of Kauaʻi because it was the first place that Pele mā came to after passing Nīhoa, Kaʻula, and

Niʻihau. Hiʻiaka backs up this claim immediately by listing the names of the places and winds of each ʻili they pass. It is here that Lohiʻau realizes that Hiʻiaka is also a kamaʻāina to his one hānau. He responds,

He keu io no kou kamaaina i nei mau wahi o Kauai nei; a kamaaina pu nohoi oe i na makani. Kuhi au o kela wahine wale no la hoi o olua ke kamaaina ia Kauai nei, eia no ka hoi o oe kekahi kamaaina.

O makou o ka poe i hanau i keia aina a nui a make a ola hou nohoi ia Kauai nei; aohe paanaau ia makou keia mau wahi, a he oki loa aku hoi na makani. Eia nae, ia oe keia, ua hele a wale waha.[28]

Because Hiʻiaka can remember and display this ʻike, Lohiʻau is compelled to confirm her as a kamaʻāina to Kauaʻi. By doing so, he points out another way that Hiʻiaka and her kaikuaʻana are pili, because they now have both demonstrated they are kamaʻāina to his home. And Lohiʻau celebrates the superior ʻike held by these two wāhine about Kauaʻi. According to Lohiʻau, many who have lived their whole lives on Kauaʻi and are buried in its dirt do not hold the same depth of ʻike that Hiʻiaka does to his ʻāina. Hiʻiaka is truly a kamaʻāina.

In addition to being significant because it adds to the theme of displaying ʻike about place and makani to prove one's claim to kamaʻāina, this passage is important because it is reproduced in the later mana attributed to Poepoe. He found this particular episode crucial enough to reproduce the same phrasing almost identically.[29] The mana attributed to both Poepoe and Hoʻoulumāhiehie demonstrate an imperative need that their readership recognize this particular path toward becoming kamaʻāina through the proper cultivation of ʻike.

This should not be surprising when we remember that Poepoe's introduction of his Hiʻiaka mana in 1908 began with a call for more rigorous study of the ʻike preserved in our moʻolelo. Just as Hiʻiaka has set the challenge and the bar for what ʻike must be possessed to fulfill the kuleana of being a kamaʻāina, Poepoe sets the bar and challenge for any moʻokūʻauhau or haku moʻolelo who hope to claim a kuleana to these moʻolelo. To Poepoe, this moʻolelo is far more than narrative and entertainment. It demonstrates the excellence of Hawaiian thought, standing as an important archive of ʻike Hawaiʻi that should be treated as such.

E hoomaopopoia, eia na poe naauao o kakou iho nei a me ko na aina
e ke apu mai nei i na moolelo kahiko o Hawaii nei, [o ko] kakou poe
opio [naauao/po] hoi, ke hoohemahema nui nei i keia kumu waiwai
nui o ka aina oiwi. Aohe huli, aohe imi, aohe no he makemake ia
mau mea. Aka, no makou iho, ke hoomau nei makou i keia hana no
ka makemake maoli e hoouluia [?] a hoomauia aku ka ike ia ana o na
moolelo a kaao kahiko o Hawaii nei i hiki ai ke malamaia e kakou,
ka lahui.[30]

Poepoe reminds his readers of the kuleana that comes with carrying and
protecting these moʻolelo. He urges us to consider the way ignorant people
have not cared properly for this ʻike that is so dear to us. He reminds us
that we are continuing these practices and sharing these moʻolelo to sustain and care for our lāhui, even while set within a territorial American
government.

Like one's kuleana to tell a particular moʻolelo, the claim to kamaʻāina
can always be challenged. Hoʻopāpā therefore becomes an important skill
to weed out those who will not honor the kuleana of our places or our
ʻike. Here too, we see the unstable and dynamic nature of what some call
an identity but what this archive demonstrates to be, in fact, a relationship. If people cannot show how they are kamaʻāina, then they cannot be
true kamaʻāina to that place or those peoples. It is specifically because
these pilina come with kuleana and authority that hoʻopāpā is an appropriate reaction to someone claiming to be a kamaʻāina to place.

Hoʻoulumāhiehie further shows how kamaʻāina becomes the premier
rank of authority when entering into a new place. Although Hiʻiaka is
indisputably the alakaʻi of her hui, Wahineʻōmaʻo is honored with the
kuleana to alakaʻi their group through the ʻāina to which she is kamaʻāina.
While, for instance, Hiʻiaka mā are traveling through Punahoa, Hiʻiaka
explains to her aikāne why she (Wahinʻōmaʻo) shall be the one to represent them.

Auhea oe e aikane? E hoolohe mai oe, oiai he maka kamaaina kou i
kahi poi o keia wahi, a he oi loa aku hoi kou kamaaina i na alii o Punahoa nei; nolaila, i ko kakou hele ana a hoea i kahi o ke alii ea, ia oe
auanei ka olelo a kaua, a o ka noho malie wale aku no kaʻu; aia no hoi

a ku ka olelo i kahi o kaʻu apana hana, aʻu no hoi e ike aku ai he hana
io ia, alaila, o kaʻu wahi no hoi ia e olelo ai a e hana ai.[31]

Because Wahineʻōmaʻo is a kamaʻāina of Hilo and therefore has a pilina
to Punahoa, Hiʻiaka instructs Wahineʻōmaʻo to speak for them when they
meet the aliʻi of that place. Here we see how even kuleana is positionally and relationally articulated. What makes Hiʻiaka a good alakaʻi to
her hui is that she recognizes the limitations of her kuleana from place
to place. She knows when and where it is appropriate for her to lead
and speak, and when she must yield to those whose pilina with place
and people are superior to her own. Time and time again in moʻolelo
o Hiʻiaka, we see this respect and accommodation of kamaʻāina, pilina,
and ʻike, whether in the company of the aliʻi of a place or in determining the order of kilu players.[32] At its simplest, then, kamaʻāina relate
to the land and her people as ʻohana, and those who travel often, like
our Wahinepōʻaimoku, are attuned to recognize the claims and the limitations of their own pilina to particular places, lest they overstep their
kuleana.

In many mana of our moʻolelo o Hiʻiaka, her malihini status is em-
phasized. This makes sense because Hiʻiaka is a moʻolelo about someone whose journey maps out all these islands—their moʻolelo, people,
and important geological features. But read through the intersection of
this moʻolelo and our ʻōlelo noʻeau, Hiʻiaka becomes less a moʻolelo about
a malihini going from place to place and more about how malihini come
to practice reciprocal pilina to places beyond the sands of their birth to
become kamaʻāina.

For those who may be thinking they have found a backdoor into Indigeneity, or a solution to their Hawaiian-at-heart dreams, it is important
to understand that while kamaʻāina reflects a *familiar* pilina to land and its
people, it does not necessarily reflect a *familial* one. This marks an important difference in the way Kānaka Maoli and settlers can and will experience what it means to be kamaʻāina to a place. Kanalu Young says it best
in *Rethinking the Native Hawaiian Past,* when describing what can and
cannot be accessed in ʻike by non-kānaka. He writes, "This is where someone who is Native Hawaiian can enter the Awāwa and take in all that a
non-Hawaiian does, but also feel something more. That something more

"A stranger only for a day. After the first day as a guest, one must help w/ the work."

is the heritage connection to ʻike kupuna as contents within pūʻolo. This is what ʻano ʻōiwi Maoli can predispose a Native Hawaiian to experience."[33] Rest assured that Trask's succinct words continue to ring true: "Hawaiʻi has only one Indigenous people: Hawaiians."[34]

Pukui translates the ʻōlelo noʻeau "Hoʻokahi nō lā o ka malihini" to mean "A stranger only for a day. After the first day as a guest, one must help with the work."[35] This reminds us that Hiʻiaka must be far more than a journeying malihini. Hiʻiaka's behavior throughout the moʻolelo asks us to take note of the ways she continues to take seriously her reciprocal kuleana as a guest while also taking on the labor to prove herself worthy as a kamaʻāina to these Kānaka and ʻāina. By following the guidance of Hiʻiaka, we too can develop and maintain ethical pilina with our places and peoples. This practice of pilina is not meant to name and claim territories as our own but to disrupt settler strategies that alienate and isolate us from our land and our communities.

You got to do the work

"Hoʻokahi nō lā o ka malihini" is a historic value that in company with the narratives in our moʻolelo rejects the settler state's preference and demand that Hawaiʻi should always be on call for visitor entertainment and hospitality. This practice, which puts "malihini"/visitors in the powerful role as buyers and Kānaka/kamaʻāina as sellers, sustains the power of the settler state by dehumanizing Kanaka Maoli bodies and culture. Our moʻolelo, however, can show us what deservedly happens to malihini who overstay their welcome by not putting in the work to develop a more respectful pilina to place and people. Today, more than ever, we must recognize the consequence of choosing to remain as malihini in our own land: complicity in maintaining oppressive structures such as settler colonialism.

Being a malihini is easy—it is literally a vacation from whatever responsibilities visitors might have where they live. But long-standing Hawaiʻi residents, and even Kānaka, can and do act like malihini too. What I am saying is that we all—Kanaka and haole—by living here have the kuleana to become more than malihini to each other and to our places. To do this is difficult but rewarding work that will transform our communities, expand our capacities, and help heal our societies. In the language of Indigenous studies, this is the work of identifying and practicing settler responsibility, or what I like to call ke kuleana malihini. If settler

Settler responsibility – ke kuleana malihini

colonialism is a structure rather than an event, then dismantling that system must begin with unpacking and understanding our diverse kuleana to 'āina and each other—moving through our time as malihini in an appropriate fashion before becoming kama'āina to our places and communities.[36] Reckoning with these difficult questions will allow Kānaka and settlers alike to recognize who our alaka'i and ali'i are, or should be, and then to support and hold them accountable.

For settlers who are seeking to establish and practice meaningful and generative pilina with our 'āina, I suggest beginning by investing in an honest pilina with the only Indigenous people of this 'āina. The only way to truly know and love our home is to know and love our people. And the only way to know and love our people is through our invitation. A part of this process is understanding and respecting when no invitation has been given.

MAI POINA

Many contemporary scholars and leaders in our sovereignty movement have articulated an important need to center our nation building in aloha 'āina.[37] They speak of a need to return to our places, to turn our hands down to the dirt and practice mālama 'āina, to reconnect with our land base. These are all important steps toward healing a Kanaka Maoli community whose values and identities have been deeply harmed by a colonial project now generations old. The truth is, however, that we cannot aloha 'āina if we don't know what aloha means. We must heal our pilina with each other just as much as we heal with our 'āina, and relearn to love in the ways that our kūpuna did—deeply, and without fear of harm or persecution.

Hi'iaka and other mo'olelo offer example after example of distinct practices of aloha between people and all the sources that feed them. Hi'iaka shows us that to be a kama'āina is to both feed and be fed, to love and be loved by place and community. She teaches us that no self-appointed leaders go unchecked or unquestioned. No human force is so supreme that it can circumvent the rules of intimacy and pilina between community and 'āina. No foreign power can fully rewrite the intimate practices of 'ohana that have existed in Hawai'i since time immemorial. But Hi'iaka is not the only mo'olelo that teaches us this vital lesson.

Scattered throughout our nūpepa archive, and in the embodied archive of our kūpuna who still remember these mele and moʻolelo, are countless narratives and melodies that inform and remind us time and time again about the great diversity and power of Kanaka Maoli intimacy. Aloha ʻāina is just one very important way we continue to practice intimacy in a Hawaiian way.

As we as Kānaka continue to struggle with how we should care for our ʻāina and govern ourselves, we must turn to these moʻolelo because they provide an abundance of models to learn from. As we attempt to enact alternatives to the status quo in Hawaiʻi, we must take up the study of our moʻolelo as vigorously as we study our kingdom and legal history. Our aupuni was one way our kūpuna imagined and practiced governance and community, but our moʻolelo offer an abundance of options. At the center of this call is a need to remember what it truly means to carry the kuleana of being a kamaʻāina to our places. Any supposed kamaʻāina without a clearly acknowledged and intensely practiced aloha and pilina to ʻāina and intimates is in danger of becoming a wandering child, without a place to call home. And without that ʻāina to which you are magnetically pulled, you cannot practice aloha ʻāina. For aloha ʻāina is not a metaphor or a political theory; rather, it is how we greet each other and the ʻāina as ʻohana, no matter how much time has passed, and also how we remember that we have kuleana here to fulfill.

The moʻolelo of Hiʻiakaikapoliopele very clearly describes many of these practices of pilina as well as the trauma and insecurity that results from their disruption. Hiʻiaka herself recognizes and even fears such trauma. As Hiʻiaka is traveling home to Hawaiʻi with her newly revived kāne, she offers chant after chant to the places she has become pili to. She repeatedly expresses her desire not to be forgotten by these places. "Mai poina oe iau," Do not forget me, she says, over and over again. When she does this, she also calls out to these places as hoa, companions with whom she has cultivated a sincere pilina (see Figure 11 for a partial list).

To be forgotten by an ʻāina that she has earned a particular pilina to would clearly be devastating for Hiʻiaka. It would mean that the ʻāina now refuses to recognize her pilina and therefore transforms her from a kamaʻāina into malihini. By composing mele after mele for each of these wahi pana, and by pleading, "Mai poina oe iau," Hiʻiaka is doing the

Place	Source
Halehau	Kapihenui, April 3, 1862, 4
	Hoʻoulumāhiehie, June 6, 1906, 4
Hapuu	Bush and Paʻaluhi, May 3, 1893, 4
	Hoʻoulumāhiehie, June 13, 1906
Haupu	Kapihenui, April 3, 1862, 4
Honouliuli	Kapihenui, April 3, 1862, 4
	Bush and Paʻaluhi, April 28, 1893, 4
Kaala	Kapihenui, February 13, 1862, 4
Kaehumoe	Bush and Paʻaluhi, April 28, 1893, 4
Kaena	Bush and Paʻaluhi, April 27, 1893, 4
Kalaihauola	Kapihenui, April 3, 1862, 4
	Bush and Paʻaluhi, May 3, 1893, 4
	Hoʻoulumāhiehie, June 13, 1906, 4
Kalalau	Kapihenui, March 13, 1862, 4
	Bush and Paʻaluhi, April 20, 1893, 4
Kamae	Kapihenui, February 13, 1862, 4
	Bush and Paʻaluhi, March 27, 1893, 4
Kanehoa	Kapihenui, April 3, 1862, 4
	Bush and Paʻaluhi, May 1, 1893, 4
	Hoʻoulumāhiehie, June 6, 1906, 4
Kapahi	Kapihenui, March 6, 1862, 4
	Bush and Paʻaluhi, April 10, 1893, 4
Keahumoe	Kapihenui, April 3, 1862, 4
Kealia	Kapihenui, April 3, 1862, 4
	Bush and Paʻaluhi, May 2, 1893, 4
	Hoʻoulumāhiehie, June 13, 1906, 4
Kinimakalehua	Kapihenui, April 3, 1862, 4
	Bush and Paʻaluhi, May 2, 1893, 4
	Hoʻoulumāhiehie, June 13, 1906, 4
Lalea	Kapihenui, March 6, 1862, 4
	Bush and Paʻaluhi, April 10, 1893, 4
Laniloa	Kapihenui, February 13, 1862, 4
Leinono	Kapihenui, April 3, 1862, 4
	Bush and Paʻaluhi, April 28, 1893, 4

(continued)

Place	Source
Leinono (*continued*)	Bush and Paʻaluhi, May 2, 1893, 4
	Hoʻoulumāhiehie, June 2, 1906, 4
	Hoʻoulumāhiehie, June 13, 1906, 4
Lihue	Kapihenui, March 20, 1862, 4
	Bush and Paʻaluhi, April 28, 1893, 4
	Hoʻoulumāhiehie, June 1, 1906, 4
Nawahineokamao	Kapihenui, April 3, 1862, 4
Nawahineokamaomao	Hoʻoulumāhiehie, June 5, 1906, 4
Nuuanu	Bush and Paʻaluhi, May 3, 1893, 4
Pohakuokauai	Kapihenui, March 20, 1862, 4
	Bush and Paʻaluhi, April 27, 1893, 4
Puukapolei	Bush and Paʻaluhi, April 28, 1893, 4
Puukua	Kapihenui, April 3, 1862, 4
	Bush and Paʻaluhi, May 1, 1893, 4
	Hoʻoulumāhiehie, June 6, 1906, 4
Puuokapolei	Kapihenui, April 3, 1862, 4
	Hoʻoulumāhiehie, June 5, 1906, 4

Figure 11. Mai Poina ʻoe iaʻu (Do not Forget Me).

important work of (re)membering her own ʻupena of intimacies, cultivated during her huakaʻi kiʻi kāne.

What this part of moʻolelo o Hiʻiaka tells us is that Kānaka Maoli not only wish to live sustainable, equitable, and fulfilling lives in relationship to each other and our lands but that we wish to be known and loved by our lands as well. Hiʻiaka reminds us that we long not to be forgotten or left behind. Our moʻolelo also remind us that when we do the work to build and maintain these relationships, being torn away from them, regardless of the cause, is serious trauma. This is the pilina that comes with aloha ʻāina. Like all other relationships, kamaʻāina is reciprocal. So therefore, this famous, oft-cited aspect of moʻolelo o Hiʻiaka reveals that our ʻāina in its own ways remembers how we aloha, honor, or dismiss her. Like our bodies, our ʻāina carry intergenerational aloha and trauma. So if I want to be remembered by Waikīkī, then I must remember Waikīkī back, and if I do not want to be refused or forgotten, then I must not refuse her. If we seek to reclaim our kuleana to call these places home, we all have more to learn about these 'āina and their mo'olelo. On an individual level, that means honoring the names our kūpuna gave to the 'āina we love.

(RE)MEMBERING KAPUA

While writing this chapter, I was directed to resources that properly account for Kaimana Beach's historic name, Kapua. By learning her name, I am coming to this place both as my new hoa and as a hoa I must heal old wounds with—a hoa with whom I must practice my pilina. In addition to the all-important structural work necessary to liberate Kānaka Maoli from the oppressive forces of settler colonialism, we must also engage in a few simple yet important practices of resurgence as Kānaka if we wish to heal ourselves and our 'āina. We must first return to the lands where we (or our kūpuna) were once kama'āina. We must fight to remember these places as they still are, beneath the scars of their development, beyond the ways they have been pimped out for economic opportunity. In my own life, this means returning to Waikīkī. With my 'ohana, I will recover and sing the old melodies and 'ōlelo of our shared kūpuna, showering Waikīkī's shoreline with our voices. These simple acts of resurgence are especially important in those places where the occupying settler state of Hawai'i and the city and county have made abundantly clear that Kānaka are not welcome. Part of our trauma of being displaced and removed from Waikīkī and our other 'āina is our awareness that they have been left alone with strangers, transformed and forgotten. To again practice our pilina, we must offer what we know best, our mo'olelo and music, back to these places. And we must say, "'A'ole mākou e poina iā 'oe," We will not forget you or refuse you again.

And when we do this, when we practice our pilina and aloha with our places, we remember some of the many ways and reasons we aloha each other. We remember the reasons we cherish a place. For my 'ohana, we remember how the sand used to feel soft and would crumble between our toes. We remember the salt of the ocean on our lips. We tell our stories and are told stories as well. And despite, or even because of, the trauma she has experienced, we accept Waikīkī, and all her shades. She is not debris, she is not hotels, concrete, or capitalism. She is the playground of our aliʻi, she is seventy-seven acres of loko iʻa producing twenty-three thousand pounds of fish per year to feed our communities.[38] She is home, and it is our kuleana to remember that. We are then (re)membered in that remembering. Our ʻupena of pilina is once more secure, unquestioned, and undeterred, and our ʻohana and lāhui are made stronger for it.

Rise Like a Mighty Wave

Ask me about The Mauna
And I will tell you about 30 Kānaka
Huddled shivering in an empty parking lot
Praying
The lāhui would answer the call
I will tell you about two nights
Cot sleeping
Directly under a sky scattered in stars
In air so clear
Every inhale is medicine

How every morning
I woke to a lāhui kanaka growing
As if we were watching Maui fish us
One by one
From the sea

Ask me about the mauna
And I will tell you
How on the third morning I watched
As 30 became 100
Then 100 became 1,000

Then 1,000 became us all
Each and every one of our Akua standing beside us

Ask me about The Mauna
And I will tell you the moʻolelo of 8
Kānaka chained to a cattle grate
And the kōkua that sat beside us
How we were never alone in the malu of our mauna
How no one is ever alone in the malu of our mauna

Ask me
And I will tell you about the hands I held
Through blistering cold
And extreme heat
How I learned love
From the subtle tilt of her temple pressed against mine
Or by the solemn promise of her eyes
How the evening before I braided prayers into her hair
Hoping they would hold

Ask me
And I will recount their names
All 38
Of kūpuna
Who showed us moʻopuna how to stand
How I wept
And wept
And wept
As I quietly held their names in my chest

Ask me
And I will sing the song of our mana wāhine
Linked arms and unafraid
Standing in the face of the promise
Of sound cannons and mace

Ask me
And I will tell you
I have been transformed here
But won't have the words to quite explain

I will say:
I don't know exactly who I will be when this ends
I don't know exactly who *we* will be when this ends
But at the very least
I'll know
This 'āina
Did everything it could to feed me
And that will be enough to keep me standing

On July 17, 2019, I watched alongside my lāhui as thirty-eight of our beloved kūpuna stood fiercely in their aloha for our 'āina and were hauled away by state and Hawai'i County enforcement officers.[1] Hundreds of thousands of people clung to their Facebook and Instagram live feeds while nearly a thousand kia'i (protectors) lined the Ala Hulu Kūpuna (Mauna a Wākea Access Road) and flooded the pāhoehoe in our tears.

Just two days earlier, on July 15, the kia'i at the Pu'uhonua o Pu'uhuluhulu had reactivated a call to our lāhui to join us in the protection of our sacred mauna when eight kia'i chained ourselves to the cattle guard on the access road, preventing the delivery of construction equipment.[2] We laid there in the malu and protection of our mauna and our lāhui for twelve hours.

The next morning, our numbers increased from a couple of hundred to a thousand brave kia'i ready to stand up and put their bodies between our mauna and any acts of desecration. We stood proud, basking in the wealth and brilliance of our people. We also stood anxious, because as our numbers grew, so did the numbers of enforcement officers, and their weaponry and machinery. As we grew to possibly the greatest activation of our people since the kū'ē petition drive in 1897, we wondered if we would be met with a force that we, contemporary Kānaka, had never before encountered.[3]

In the wake of our rising wave, the state assembled its army of enforcement officers pulling from at least six separate agencies.[4] And while these officers collected their weapons, our Kumu, masters of ceremony, led us in the kāhea of our akua.[5] At this time, the state revealed that in the face of all our mana and abundance, it had only force and violence to offer us.

When July 17, 2019, arrived, our lāhui was prepared. As police took our kūpuna, one by one, each empty seat was quickly filled by another kupuna ready to take a stand until no elders remained. The rest of us, their moʻopuna, gave the officers only our silence. Not even the satisfaction of our wailing grief would surround them. And as our silence grew, so did our mana. When the final kūpuna were hauled away, their place flooded with hundreds of mana wāhine, supported by our kāne at our backs. And again, our people controlled the road, controlled our destiny, and continued to protect our ʻāina.

When we, mana wāhine, took the road, we remembered the teachings of our kūpuna, we sang our mele, chanted our oli, while some even danced our hula. We offered aloha and care to the police officers who struggled before us. We reminded them that we stood there for our children, and *their* children. But most of all, we held tightly onto each other. We insisted that we would protect our lāhui as fiercely as we would protect our mauna. We understood in that moment how the two were the same.

The next morning, the number of kiaʻi who gathered at Puʻuhuluhulu and the Ala Hulu Kupuna had tripled, and day by day we continued to grow as three to five thousand Kānaka and allies answered the call to kiaʻi our mauna. The wealth of our mana resounded across the pae ʻāina. Meanwhile, the state cowered in its incompetence, spending more than eleven million dollars in its threat to remove us from our ancestral lands.

Today our kiaʻi continue to govern the Ala Hulu Kūpuna with aloha ʻāina, in strict Kapu Aloha. Our people are rising like a mighty wave, and what we have accomplished cannot be cast aside.[6] In fewer than three months, our movement brought thousands of people to the mauna physically (and hundreds of thousands virtually). Most of these kiaʻi had never stood in the malu of Mauna a Wākea before. That's thousands of people who had never had the opportunity to develop an intimate pilina to one of our most sacred ʻāina. Through our collective ea, and our commitment to aloha ʻāina, we brought these Kānaka home.[7]

And in doing so, we have cultivated in our people an intimacy with a part of our ʻāina we had been strategically estranged from. We have given

Kānaka something back that was taken away from us. Kānaka living around the world are not just reconnecting to Mauna a Wākea but also taking these lessons of aloha and pilina to their home communities. This movement and the sacrifice of our kūpuna prepared us for such a strong and unrelenting commitment.

Therefore, as we continue to grow, we will remember that it was this very intimacy of aloha ʻāina that pulled islands out of the depths of the sea, that called upon the great koa of our history to fight against a variety of oppressive forces, and that mobilized Kanaka opposition to U.S. imperialism and annexation. The intimacy of aloha ʻāina carried fifteen thousand Native Hawaiians to march to the ʻIolani Palace in 1993 in recognition of one hundred years of being a stolen kingdom. Twenty-five years later, in 2018, aloha ʻāina called another twenty thousand of us to return to that march to celebrate the vibrancy of our resilience and resurgence.

More recently aloha ʻāina called eight Kānaka Maoli to chain ourselves to a cattle guard and later inspired thirty-eight kūpuna to face arrest at the Ala Hulu Kūpuna two days later. It was that same aloha ʻāina that then resulted in upward of five thousand kiaʻi joining us at any given time at the Ala Hulu Kūpuna to protect our mountain. And it is putting this intimate aloha ʻāina to action today that has resulted in similar uprisings in our communities in Waimānalo (Hūnānāniho), Kalaeloa, and Kahuku and will surely empower the continued rising of our kiaʻi on Maui (Nā Wai ʻEhā, and Kauaʻula) and Kauaʻi (Save Hanapēpē Salt Ponds).

The power of memory and remembering our past and the pilina that we have been reclaiming is still so very important to this movement because our moʻolelo and kūpuna teach us that it is our pilina to our ʻāina and to each other that gives us the kuleana and mana to govern. We should celebrate the many ways our people are returning to an aloha ʻāina that is not simply political but also deeply intimate and emotional. Our growing intimacies shared between each other and our ʻāina is our greatest wealth. That is one of the lessons we learn at Mauna a Wākea, Hūnānāniho, Kalaeloa, and Kahuku every day.

I believe it is only a matter of time until the Thirty Meter Telescope corporation packs up its bags and departs our beautiful home. And on that day, we will have succeeded in protecting our Mauna from this specific act of violence. But perhaps we should also remember we are not simply standing in opposition to desecration; rather, we are fearlessly committed to protecting our humanity and our ability to live, breathe, think, and act as our kūpuna have for generations. What if protecting ʻāina is what makes us Kanaka in the first place? What if that is the wealth and lesson of our ancestors that we cannot afford to lose?

CHAPTER SIX

Kū Kia'i Mauna

◆ ◆ ◆ ◆ ◆ ◆

*How Kapu and Kānāwai Are Overthrowing
Law and Order in Hawai'i*

The mo'olelo of the desecration of Mauna a Wākea (Maunakea, the Mauna) begins in 1968 when the State of Hawai'i via the Board of Land and Natural Resources (BLNR) issued a sixty-five-year general lease for 13,321 acres of ceded lands at the summit of Maunakea to the University of Hawai'i (UH) to build one observatory.[1] Following its construction, developers planned and built a number of observatories and auxiliary buildings without permits. As an answer to public protest and outrage, the BLNR issued permits (after the fact) for the unauthorized structures. By 1983 the Mauna Kea Complex Development Plan was finalized, approving up to thirteen telescopes by the year 2000. Importantly, this sixty-five-year master lease could be vacated at any time by the state for failure to properly care for or manage the Mauna.[2]

In 1998 the Hawai'i state auditor released a report documenting thirty years of mismanagement of the summit by both UH and the BLNR. The audit did little to stall the further development of Maunakea; in fact, in the next year, two additional telescopes were constructed. At this time, Kānaka Maoli and allies who stood in opposition to the continued degradation of the Mauna continued to use bureaucratic means toward lodging and documenting our opposition. Ultimately the impact of the ongoing development of the summit resulted in an Environmental

149

Impact Assessment (EIS) that documented the astronomy activity having caused "significant, substantial and adverse" harm.[3] However, rather than stall or slow further development following the publication of the EIS, the BLNR moved forward to approve a "Comprehensive Management Plan," which made possible the construction of an unlimited number of observatories and auxiliary structures.[4]

This is the corrupt history the Thirty Meter Telescope (TMT) Corporation walked into when it applied for a permit in 2010 to build what would be the largest and most devastating structure built within the conservation use district of Maunakea's summit. During a string of court hearings, public opposition to the project and overall continued mismanagement and desecration of the Mauna grew and was documented.[5] This ultimately culminated in a number of standoffs between Kānaka Maoli, allies, and state law enforcement during numerous demonstrations to block the delivery of construction equipment to the build site. Across numerous demonstrations since 2014, at least eighty kiaʻi (including thirty-eight kūpuna in 2019) have been arrested in their ongoing protection of our Mauna.

On July 12, 2019, approximately three hundred Kānaka and allies gathered in Kona, Hawaiʻi, to reestablish a plan to obstruct the construction of the TMT. That evening, thirty or so Kānaka caravanned to Puʻuhuluhulu (just across the road from the Maunakea Access Road) in the dark of night to hold space and prepare for a standoff with Hawaiʻi law enforcement. Two days later, with the blessing and support of the Royal Order of Kamehameha, we kiaʻi ceremonially established a puʻuhonua (place of refuge) at Puʻuhuluhulu and called upon the greater lāhui to seek refuge with us and join in our collective resistance to the desecration of our sacred Mauna a Wākea. While our numbers have varied from our humble thirty to approximately five to seven thousand on any given day, our kiaʻi remained at the puʻuhonua until the onset of the covid-19 pandemic.

The current and ongoing movement to protect Mauna a Wākea is born out of the strength of those who have stood in protection of our sacred sites for generations. It is also born out of a sincere and serious opposition to the injustice outlined here. It is important to call attention to the pilina between the overall mismanagement of the Mauna to a larger practice of mismanaging Indigenous lands under the occupying jurisdiction

Biggest threat: live in abundance in the face of a society that is drowning in scarcity

of the settler state. The rise of our lāhui today has everything to do with the fact that more and more of our people are being educated and engaged to take up their kuleana in overturning this long history of injustice. It would be foolish and insincere of me to limit the scope and impact of this movement to the fight to obstruct the construction of a Thirty Meter Telescope. While the TMT has become the material opponent we have directed our energies toward defeating, it is clear, through every stage of protest, demonstration, and public comment period, that our aim as Kānaka reaches far beyond the blocking of a single development project.

This too can be said of the State of Hawai'i and its unwavering and overzealous support of the TMT project. Perhaps the early years of this struggle could be boiled down to a simple disagreement over appropriate sites for development; however, the fight over Maunakea today is certainly not simply about a telescope or even more broadly about development. 'A'ole, this battle has grown into something much larger for both the occupying State of Hawai'i and our lāhui.

That the State of Hawai'i has spent more than $11 million in its functioning as private security for the TMT project is not so much demonstrative of its sincere investment in the building of a telescope.[6] Rather, this all-in approach by the state demonstrates the way the Pu'uhonua o Pu'uhuluhulu and our growing grassroots power pose a serious threat to business as usual in Hawai'i. As a living alternative to the settler society that the majority of Kanaka and Hawai'i residents participate and live in today, the Pu'uhonua o Pu'uhuluhulu offers an alternative calculus. While not completely free from the seduction of capitalism, patriarchy, and Christian morality, the Pu'uhonua o Pu'uhuluhulu represents the potential of a governing formation rooted in aloha 'āina, sustainability, and Kanaka-led cooperation. This is certainly the biggest threat we pose to the State of Hawai'i: we live in abundance in the face of a society that is drowning in scarcity.

In addition to demonstrating an alternative, the kia'i on Maunakea and across the pae 'āina (Hawaiian Islands) have eloquently and successfully challenged the governing jurisdictions of our occupying forces on multiple levels. Since the very onset of this movement to protect Mauna a Wākea, kia'i have challenged the settler state jurisdiction over the proposed development site. In the macro sense, following the work of Keanu Sai, many Kānaka have argued that since there was never a treaty of annexation, Hawai'i remains an illegally occupied kingdom, which, in addition to making all operations of the State of Hawai'i illegal, nullifies any jurisdiction on the state's part to negotiate with internationally funded corporations over any development projects, including the TMT.[7] Following the work of scholars such as Haunani-Kay Trask and Mililani Trask, other Kānaka have continued to assert that the summit of Mauna a Wākea consists of kingdom and Crown lands that were seized during the overthrow and that questions of sovereignty and self-determination to these and other lands need to be addressed before moving forward with such a project.

More recently the battle to protect Mauna a Wākea has demonstrated the imperfection and vulnerability of the occupying settler state of Hawai'i. When it became public knowledge that the lands beneath the pu'uhonua and the Ala Hulu Kupuna (the Maunakea Access Road) were under the jurisdiction of the Department of Hawaiian Home Lands (DHHL), questions of the legality of the arrest of beneficiaries on that same road were brought to the fore.[8] Each and every one of these challenges to the settler jurisdiction over 'āina in Hawai'i has not been enough, at this point, to terminate the TMT project; however, together they raise serious questions about governance, legality, and jurisdiction.

Since jurisdiction is so hotly contested in this issue, reconsidering the very meaning of the term via an analysis of its etymology would prove useful in this case. In "Jurisdiction: Grounding Law in Language," Justin Richland reminds us that although jurisdiction is often a concept that "demarcates law's territorial scope, and thus the bounds of state sovereignty," there is a deeper history and meaning to the language of jurisdiction.[9] Richland writes,

> Sociolinguist Emile Benveniste (1973) offers an etymology of the word jurisdiction as combining the Latin roots for law (juris) and speech (dictio) in a way that simultaneously points up the performative character of legal speech (speaking the law) and makes reference to the ideational content of that speech (law's speech). For contemporary scholars, this double sense of jurisdiction suggests the reflexive, metalinguistic

qualities by which law (and its social force) is spoken into existence not only in foundational legal speech acts—such as preambles of constitutions—but also in more mundane moments, such as when litigants petition a court to decide on its authority to hear their case, or in the opening statements of legislation, regulatory opinions, or executive orders that recite boilerplate language.[10]

Richland and Benveniste encourage us to see beyond the imagined rigid borders of state sovereignty and pay heed to the way jurisdiction is created and upheld by "speaking the law." This reading of jurisdiction makes profound sense to me as a Kanaka raised on the famous 'ōlelo no'eau "i ka 'ōlelo no ke ola i ka 'ōlelo no ka make" (in language/speaking, there is life and death). In this way, while we Kānaka continue to live in a society where rights over land, development, and progress are so heavily contested, our charge as we continue to speak, dance, and chant the law daily is increasingly dangerous to the maintenance of the settler state.

As for now, the occupying settler state of Hawai'i has responded to these challenges by simply highlighting the lawlessness of the kia'i to occupy the Mauna and obstruct the road. Various enforcement agencies have threatened the kia'i with charges like obstruction, trespassing, and obstructing a government operation at different junctions. The irony of arresting Kānaka Maoli on lands specifically set aside for their betterment is outrageous enough that I probably need not elaborate. But ultimately what has come to a head in this movement is that the state has put all its eggs in one basket, hoping that the insidious invisibility of settler colonialism will rule powerfully enough that the general public will fail to recognize the irony of an illegal occupying state calling Indigenous protectors on Indigenous land lawless. The state's only argument thus far for the progression of this project is that it has "followed the law." For those wanting a more detailed analysis of the incredible number of laws that have been broken in the pursuit of this and every telescope on Mauna a Wākea, I suggest consulting the website of KAHEA: The Hawaiian-Environmental Alliance.

However, this chapter and to a greater extent this book are not about what does and doesn't fall under the category of what is lawful. This book is a challenge to all settler structures we have taken for granted in the violent reorganizing of our lives as ʻŌiwi peoples. When settlers cite the law for their benefit, they fail to recognize that laws are no more sacred than any other moʻolelo, and therefore in Hawaiʻi we have record after record of other moʻolelo to order our lives around. In short, to be lawless as Kānaka under settler colonialism or belligerent settler occupation does not necessarily mean we are without discipline and order.

When we come to the law as a moʻolelo, or something we must speak, ever evolving with many mana, and with as much mana as we choose to recognize as a collective, we destabilize the assumed preeminence of Western law in the settler occupation of Hawaiʻi. We begin to make way for conversations about where else we might find justice and order if not from the U.S. and state constitutions or the thousands of statutory laws that currently govern our settler society. Hawaiʻi Kingdom scholars such as Kamana Beamer might, in this instance, point us to kingdom constitutions as alternatives to the current Hawaiʻi State Constitution.[11] But whether or not our kingdom constitutions and statutes represent the brilliant ingenuity of our kūpuna, the question still remains: Are there other ways to create order, ethics, and justice in a society without what we conceive as laws today? And if there are, are our people rising in the image of something grand and old that is intimately documented in our moʻolelo? On both accounts, I believe the answer is yes.

KAPU, KĀNĀWAI, AND HAWAIIAN "LAWLESSNESS"

Questions around the possible irrelevance of the rule of law in Hawaiʻi are important in a time where the faithful adherence to law and order forms the central justification for the removal of Indigenous peoples from our lands, from our posts protecting ʻāina, and from our practicing and visioning of decolonial futures in Hawaiʻi. In this chapter, I dive into the center of this conflict by outlining the ways the kiaʻi of Mauna a Wākea are returning to a different and older system of order and accountability rooted in the teachings of our moʻolelo and ʻāina. I continue to rely on our moʻolelo, like that of Hiʻiakaikapoliopele and others, to form the foundation of this analysis.

In the moʻolelo of Hiʻiakaikapoliopele, there are three main terms used to create and maintain formal agreements and conditions of behavior (i.e., what the state calls "law and order"): kapu, kānāwai, and kauoha.

Kapu doesn't necessarily mean keep out;
it mems be intentional about relation
to sacred
KŪ KIA'I MAUNA   155

These terms and the way our kūpuna adhered to an appreciation of their sacredness ordered our world in a way that is unintelligible to the settler state. As we've seen in the previous chapters, our mo'olelo offer a map showing how to return to practicing a bit of that radical unintelligibility. As with all the other Hawaiian-language terminology used throughout this book, these terms cannot be easily glossed by English substitutes. When thinking specifically about language crucial to questions of governance, these complications in translation become even more apparent.[12] To mitigate this problem, I have provided, as I have previously, a compilation of translations from our most-trusted Hawaiian dictionary sources (see Figure 12), followed by an engagement with the definitions through our mo'olelo o Hi'iaka and our current movement to kia'i 'āina in Hawai'i.

In Hawai'i today, the term *kapu* is most often misunderstood as "keep out." The word appears on many fences as signs warning of danger and prosecution should people break these boundaries. Significantly, signs marked with kapu have, in the past century, been used to restrict access of Hawaiians to our own lands and resources. However, historically, kapu on 'āina would have been marked with Hawaiian adornments to signal the land and boundaries of an ali'i's 'āina. Importantly, kapu doesn't necessarily mean keep out. Rather, kapu marks the sacred, and coming in proximity or under kapu requires that one intimately account for one's relationship to the sacred.

The definitions collected here reflect some of the nuances behind this term. The authors generally agree that these "prohibitions" are not secular or arbitrary but rooted in an ancestral recognition of the relationship between 'āina, our bodies, and the sacred. In contemporary Hawai'i, the settler state has reduced kapu from marking the sacred to protecting individual commodities and property. In the appropriation of kapu by the settler state, they reduce its meaning to mark a prohibition, an impasse, an obstruction. However, in our older mo'olelo, kapu force us to reckon with our pilina to each other, the 'āina we are fed by, and our governing structures. Understanding a kapu requires understanding your specific pilina and orientation to that which is sacred.

Today, the word *kānāwai* has been similarly appropriated by the state to describe the same laws and statutes that enable the removal of Kānaka

Term	Definition	Source
kapu	nvs. Taboo, prohibition; special privilege or exemption from ordinary taboo; sacredness; prohibited, forbidden; sacred, holy, consecrated; no trespassing, keep out. hoʻo. kapu To make taboo, prohibit, sanctify consecrate, forbid.	Pukui and Elbert
kapu	s. A general name of the system of religion that existed formerly on the Hawaiian Islands and which was grounded upon numerous restrictions or prohibitions keeping the common people in obedience to the chiefs and priests but many of the kapus extended to the chiefs themselves. The word signifies 1. Prohibited; forbidden. 2. Sacred; devoted to certain purposes. Nah. 6:7. 3. A consecration; a separation. (See Hawaiian History and D. Malo on Kapus.) Eha na po kapu ma ka malama hookahi there were four tabu nights (days) in a month: 1st kapuku 2d kapuhua 3d kapukaloa 4th kapukane.	Andrews
kapu	1. The system of religion that existed formerly in Hawaii. It was based upon numerous restrictions or prohibitions keeping the common people in obedience to the chiefs and priests but many of the tabus extended to the chiefs themselves: Eha na po kapu ma ka malama hookahi there were four tabu nights (days) in a month: First Kapuku; second Kapuhua; third Kapukaloa; fourth Kapukane. 2. A restriction; a restraint; a consecration; a separation. 3. Any restrictive or prohibitory order.	Parker
ka-na-wai	nvs. Law, code, rule, statute, act, regulation, ordinance, decree, edict; legal; to obey a law; to be prohibited; to learn from experience. *Fig.*, ti leaves, as used in religious ceremonies as a plant respected by spirits. Since some early laws concerned water (wai) rights, some have suggested that the word kānāwai is derived from wai, water; this seems doubtful in view of the many ancient edicts of gods that have no relation to water (also cf. *wai* 4 and derivatives).	Pukui and Elbert
kanawai	s. *Ka*, preposition, of belonging, relating to, &c., *na*, sign of the plural, and *wai*, water. LIT. What belongs to the waters, i.e., rights of water. N.B.—The ancient system of regulations for water courses contained almost everything the ancient	Andrews

Term	Definition	Source
	Hawaiians formerly had in common in the shape of laws; hence the name *Kanawai* has in more modern times been given to laws in general. 1. A law; an edict; a command of a chief. 2. Still more modern, a legislative enactment.	
kānāwai	[Ka, preposition, of belonging, relating to; na, sign of the plural, and wai, water.] 1. Lit. What belongs to the waters, that is, rights of water courses contained almost everything the ancient Hawaiians formerly had in common in the shape of laws; hence the name kanawai has in more modern times been given to laws in general. 2. A law; an edict; a command of a chief. 3. More modern meaning, a legislative enactment.	Parker

Figure 12. Defintions of kapu and kānāwai from Pukui and Elbert, *Hawaiian Dictionary*; Andrews, *Dictionary of the Hawaiian Language*; and Parker, *Dictionary of the Hawaiian Language*.

from our 'āina. And unfortunately, this marriage of terms is reflected in the accepted definitions across all the main Hawaiian dictionaries. As such, law and statute are the most common English glosses for the term *kānāwai,* and although it is clear that the term was appropriated in the nineteenth century to be applied to kingdom constitutions and statutes, we must remember that kānāwai are an institution that predates Western law in the islands.[13] Andrews's and Parker's definitions for kānāwai are nearly identical and comment most directly on this phenomenon. Both Andrews and Parker cite kānāwai as "the ancient system of regulations for water courses [that] contained almost everything the ancient Hawaiians formerly had in common in the shape of laws."[14] In the case of this book, it is important that we not overly entangle the relationship between laws and kānāwai and remember to analyze kānāwai from within its own context, that is, within its own mo'olelo. Therefore, rather than simply glossing these terms, it would serve the reader to understand that kapu can often describe the overall structure and system, while kānāwai work under the system of kapu to maintain our particular society and system.

The ʻAi Kapu is certainly the most commonly known and referred to kapu of ka wā ma mua (the time before). Importantly, this kapu was inherited by our people from our akua, Papa and Wākea. Under this kapu, specific kānāwai were to be followed. Specifically, kāne were to prepare two imu (underground ovens) and cook foods for themselves and wahine separately. This was done to ensure that foods forbidden to kāne and wāhine were not contaminating the foods allowed to them.[15] Like many of the kānāwai of that period, failing to abide by them could result in death. The kapu applied to Kānaka of every kūlana, including the mōʻī and aliʻi themselves. The ʻAi Kapu is a kapu that our Kānaka adhered to for generations before it was eventually dismantled by Liholiho under pressure from his mothers Keōpūolani and Kaʻahumanu by sharing a meal together after the death of Kamehameha.

The ʻAi Kapu was an important system that mediated the pilina and the boundaries between kāne, wahine, and māhū.[16] However, its strategic abolition came at a time when it seemed as if the old systems were proving to be ineffectual to maintain the health and wellness of the people. In abolishing this kapu, Keōpūolani, Kaʻahumanu, and Liholiho were perhaps responding to the great dying of their people.[17] It is not beyond reason to assume that perhaps they imagined that these kapu were no longer serving them and therefore needed to be rethought.[18] This moʻolelo helps offer context to the operational structure of kapu in ʻōiwi society.

In the moʻolelo of Hiʻiakaikapoliopele, the Pele ʻohana certainly operates according to a system of strict kapu under which kānāwai also mediate an ʻŌiwi ordering. Often when kapu are mentioned, we are referred to specific ʻāina, aliʻi, and akua. Pele is known as ka Wahinekapu, demonstrating that in this particular moʻolelo, she is both that which is marked as sacred and she who enforces the kapu.[19] Kīlauea is also called ka Wahinekapu, therefore demonstrating Pele's intimate pilina to her home and that her ʻāina also fall under the same kapu as her body.

Like any kapu, under the recognition of this particular system are a set of kānāwai.[20] In Pualani Kanakaʻole Kanahele's book *Ka Honua Ola: ʻEliʻeli Kau Mai*, she discusses this set of kānāwai as protocols outlining appropriate behavior. Within the example of the moʻolelo of Hiʻiakaikapoliopele, oftentimes these kānāwai articulate appropriate protocols for safely approaching and interacting with the kapu territory/body of Pele.

E ho'i, e komo i kou hale

'O Kapō'ulakīna'u, he ali'i
E ho'i, e komo i kou hale
'O Ke'alohilani
E 'au'au i kou ki'o wai kapu
'O Pōnahakeone
E inu i kou pū 'awa hiwa
'Awa papa a ke akua
I kānaenae no Moehaunaiki ē
Hele a'e komo
I ka hale a Pele
Ua huahua'i Kahiki, lapa uila
Pele ē hua'ina ho'i
Hua'ina a'e ana
Ka mana o ko'u akua i waho lā ē
O kūkulu ka pahu kapu a ka leo
Ho'okikī kānāwai
He Kua'ā Kānāwai
He kai'okia kānāwai
He ala muku no Kāne me Kanaloa
He kīho'iho'i Kānāwai
No Pele, no ko'u akua lā ē[21]

In the mele "E ho'i, e komo i kou hale," the chanter fulfills two purposes: "defining the ceremonial approach to the crater to visit the fiery deity, Pelehonuamea," and defining the natural laws surrounding the volcano and the existence of Pele.[22] Therefore, the mele delineates a sequence for the protocol for the safe adherence to these kānāwai in the presence of Pele and Kīlauea's powerful kapu. In the final eight lines of the oli, the chanter announces the kānāwai that "preserve the birthing state of the land and to maintain the functions of Pele."[23] Adhering to these kānāwai allows for sustainable maintenance of pono. Should anyone disregard these kānāwai, the functions of Pele's creation of land and Hi'iaka's restoration would be disrupted and result in extreme disorder. Kanahele reminds us that all akua and ali'i have kānāwai to "preserve their omnipotence and protect the people and environment."[24] The kānāwai themselves reveal the pilina between the akua, the ali'i, and their function in society (e.g., Pele creates land). These kānāwai help us navigate safely in what would otherwise be an incredibly dangerous process of creation.

The final eight lines of this mele have been adapted into the standard repertoire of the daily protocol observed at the Ala Hulu Kupuna since the first week of the consecration of the Pu'uhonua o Pu'uhuluhulu. Our kia'i are therefore taking the time, three times a day, to rearticulate the kānāwai that order our behavior and protocol while in the presence of our akua and each other at the Pu'uhonua. When we do so, we create, mark, and maintain our jurisdiction to that 'āina by "speaking the law" upon that 'āina three times a day. Similar to the way the Kānaka in the Hi'iaka mo'olelo honor Pele's kapu through the articulation of kānāwai that order their interaction in her realm, these 'ōlapa are honoring and upholding the system of kapu on the mauna (kapu aloha) that require all kia'i to recognize and adhere to the kānāwai often reiterated by Kumu Pua Case, "Sacred Mauna, Sacred Conduct."

The articulation of an alternative governing body and practice at the Pu'uhonua demonstrates in many ways that Pele and her 'ohana are not the only lāhui that operate under a system of kapu. In the face of laws and statutes that do not serve the sustainability of our people, our Kānaka on the Mauna and across the pae 'āina are abandoning those settler laws and leading ourselves by a strict directive of Kapu Aloha.

Often misinterpreted by skeptics as passivity, Kapu Aloha, as Kumu Luana Neff articulates, is a firm commitment to pono. This pono is not simply righteousness (whatever that might be imagined to be) but balance with each other as kia'i and with our natural relations. When we kia'i block the passing of construction vehicles with the power of our collective bodies and voices, we too are recognizing the pilina between the kapu and sacredness of our bodies and the sacredness of the 'āina we wish to protect. Grounded in the principles and teachings of nonviolent direct action, and committed to a sacred bond of aloha, kia'i engage in a movement and strategy that are crucially rooted in the 'āina, which we fiercely protect.

Importantly, while the "sanctity" of the law requires that kia'i clear the roads to make way for "lawful progress," Kapu Aloha reminds kia'i that

kū'ē + kūkulo

Western laws are merely one mo'olelo—which are perhaps in this instance not relevant to the 'āina on which they are currently being told. Any good storyteller knows that a story is only as valuable as it is relevant.

Just as the great dying of our people may have symbolized to our ruling class in the nineteenth century that the specific system of kapu of that time (the 'Ai Kapu) was ineffectual to support the survival of our lāhui, the laws and statutes of our occupying settler governments have also proven to be antithetical to our health and well-being as Kānaka. Therefore, we do not abandon the laws of our occupiers strictly in pursuit of defiance (although we certainly do defy them) so much as we are centering ourselves in the practice of creating and maintaining a system that leads to our collective ea (sovereignty, life, well-being). In essence we embody a commitment to create 'Ōiwi futures in Hawai'i by using what Andre Perez has coined as a Hawaiian philosophy of change, "kū'ē and kūkulu."[25]

Pele and Hi'iaka are certainly not the only mo'olelo that we Kānaka gather strength from in our collective rising. As the story goes, during an expansion expedition in Puna, Kamehameha Pai'ea's foot was caught in the pāhoehoe (lava rock) while chasing after a couple of lawai'a (fishermen) from the area. While Kamehameha was trapped, one of the lawai'a took his paddle and struck it so forcefully against the head of the future mō'ī (supreme ruler) that the paddle was shattered. Rather than killing the mō'ī, the lawai'a ran off. Such an offense and violation to the mō'ī could have easily resulted in these fishermen being put to death. However, when the lawai'a was brought before the mō'ī, Kamehameha instated the Kānāwai Māmalahoe (the kānāwai of the splintered paddle).

E nā Kānaka,
E mālama 'oukou i ke akua
A e mālama ho'i ke kanaka nui a me kanaka iki;
E hele ka 'elemakule, ka luahine, a me ke kama
A moe i ke ala
'A'ohe mea nāna e ho'opilikia.
Hewa nō, make.[26]

In the mo'olelo, Kamehameha grants all Kānaka the right to exist without fear of harm. In this kānāwai, the ali'i calls for his people to first care for the akua, Kūkāʻilimoku, and from that guidance to also care for the people great and small and those young and old. In the final lines, he orders that all Kānaka be allowed to lie and sleep in the streets without any disturbance to them. This kānāwai is often referred to as Hawaiʻiʻs first human rights law, and many turn to the moʻolelo as a metaphor for how our leadership should protect and serve its communities. This has resulted in the State of Hawaiʻi appropriating this moʻolelo via a splintered-paddle image centering the Honolulu Police Department (HPD) badge worn by every HPD enforcement officer.

But this moʻolelo is not simply a metaphor we should draw upon and extrapolate toward a settler state's enforcement practice. This moʻolelo is not just Hawaiian wrapping paper we can dress mechanisms of settler state violence in to call their practice pono. This moʻolelo is a kānāwai whose power lies indisputably upon the ʻāina it was birthed from. This moʻolelo reminds us that kānāwai can give and take life—making it at least as powerful as any state or city statute.

Today, as thousands of Kānaka Maoli gather upon Ke Ala Hulu Kupuna (Maunakea Access Road) in the protection of Mauna a Wākea, we reflect upon this moʻolelo and its kānāwai as we carefully negotiate the pāhoehoe terrain that encircles us. As we consider this moʻolelo, we have built and developed institutions that support our adherence to its kānāwai. With the creation of the Hui Kākoʻo Kūpuna, the Mauna Medics Hui, the Kapu Aloha kiaʻi, and even the Puʻuhuluhulu University, the ea and well-being of each and every Kanaka upon Maunakea is seriously considered and invested in just as Kamehameha instructed. As such, the movement to protect Maunakea is not only a movement to protect our ʻāina; it is a movement that is rapidly growing because of our investment in our protection of each other upon our ʻāina.

Therefore, when eight of us kiaʻi chained ourselves to the cattle guard on the Maunakea Access Road on July 15, 2019, to block the movement of construction vehicles, the threat of our arrest and removal was not only offensive in the face of the settler state's complete lack of jurisdiction over the ʻāina that we were chained to but also offended a kānāwai as tangible as the crest worn by Hawaiʻiʻs largest enforcement agency. As we chained ourselves to that guard, we held the words of Kamehameha within our bones. We knew that as Kānaka we had the kuleana to lie in the streets without fear of harm. When we asserted ourselves based upon that kuleana, carrying our moʻolelo carefully within us, we challenged the TMT's movement of construction vehicles as well as the occupying settler state of Hawaiʻi's marriage to its rule of law. We lodged this challenge not in a state of chaos or lack of order but within the organized adherence to our kānāwai that have existed hundreds of years before the State of Hawaiʻi took its first stolen breath.

And for every evening since we chained ourselves to the guard, some of the most powerful and fragile members of our lāhui literally sleep in the Ala Hulu Kupuna in freezing temperatures while our young devote themselves to caring for their well-being and safety. The irony here, of course, is that by our kānāwai, the protection of our ʻāina and kūpuna is the kuleana of our leadership, who instead spend their time planning our removal and the safe passage of construction equipment. This demonstrates to us Kānaka once again that the state's god is capitalism, the first thing it must protect. But we Kānaka today are remembering our akua, our ʻāina, and each other. And we will continue to mālama what the state will not.

KAUOHA

Time and time again we should remember that our generation is not the first to look to these moʻolelo for guidance on our governance and leadership. In fact, Bush and Paʻaluhi emphasize the governance aspect of the ʻohana pilina more than any other authors studied for this book. As I mentioned in chapter 2, throughout this mana, the allusions to lāhui, governance, and aliʻi continue with reference to Pele and her ʻohana. In the first issue of their mana of Hiʻiakaikapoliopele, Bush and Paʻaluhi explicitly refer to the Pele "lahui" and their migration.

Ma ka moolelo maoli, ua oleloia he ohana nui o Pele a me kona mau kaikaina a me kona mau kaikunane. Ua pae ae lakou ma ka Mokupuni o Hawaii i ka wa kahiko, o Pele ke alii a pau o keia ohana a me na kanaka malalo ona, a ua hookahua iho ko lakou noho ana ma ke alo o Maunaloa. Ua kuee aku na kamaaina, aka, no ka ikaika o keia poe ua lanakila lakou ma mua o na kamaaina, a mamuli o ka ui o na wahine o keia lahui a me na kane, ua hooki pu iho la ke kue o na kamaaina i ka poe malihini.[27]

We learn from this passage that Pele is the "alii" of her 'ohana and her siblings are therefore her maka'āinana. In Bush and Pa'aluhi's mana of Hi'iaka, the Pele 'ohana is not merely on a journey from Kahiki; rather, Pele and her lāhui are on a "huakai nai aina" (a journey to conquer and rule a new land). As a result, their migration to Hawai'i was challenged by the kama'āina at first, until Pele could prove herself a worthy ali'i.[28]

Just days before the illegal overthrow of the Kingdom of Hawai'i, Pele and her 'ohana sailed through the pages of *Ka Leo o ka Lahui,* displaying a different kind of governance and hulihia than the usurping threat of force about to be experienced in Hawai'i. According to the authors, Pele and her siblings traveled together on their journey to conquer new land.[29] As the authors mentioned previously, the kama'āina's resistance to this new 'ohana was short lived, as Pele and her 'ohana proved themselves to be worthy through their strength and beauty.[30]

In this particular mo'olelo, one of the ways Pele demonstrates her leadership is through her ability to offer kauoha to her kaikaina. While kauoha is not a common term heard on Mauna a Wākea these days, it is one that is central to the organization of power and in Hi'iakaikapoliopele mo'olelo, and therefore it has important insight for Kānaka today when developing a Kanaka Maoli political theory of leadership (see Figure 13).

As the hānau mua, Pele is entrusted with the kuleana to offer kauoha to her siblings and to other Kānaka in her lāhui. But Pele's power to offer

Term	Definition	Source
kau.oha	nvt. Order, command, demand, testament, decree, precept, will, message, statement; to order, command, direct, send for, subscribe, dictate, assign, decree, entrust, bequest, commit into the hands of; to summon, to order, as groceries or goods. Kauoha 'ia, entrusted, as to God's power. Ma ke kauoha, legal notice. 'Ōuli kauoha, sign of the imperative. He kauoha na ka 'aha, a judicial decree. Ke'ehia i ka ho'ounauna, ke'ehia i ke kauoha (prayer), trample on the evil messenger, trample on the evil order. Make kauoha 'ole, die intestate, without a will. Keiki kāne lawe kauoha, messenger boy.	Pukui and Elbert

Term	Definition	Source
kau-o-ha	v. 1. To give a dying charge; to make a bequest or a parting charge. *Isa.* 38:1. Hence, to make a will. NOTE.— Ancient wills, of course, were verbal; now, by law, they must be written. 2. To give a charge on any subject; to command; to put in charge or trust, as one dying or going away; *kauoha* ae la oia (o Kamehameha) ia Kauikeaouli e noho i alii no Hawaii nei, he (Kamehameha) *gave in charge* to Kauikeaouli to reign as king over the Hawaiian Islands. 3. To commit into the hands of another. 1 *Pet.* 4:19. 4. To give orders concerning a person or thing. *Kin.* 12:20. 5. To commit to paper, i.e., to write down; nolaila, ke *kauoha* aku nei au i ko'u manao ma keia palapala, i ike oe i ko'u manao.	Andrews
kau-o-ha	s.1. A will, verbal or written; a command; a charge; a dying request. 2. A covenant; a commission; a judicial decision. 3. A determination; a decree. 4. Beggary.	Andrews
kauoha	n. 1. A will, verbal or written; a command; a charge; a dying request. (A written will is now called palapalakauoha or palapalahooilina.) 2. A covenant; a commission; a judicial decision. 3. A determination; a decree.	Parker
kauoha (kă'u-ō'-ha)	v. 1. To give a dying charge; to make a bequest or a parting charge; hence, to make a will. (Ancient wills, of course, were verbal.) 2. To give a charge on any subject; to command; to put in charge, as one dying or going away: kauoha ae la oia (o Kamehameha) ia Kauikeaouli e noho i alii no Hawaii nei; he (Kamehameha) gave in charge to Kauikeaouli to reign as king over the Hawaiian islands. 3. To commit into the hands of another. 4. To give orders concerning a person or thing. 5. To write down; nolaila, ke kauoha aku nei au i ko'u manao ma keia palapala, i ike oe i ko'u manao.	Parker

Figure 13. Definitions of kauoha from Pukui and Elbert, *Hawaiian Dictionary*; Andrews, *Dictionary of the Hawaiian Language*; and Parker, *Dictionary of the Hawaiian Language*.

kauoha is not unilateral. In fact, early in the moʻolelo, the sisters set the stage for future conflict when Pele and Hiʻiakaikapoliopele offer each other kauoha, demonstrating that while Pele is certainly the aliʻi of her ʻohana, Hiʻiaka has mana that is worth recognizing as well. After agreeing to take on the dangerous task of going out to retrieve Lohiʻau, Hiʻiaka commands of Pele that she not harm or disturb her beloved Hōpoe.

Kauoha mai hoi o Hiiakaikapoiliopele i ke kaikuaana. Ke kii nei au i ke kane, a kaua, ke noho nei hoi oe, a i ai hoi oe i kahi nei o kaua, e ai no oe ma na wahi o kaua a pau, a o kuu moku lehua nei la, mai ai oe malaila, ae mai la o Pele. Olelo hou aku la no o Hiiakaikapoli-opele, i noho oe a, kuia e ko la inaina, i ai oe i uka nei, a i iho oe i kai o Puna e ai ai, ai no oe ma na wahi a pau o puna, o kuu aikane, mai ai oe, ae mai la o Pele i na kauoha a pau o ke kaikaina. No ka mea ua maikai ia mau mea i ko Pele manao, e like hoi me ka Pele kauoha iaia nei.[31]

In the kauoha, Hiʻiaka reminds her elder sister that she will go out to fetch Lohiʻau. In return, while Pele stays behind, she is free to rule and send her fires out to any of the lands they share *except* the lehua grove belonging to Hōpoe. Hiʻiakaikapoliopele repeats herself for emphasis that all of Puna shall be Pele's to devour save for that ʻāina of Hiʻiaka's beloved aikāne, Hōpoe. Following Hiʻiaka's command, both sisters agree to the kauoha set between them, and Hiʻiaka embarks on her journey.

However, as we know, Pele does not keep up her part of the kauoha. And instead, while Hiʻiaka is returning home from Hāʻena, Pele sends her fires into Keaʻau and kills Hōpoe. This act is the center of the major conflict of this moʻolelo. As the hānau mua, the Pele ʻohana kāne and wāhine are subject to Pele's leadership, and the hoahānau stay relatively balanced and stable in this regard. But it is Pele's breaking of these kauoha between herself and her pōkiʻi that overthrows the system of leadership in Kīlauea late in the moʻolelo.

Hiʻiaka responds to Pele's treason by vowing to sleep with Lohiʻau at the edge of the crater, where Pele will have a front-row view of her sister's disobedience. When Pele sees this, her anger at her punahele grows, and so she commands the other Hi'iaka sisters to descend upon Hi'iaka, Lohi'au, and Wahine'ōma'o and to kill them with the raging fires of Pele.

Pele's kauoha that her younger sisters use her fires to kill Lohi'au and Hi'iaka is not just a command of an elder sister but the command of their ali'i. As with other ali'i, Pele's power, leadership, and kuleana to rule are protected as long as she leads and rules in ways that are pono. When Pele defies Hi'iaka's kauoha to protect Hōpoe and sends her raging fires into Hōpoe's ulu lehua at Kea'au, Hi'iaka's retaliation is not only understood by her 'ohana but justified and supported. As a result, when Pele sends her other Hi'iaka sisters to kill Lohi'au and their pōki'i haku, Hi'iaka-ikapoliopele, none of the sisters take her command to heart.

Ho'oulumāhiehie expresses this conflict with the following passage: "A ia wa oia i huli ae ai a kena mai la i na kaikaina Hiiaka ona, e pii lakou e kuni i ke kane a ke kaikaina i ke ahi, Aohe Hiiaka i hoolohe iho i keia kauoha a ua Pele nei."[32] In this mana of the mo'olelo, Pele instructs the Hi'iaka sisters to climb the crater and kill Hi'iaka and their kāne, Lohi'au. But we learn immediately that not one of these sisters took seriously the command of their kaikua'ana.

A hiki ua poe Hiiaka nei iluna i kahi a Hiiaka ma e ku ana, pane mai la o Hiiaka-i-ka-alei i ka pokii kaikaina.

Hemo ka piko la e ka hoahanau. Eia makou mamuli o ke kauoha a ke kaikuaana haku o kakou. A i pii mai la makou e hooko i kana kauoha . . .

O ka huna o ke ahi ka makou e hoopa ae i ko kane, a o ka nui o ke ahi, ea, me makou no ia. He keu kau a ke kane ui. "Pali ka hoi ke kua; mahina ke alo—O ke ku no a ua kanaka ui."[33]

Instead, when the Hi'iaka sisters reached their pōki'i (Hi'iakaikapoliopele) and their kāne (Lohi'auipo), they acknowledged that the umbilical cord was severed ("hemo ka piko") between them and vowed not to send all their fire to Lohi'au and their pōki'i.

All the Hi'iaka sisters were raised to know Pele as their kaikua'ana, their haku (leader/guide), and their ali'i. All Hi'iaka sisters know that to defy any ali'i is a crime punishable by death. However, rather than participate blindly in the injustice Pele has put in motion, first by killing Hōpoe and then by deciding to kill Lohi'au and Hi'iakaikapoliopele, these kaikaina of hers—these makaʻāinana, these commoners—resist her command. Though these kaikaina are ultimately not killed for their rebellion, it is important to note that they resist knowing that death is the likely consequence.

Much like the phrase "Mō ka piko la," the Hiʻiakas' declaration "Hemo ka piko la" announces broken ties within this ʻohana.[34] It is this conflict, this severing of the ʻohana ties through the unjust acts of the kaikuaʻana (Pele), that informs these kaikainaʻs decision to disobey her commands. Without that piko, that umbilical cord or aho shared between them as hoahānau, binding them together in a sacred ʻupena of intimacy, Pele is no longer a worthy aliʻi or kaikuaʻana. And as the piko is seen to be severed, so is their loyalty to her. This is what allows the Hiʻiaka sisters to spare Hiʻiakaikapoliopele. This part of the moʻolelo reveals an important quality of leadership. Leadership is not at all a position that can be named and claimed; rather, leadership is a relationship that must be cared for and tended to. To ignore the relations that allow one to lead ultimately disempowers the leader, making them vulnerable to rebellion and uprising.

We can consult the rules that govern the Pele ʻohana as a lāhui when attempting to imagine alternative norms for governance in our current aupuni. What makes the Pele lāhui distinct from patriarchal forms of governance is not a lack of violence or a lack of hierarchy but its status as a system in which violence and hierarchies are checked when abused. Although she is the most powerful member and the mōʻī of her ʻohana, Pele is not free from scrutiny and resistance. Peleʻs kuleana to rule requires that her pilina to her subjects (ʻohana) must be cared for and maintained. When those pilina are defiled, severed, or taken for granted, Peleʻs capacity to lead is weakened, making her vulnerable to attack or kahuli (overthrow).

When we honor leadership as a relationship, it follows that the more intimate the relationship you have to a place, the more empowered you are to make decisions on behalf of that place. Therefore, it is not simply Peleʻs breaking of a kauoha that challenges her right to rule; in breaking Hiʻiakaʻs kauoha, she has destroyed the pilina between her and her sister, which ultimately leads to her power being questioned and resisted. In our contemporary battles with "leadership" in Hawaiʻi, the question of pilina is at the center of our challenge to the "state."

PĪPĪ HOLO KA'AO

My time with Hi'iakaikapoliopele and Mauna a Wākea led me to the understanding that the nature of our governance and leadership is depicted and preserved through our extensive archive of mo'olelo and mele. As Kānaka 'Ōiwi, we've been strategically colonized into a different "natural" ordering of society. These mo'olelo offer the powerful reminder that there is nothing natural about this "state" and its violence against us.

That all but four of the known published mana of our mo'olelo o Hi'iaka were published during or after the illegal overthrow of the Hawaiian Kingdom should not be lost on the reader. Hi'iakaikapoliopele moves through a time of hulihia, and our people too were enduring a hulihia of their own while this mo'olelo was being republished throughout the nineteenth and twentieth centuries; that is what made its publication so very relevant. Our kūpuna faced these hulihia bravely while choosing to author and publish, over and over, a mo'olelo that so intimately discusses the politics of 'ohana, leadership, and governance.[35] These mo'olelo were reminders and guides to our kūpuna on how to remain steadfast in the love and protection of our 'āina and values.

Neither should it be lost on us that our mo'olelo stress the importance of pilina to leadership and governance. Because the provisional government in 1893 had no pilina to the "governed" Kānaka, publishing mo'olelo such as Hi'iakaikapoliopele would have continually called attention to that absence of pilina and kuleana. As for today, we too are living in a similar time of hulihia. Therefore, it is essential that we turn to mo'olelo like Hi'iaka as the cornerstone of how we will lead ourselves into the future. Therefore, just as my kūpuna have before me, I present us this mo'olelo of Hi'iakaikapoliopele in this specific and intentional time to offer us guidance in an enduring of injustice, violence, and transformation.

As we conclude the journey of this book together, let us not forget the ways Hi'iaka called out to the 'āina she departed, on her journey back to Kīlauea, begging that she not be forgotten. Mai poina 'oe ia'u, she said, over and over, until it became the subtle chorus of her return home. Hi'iaka's call to her 'āina was a mutually binding kuleana, one that called her to also hold steadfast in the recollection of her 'āina aloha in return. In the face of colonialism and many unnamed violences thrust against us Kānaka,

[handwritten annotation: Without mana, what else could they bring but force?]

we have struggled to uphold our end of that agreement, while at the same time some of our loved ones have died in their pursuit of this kuleana.

But the fact remains that the thirteen telescopes on Mauna a Wākea demonstrate quite viscerally the ways colonialism has been successful in Hawaiʻi to force our forgetting of ourselves and our places. Each and every one of those buildings is a scar upon our ʻāina and a mark of our weakened memory and our neglect. Of course, we did not all forget the great and important pilina we had to this sacred ʻāina. And most important, today our lāhui is rising in our remembrance. Today we call out to Mauna a Wākea and all our ʻāina under threat and commit to protecting the sacred pilina between us. When we do so, we know we are not so much protecting our ʻāina as much as our ʻāina is giving us the opportunity as Kānaka to reclaim our humanity as ʻŌiwi by living in pilina and pono with her.

In this book, I have offered moʻolelo that are meant to challenge our notions of how we ought to live in this world. As such, we must remember that our battle to protect Mauna a Wākea from further violence is also a moʻolelo. When our moʻopuna face the greatest challenges of their times— climate change, overpopulation, and growing state violence—I hope they take our moʻolelo as kiaʻi of Mauna a Wākea side by side with that of Hiʻiaka. I hope they dive deep into the well of knowledge of our kūpuna to find solutions that are rooted in Kanaka ʻŌiwi visions of justice and ea. I hope that our stand today is enough to show them the value of doing so.

Either way, today our people are growing in our fierce protection of our ʻāina. That alone is worthy of celebration. Our Kānaka are rising at Mauna a Wākea, Kalaeloa and Kahuku, Hūnānāniho, Nā Wai ʻEhā, Kauaʻula, Hanapēpē, Pōhakuloa, Kahoʻolawe, and across the pae ʻāina.[36] At the Puʻuhonua o Puʻuhuluhulu and other places under direct attack of settler state violence, we remain vigilant of the force they will bring against us. We know that when the police return, they will bring their riot gear, guns, tasers, sound cannons, and batons. Without mana, what else could they bring but force? But we will bring our mele, our oli, our hula, and our moʻolelo. We will be equipped with these weapons of aloha ʻāina because our kūpuna left them for us and for this explicit purpose. The state will have its laws and its violence, but we will have our pilina to each other and our ʻāina, knowing for sure that so long as we stand in this way, we will never be defeated.

'Ōlelo Pīna'i: Epilogue

My grandmother Clara Ku'ulei Kay, Granny Groovy, a beautiful mo'opuna of Kona Chiefs, lived out her final days in the center of Pele's poli. A godly woman, she believed in and practiced kindness and aloha, and also like her mother-in-law, she believed fiercely in Iesū. My 'ohana would spend our thanksgivings with her in Volcano. Granny Groovy's home was tucked away in the forest, and we spent most of our hours as children getting lost between the 'ōhi'a and kupukupu.

When we visited our kūpuna, we slept in what I would later come to know as one of Pele's many poli. Those visits were full of fresh papaya, Portuguese bean soup, laughter, and music. As the primary caretaker of my 'ohana's 'upena of pilina, Granny Groovy was the center of any 'ohana gathering. While she was alive, there was not a single Thanksgiving holiday that didn't involve a massive gathering of Osorios.

When I was eight years old, I went to visit Granny Groovy alone. Forty years after my father walked back along that long, quiet, and devastating trail from Kīlauea Iki, I took my first solo airplane trip to Volcano for the summer. Granny Groovy and I gardened, ate papaya, said grace, strung lei—and hiked to Kīlauea Iki. We saw what was left after Pele's path had cut through the forest, marveled at Pu'u Pua'i, and felt the heat of Pele's kiss on our cheeks.

I did not ask about Pele. I did not think I was allowed to. I only watched, listened, and felt her presence. This is how I know that sometimes silence can be passed down through generations until it becomes tradition.

Years later, I remembered another detail of that trip. Hanging on my grandmother's living room wall was a simply framed photograph of another green-and-white home in Volcano. Nailed to the front was its name, a single word: Hi'iaka. I came to learn that the house belonged to my great-grandmother Eliza. When the summer heat became a burden, Eliza and Emil, my great-grandparents, would leave Hilo for Volcano to stay in this home, Hi'iaka.

It is unfortunate that I did not know our mo'olelo better at that time. Like my father, I might have asked about Pele. But now, in my (re)membering his mo'olelo and mine, I realize that I have spent much of my life gathering the courage and the kuleana to ask about Pele.

I am telling you this part of the mo'olelo now because I think it's important to know how my 'ohana continued to recognize their Pele 'ohana long after they had become Christians. And especially Eliza; too challenged by the thought and power of Pele to discuss her with my father, her grandson, she still found refuge every summer in Pele's poli, Hi'iaka.

A true Honolulu girl, I got homesick and flew home after only a couple of weeks in Volcano. But given what has happened since, I think that something must have been planted in me during those days living in Pele's poli, Hi'iaka. Sometimes a single seed can produce a forest of rumbling lehua trees.

Granny Groovy died less than six months later. The poli I had known, loved, and was held in was gone. But now I am thinking about what makes a poli and what kind of poli I want to be, what I will hold, protect, and nurture.

When Granny Groovy died, I was broken and felt abandoned. So I left her god, Eliza's god, my father's god, and went searching for my own. I eventually found 400,000. Two thanksgivings after Granny Groovy's passing, my 'ohana returned to Hawai'i. From the time my parents had started a 'ohana, it was the longest gap between visits for any of us. It was also the first time my father would return to his one hānau and not be called into his mother's poli.

During this trip, my father, my mother, my two siblings, and I made the drive to Kīlauea Iki. I wanted to remember the feeling of heat on my cheeks. I was missing my kupuna and wanted some reminder of her embrace. We took the long hike on Devastation Trail.

And I am mesmerized. I trace Pele's stretch marks across the hillside's spine. Her dark skirt wraps handfuls of small kīpuka—reminders of what can survive the destruction of creation. I will cherish them, as memories themselves of what once was and what can be again. My mother; my brother, Duncan; and my baby sister, Hali'a, take off before us. I take my time with Pele. I learn her curve. Standing with my father, we trace her story—our story—in quiet. I do not know what he is thinking, only that we are both captured by the power of this 'āina. We walk slowly, overwhelmed by the dark pō surrounding us: My father thinking of his mother. Me thinking of all the luahine in my 'ohana. Hi'iaka.

This is where and when he tells me that when he dies, he does not want to join Granny Groovy in the ocean. He would like to be scattered here, somewhere along the black and darkening devastation. I grab his hand and we stand there, in silent awe of this mo'okū'auhau we are simultaneously creating and being created out of.

Today I wonder if he was also thinking about the first time he took this walk with his grandmother, engulfed in a different kind of stillness. I wonder if this place will always be marked in quiet for us, and if we'll ever be able to tell the difference between reverence and silence.

Like the mana of mo'olelo I have studied, these are just some of the stories I encounter when I study my mo'okū'auhau. Sometimes being a storyteller involves listening to all the mo'olelo you're offered. Sometimes it is about sitting at home, alone, piecing puzzles together. Sometimes it's about returning to Kīlauea to read these words aloud to your kūpuna while all her elements resound in aloha around you. Either way, you all know by now that this is the mo'olelo of a young wahine born into a mo'okū'auhau of mo'olelo, who grew up to look for Hi'iaka, and her aloha in everything around her. This is a mo'olelo of being rewarded, time and time again, by more and more stories to share.

I did not grow up knowing Pele as my kupuna or being able to recognize her many hō'ailona. So in my maturing, I didn't learn everything Pele could teach me. But you can bet my children will. And hopefully so will yours. In (re)membering what we know, nothing is ever exhausted. There is still so much to recall, so much to piece back together, one mo'olelo at a time. This is how we (re)member, how we bring our tattered 'upena back together and spin the frayed and torn aho into a line to cast into our past, our future, and create all the possibilities that our kūpuna deserve. And this is only one of the many pilina we as Kānaka were born to practice.

Mahalo for being a part of my 'upena, a ke aloha nō e ku'u hoa o kēia mau mo'olelo a pau. 'Auhea 'oe, e ho'i mai kāua.

'A'ole i pau.

Notes

ʻŌLELO MUA

1. Trask, *Light in the Crevice Never Seen*, 55; Kalahele, "Make Rope," 29; Goodyear-Kaʻōpua and Kuwada, "Remaking the ʻAha."

GATHERING OUR STORIES OF BELONGING

1. For instance, Hui Aloha ʻĀina was also known as the Hawaiian Patriotic League.

2. Pāʻūopalaʻā is often reffered to in other versions as Pāʻūopalaʻe.

3. As a gloss, aikāne can be described as same-sex intimate partners. However, understanding aikāne is a complicated task that I take on more fully throughout the course of this book.

4. Johnson, "Mauna Kea Series."

5. Finley, "Decolonizing the Queer Native Body."

1. ALOHA ʻĀINA AS PILINA

1. Silva, *Aloha Betrayed*, 11.

2. Silva, *Power of the Steel-Tipped Pen*, 4.

3. "Elua inoa i kapa ia ma ka mokupuni, he moku ka inoa, he aina kahi inoa, ma ka moku ana ia ke kai ua kapa ia he moku, a ma ka noho ana a kanaka, ua kapa ia he aina ka inoa." Malo, *Ka Moolelo Hawaiʻi*, 10.

4. Chapter 3 defines and elaborates upon the ʻupena of pilina as the distinct, diverse web of relations between Kānaka represented in our moʻolelo o Hiʻiaka. These pilina are transitively articulated and practiced, compounding the possibilities of pleasure and kuleana. For example, Lohiʻau as "kela kane a kakou" (that kāne of ours) creates an ʻupena of pilina between Pele and her kaikaina that makes

compounded states of pleasure and accountability not offered by heteropaternal monogamy possible.
 5. Grimshaw, *Paths of Duty*, 6–9.
 6. Silva, *Power of the Steel-Tipped Pen*, 7.
 7. Dudoit, "Against Extinction"; Trask, "Decolonizing Hawaiian Literature"; hoʻomanawanui, "Pele's Appeal"; McDougall, "'O ka Lipo o ka Lā, 'O ka Lipo o ka Pō"; Silva, "Hawaiian Literature in Hawaiian"; Goodyear-Kaʻōpua, Hussey, and Wright, *Nation Rising*.
 8. Silva, "Hawaiian Literature in Hawaiian," 103.
 9. Trask quoted in Dudoit, "Against Extinction," 11.
 10. Silva, *Aloha Betrayed*, 12.
 11. Aiu, "Neʻe Papa I Ke Ō Mau."
 12. Mookini, *Hawaiian Newspapers*, 4.
 13. "Ke Aloha Aina, Heaha ia?," *Ke Aloha Aina*, May 25, 1895, 7.
 14. "Ke Aloha Aina, Heaha ia?," 7.
 15. Maile Arvin, Eve Tuck, and Angie Morrill define heteropatriarchy as the state of affairs in which "heterosexuality and patriarchy are perceived as normal and natural, and in which other configurations are perceived as abnormal, aberrant, and abhorrent." Arvin, Tuck, and Morrill, "Decolonizing Feminism," 13. Andrea Smith calls it "the building block of US empire." A. Smith, "Heteropatriarchy," 71. Heteropaternalism is defined by Arvin, Tuck, and Morrill as "the presumption that heteropatriarchal nuclear-domestic arrangements, in which the father is both center and leader/boss, should serve as the model for social arrangements of the state and its institutions." Arvin, Tuck, and Morrill, "Decolonizing Feminism," 13.
 16. McDougall, "'O ka Lipo o ka Lā, 'O ka Lipo o ka Pō," 74.
 17. Hoʻomanawanui, *Voices of Fire*, 98.
 18. Hoʻomanawanui, 165.
 19. McDougall, "'O ka Lipo o ka Lā, 'O ka Lipo o ka Pō," 276.
 20. Although not in any formal publication, this manaʻo was first coined by Kanaka Maoli scholar/activist/organizer Andre Perez. Perez describes kūʻē and kūkulu on record in an Office of Hawaiian Affairs Board of Trustees meeting on June 29, 2017, as our "philosophy of change," which requires Kānaka be as attentive to both building and creating as we are to resisting. Perez, "Public Testimony."
 21. Davis, "Freedom Is a Constant Struggle."
 22. Allen, *Sacred Hoop*; Jaimes, "'Patriarchal Colonialism' and Indigenism"; Teaiwa, "Bikinis and Other S/pacific N/oceans"; Trask, *From a Native Daughter*; Arvin, Tuck, and Morrill, "Decolonizing Feminism"; Goodyear-Kaʻōpua, "Domesticating Hawaiians"; Finley, "Decolonizing the Queer Native Body"; see also Akaka et al., *Nā Wāhine Koa*.
 23. Allen, *Sacred Hoop*, 33.

24. Jaimes, "'Patriarchal Colonialism' and Indigenism," 59.

25. Trask, *From a Native Daughter,* 91.

26. Hoʻomanawanui, "Mana Wahine, Education and Nation-Building," 209.

27. Trask, *From a Native Daughter,* 92.

28. Trask, 94.

29. Arvin, Tuck, and Morrill, "Decolonizing Feminism."

30. Hall, "Navigating Our Own 'Sea of Islands,'" 16.

31. Million, *Therapeutic Nations Healing*; Simpson, *As We Have Always Done*; Goeman, *Mark My Words*; TallBear, *Native American DNA.*

32. Arvin, Tuck, and Morrill, "Decolonizing Feminism," 9.

33. Allen, *Sacred Hoop.*

34. Arvin, Tuck, and Morrill, "Decolonizing Feminism," 14.

35. Arvin, Tuck, and Morrill, 14.

36. Arvin, Tuck, and Morrill, 15.

37. Kauanui, *Hawaiian Blood.*

38. Kameʻeleihiwa, *Native Land and Foreign Desires*; Arista, *Kingdom and the Republic*; Osorio, *Dismembering Lāhui*; Kauanui, *Paradoxes of Hawaiian Sovereignty.*

39. According to the 1993 documentary *Act of War,* between 1778 and 1893, the Kanaka Maoli population fell from approximately 800,000 to 30,000.

40. Morgensen, *Spaces between Us,* 2.

41. Finley, "Decolonizing the Queer Native Body," 33.

42. Morgensen, *Spaces between Us.*

43. Finley, "Decolonizing the Queer Native Body," 34.

44. Rifkin, *When Did Indians Become Straight?,* 25.

45. Hoʻomanawanui, "Mana Wahine: Feminism," 28.

46. Trask, *From a Native Daughter.*

47. Goodyear-Kaʻōpua, Hussey, and Wright, *Nation Rising,* 3.

48. Goodyear-Kaʻōpua, Hussey, and Wright, 4.

49. The Hawaiian stands firmly in the present, with his back to the future, and his eyes fixed upon the past (Kameʻeleihiwa, *Native Land and Foreign Desires,* 22).

50. Morgensen, *Spaces between Us,* 25.

51. Driskill et al., *Queer Indigenous Studies.*

2. HAWAIIAN ARCHIVES, ABUNDANCE, AND THE PROBLEM OF TRANSLATION

1. Da Silva et al., "Decolonial Love and Loving."

2. Nogelmeier, *Mai Paʻa i ka Leo,* xii.

3. Wong, "Authenticity and the Revitalization of Hawaiian"; Kuwada, "To Translate or Not to Translate."

4. Arista, "Davida Malo, a Hawaiian Life"; Silva, *Power of the Steel-Tipped Pen.*

5. Venuti, *Scandals of Translation,* 165; Bassnett, *Translation Studies*; Niranjana, "Introduction"; Venuti, *Scandals of Translation*; Silva, *Aloha Betrayed*; Bacchilega, *Legendary Hawaiʻi*; Tymoczko, "Translation, Resistance, Activism"; Spivak,

"Politics of Translation"; Brisset, "Search for a Native Language"; Shankar, "'Problem' of Translation."

6. Bacchilega, *Legendary Hawaiʻi*, 14.

7. Bacchilega, 15.

8. McDougall, "'O ka Lipo o ka Lā, 'O ka Lipo o ka Pō"; McDougall, *Finding Meaning*; Bacchilega, *Legendary Hawaiʻi*.

9. Kuwada, "To Translate or Not to Translate," 56.

10. A number of scholars have addressed this issue. See hoʻomanawanui, "Pele's Appeal," 84–103; hoʻomanawanui, *Voices of Fire*, 33–64; and Silva, "Hawaiian Literature in Hawaiian," 102–17.

11. Wong, "Authenticity and the Revitalization of Hawaiian," 102.

12. Shankar, "'Problem' of Translation," 141.

13. Wong, "Authenticity and the Revitalization of Hawaiian."

14. There are earlier full academic translations of moʻolelo that presented the ʻōlelo Hawaiʻi side by side with the English translations, beginning with Martha Warren Beckwith's translation of Haleʻole's *Lāʻieikawai* (1997), followed by Frances Frazier's translation of Piʻilani's *Kaluaikoʻolau* (*True Story of Kaluaikoʻolau*, 2001), and proceeding right up to Awaiaulu Press's two-volume edition and translation of Hoʻoulumāhiehie's *Ka Moʻolelo o Hiʻiakaikapoliopele* (*The Epic Tale of Hiʻiakaikapoliopele*, 2007), translated by Puakea Nogelmeier. While not perfect, these texts were committed to the premise that access to the text in its original language is essential.

15. On translation refusal, see Aiu, "Neʻe Papa I Ke Ō Mau."

16. Wendt, "Towards a New Oceania," 71.

17. Hoʻoulumāhiehie was a pen name for Poepoe, often used when he was authoring material that wasn't entirely his own. For a detailed discussion of this attribution, see Silva, *Power of the Steel-Tipped Pen*, 141. The mana of *Ka Moolelo o Hiiakaikapoliopele* first began in *Hawaii Aloha*, but when that paper was discontinued, it was taken up in Poepoe's *Ka Naʻi Aupuni*. Hoʻoulumāhiehie, *Ka Moʻolelo o Hiʻiakaikapoliopele*, 431.

18. Hoʻomanawanui, *Voices of Fire*.

19. McDougall, "'O ka Lipo o ka Lā, 'O ka Lipo o ka Pō," 276.

20. McDougall, 276.

21. Hoʻoulumāhiehie, "He Moolelo Kapu Loa," *Ka Naʻi Aupuni*, May 24, 1906, 1.

22. Silva, *Power of the Steel-Tipped Pen*.

23. Mookini, *The Hawaiian Newspapers*; Chapin, *Guide to Newspapers of Hawaiʻi*.

24. Silva, *Aloha Betrayed*, 73.

25. Silva, 85.

26. Joseph Kanepuu, letter, *Ka Hoku o ka Pakipika*, October 30, 1862, 1.

27. Silva, *Power of the Steel-Tipped Pen*, 7.

28. Hoʻomanawanui, "Pele's Appeal," 436.

29. The recorded editors of *Ka Leo o ka Lahui* were J. W. Mikasobe, 1889; F. Meka, 1890; John E. Bush, 1891 and 1894; Kaunamano, 1893; S. P. Kanoa, 1896; and Thomas Spencer, 1896. Mookini, *Hawaiian Newspapers*, 27.

30. Mookini, *Hawaiian Newspapers*, 27.

31. Chapin, *Guide to Newspapers of Hawaiʻi*, 54.

32. John E. Bush, "Olelo Hoakaka," *Ka Leo o ka Lahui,* January 5, 1893, 1.

33. Bush, January 6, 1893, 1; this passage is also found in Silva, *Power of the Steel-Tipped Pen*, 5.

34. Bush, "Olelo Hoakaka," January 5, 1893, 1.

35. Hoʻomanawanui, "Pele's Appeal," 436.

36. Silva, *Power of the Steel-Tipped Pen*; Mookini, *Hawaiian Newspapers.*

37. Hoʻoulumāhiehie, "Ka Moolelo o Hiiakaikapoliopele," *Ka Naʻi Aupuni,* June 1, 1906, 3.

38. Silva, *Aloha Betrayed,* 76.

39. Hoʻomanawanui, "Pele's Appeal," 437.

40. Hoʻoulumāhiehie, June 16, 1906, 3; July 7, 1906, 3; September 24, 1906, 3; May 24, 1906, 4; June 8, 1906, 4.

41. Hoʻoulumāhiehie, May 24, 1906, 4.

42. Mookini, *Hawaiian Newspapers*; Chapin, *Guide to Newspapers of Hawaiʻi.*

43. Silva, *Power of the Steel-Tipped Pen.*

44. Hoʻomanawanui, "Pele's Appeal," 437.

45. Joseph Mokuʻōhai Poepoe, "Ka Moolelo Kaao o Hiiakaikapoliopele," *Kuokoa Home Rula,* January 10, 1908, 1.

46. Poepoe, 1.

47. Poepoe, 1.

48. Hoʻoulumāhiehie, December 26, 1905, 1.

49. Bush, "Olelo Hoakaka," January 5, 1893, 1.

50. Hoʻoulumāhiehie, July 6, 1906, 3.

51. Hoʻoulumāhiehie, 3.

52. Poepoe, January 7, 1910, 4.

53. Hoʻoulumāhiehie, December 11, 1905, 1.

54. Hoʻoulumāhiehie, June 19, 1906, 3.

55. Hoʻoulumāhiehie, 3.

56. "Ua like a ua like ole paha kekahi mau makani me ko ka mea i ikeia ma ka moolelo o Kuapakaa. O keia nae na mea i loaa i ka mea kakau ma keia moolelo Hiiaka, i kopeia mai e ia mai ka buke mai a J. W. Naihe o Kohala, a mai ka buke mai hoi a D. K. Waialeale. A he mahele no hoi keia i ike ole ia ma na moolelo Hiiaka i hoolahaia mamua aku nei.

A maanei ke nonoi aku nei ka mea kakau i ka hoaʻloha heluhelu, e haawi mai i kana mau hoomanawanui ana no keia nee ana aku o ka moolelo o Hiiaka-i-kapoli, oiai e nee aku ana keia mahele o ka moolelo ma na inoa aina a me na inoa makani a puni o Kauai, a he kulana panoonoo no ia o ka moolelo; aka, aole hiki i ka mea kakau ke alo ae i keia haawina, no ka mea, ua hookumuia keia moolelo mamuli o ka manao ana o ka mea kakau e pau pono na mea a pau—ke au-nui a me ke au-iki—o keia moolelo, no ka pomaikai o ka hanauna hou o Hawaii nei ma keia hope aku." Poepoe, April 24, 1908, 1.

57. "A o keia kahea hai kupuna a Hiʻiaka i hoikeia ae la, ua ikeia no ia ma ke mele 'koihonua' o Kualii, ka Moi o Oahu nei, pela no me ke mele 'koihonua' o Kaumualii, ke alii o Kauai, oia hoi o 'Ke Kala Kumalohoia' a o ke mele no nae hoi ia i oleloia ai, no Kualii no ia 'koihonua.'" Hoʻoulumāhiehie, September 24, 1906, 3.

58. "A ua hoikeia no keia papa-kuau-hau a Hiiaka i kahea ai maloko o ka Moo–kuauhau Kumulipo. A ke kaua nei keia kau a Hiiaka, i ka o aio [sic] o keia mahele kuauhau e pili ana ia Paliku, a loaa mai o Haumea, oia no hoi o Papa, wahine a Wakea." Hoʻoulumāhiehie, 3.

59. Poepoe, February 14, 1908, 3.

60. Poepoe, January 31, 1908, 1.

61. "Breaking the fourth wall" is the theater term for when the actors speak directly to their audience.

62. Hoʻomanawanui, *Voices of Fire,* 42.

63. Silva, *Power of the Steel-Tipped Pen,* 151.

64. "Hoa. 1. n. Companion, friend, associate, colleague, comrade, partner, mate, peer, fellow, antagonist (if followed by a word such as kaua or paio). Cf. *hoahānau, hoa hele, hoaloha, hoa paio,* and saying, *cold 1.* Kona hoa, his friend. Hoa a ka Hale o nā Lunamakaʻāinana, member of the House of Representatives. hoʻo. hoa To make friends. (PPN soa.). 2. nvt. To tie, bind, secure, rig; rigging, lashing. See *hoa waʻa.*" Pukui and Elbert, *Hawaiian Dictionary,* 73.

65. Hoʻoulumāhiehie, June 19, 1906, 3; also found in Poepoe, April 24, 1908, 1.

66. "Ke makemake nui nei ka Ahahui Moolelo HAWAII LANI HONUA, e hoʻuluulu a e hoakoakoa pono i na moolelo, na mele, na kuauhau a me ano nui o ke au kahiko o Hawaii nei, no ka pomaikai o ka hanauna opio o 'Hawaii Aloha.'" Hoʻoulumāhiehie, July 6, 1906, 3.

67. Hoʻoulumāhiehie, September 24, 1906, 3.

3. THE EA OF PILINA AND ʻĀINA

1. Hoʻomanawanui, "Pele's Appeal," 436–38; Charlot, "Pele and Hiʻiaka," 55–57.

2. McDougall, "'O ka Lipo o ka Lā, 'O ka Lipo o ka Pō"; hoʻomanawanui, "Pele's Appeal."

3. Elbert, *Spoken Hawaiian,* 52. For a much more detailed analysis of possessives and ʻōlelo Hawaiʻi syntax, see C. M. Baker, "A-Class Genitive Subject Effect."

4. Makuahine is given as Kahinalii (Poepoe) in some versions and Haumea (Bush and Paʻaluhi) in others. Makuakāne is given as Kanehoalani (Poepoe),

Kuahailo (Bush and Paʻaluhi), or Kamanuwai (Kapihenui). Poepoe, "Ka Moolelo Kaao o Hiiakaikapoliopele," *Kuokoa Home Rula,* January 10, 1908, 3

5. Poepoe, 3.

6. Hoʻoulumāhiehie, "Ka Moolelo o Hiiakaikapoliopele," *Ka Naʻi Aupuni,* July 3, 1906, 3.

7. With the exception of the Poepoe version, in which Laka and Ehu also join Pele on her huakaʻi ʻimi kāne.

8. Pukui, Haertig, and Lee, *Nānā I ke Kumu,* 167.

9. Pukui, Haertig, and Lee, 127.

10. Pukui and Elbert, *Hawaiian Dictionary,* 128, 377; Andrews, *Dictionary of the Hawaiian Language,* 257, 508; Parker, *Dictionary of the Hawaiian Language,* 260, 612.

11. Hoʻoulumāhiehie, June 29, 1906, 3; parallel passage found in Poepoe, June 5, 1908, 1.

12. Kapihenui, "He Moolelo no Hiiakaikapoliopele," *Ka Hoku o ka Pakipika,* December 26, 1861, 1.

13. Kapihenui, January 2, 1862, 1.

14. Unlike English and other European languages, ʻōlelo Hawaiʻi does not have gendered pronouns. Rather, we use an extensive set of exclusive and inclusive pronouns that help demonstrate inclusivity and exclusivity in relation to the speaker. Elbert, *Spoken Hawaiian,* 20; Pukui, Haertig, and Lee, *Nānā I ke Kumu.*

15. Parker, *Dictionary of the Hawaiian Language,* 133.

16. Osorio, *Dismembering Lāhui,* 24–43.

17. Pukui and Elbert, *Hawaiian Dictionary,* 116.

18. Hiʻiaka and Kahuanui are mentioned as kaikoʻeke by Poepoe, Hoʻoulumāhiehie, and Kapihenui. Lohiʻau and Nakoaola, and Lohiʻau and Lonomakua are mentioned as kaikoʻeke by Kapihenui.

19. Morgensen, *Spaces between Us.*

20. Aikāne relationships also appear in the following moʻolelo: "Moolelo no Pamano," "Mokulehua," "He Moʻolelo no Umi Kekahi Aliʻi Kaulana o Ko Hawaii Nei Pae Aina," "Ka Manu Uliuli," "He Kaao No Ka Poe Ilihune e Noho Ana ma Nuioka," "Ka Moolelo o Kepakailula," "Ka Moolelo no Kamehameha I," "No ka Noho ana o ke Au o ka Moi Liholiho Kamehameha II," "Ka Moolelo no Kailiokalauokekoa," and dozens more.

21. Bishop Museum Archives, Kealanahele, Mekela, Interviewee HAW 55.3.1 (Track 6).

22. Kamakau, *Ke Aupuni Mōʻī*; Kamakau, *Ke Kumu Aupuni*; Kamakau, *Ruling Chiefs of Hawaii*; Hoʻoulumāhiehie, *Kamehameha I.*

23. Pukui and Handy, *Polynesian Family System,* 73.

24. Poepoe, July 31, 1908, 1. Kanaka Maoli took very seriously the practice of naming places and people. That Hiʻiaka has the mana to formally change

Nānāhuki's name speaks deeply to the intimacy they share together. Pukui describes many of the practices surrounding Hawaiian naming in her coauthored books *Nānā I Ke Kumu* (vol. 1) and *The Polynesian Family System in Ka-ʻu, Hawaiʻi*.

25. Poepoe, July 31, 1908, 1.

26. Hoʻoulumāhiehie, July 12, 1906, 3.

27. Poepoe, June 12, 1908, 1.

28. Hoʻoulumāhiehie, November 30, 1906, 4.

29. Hoʻoulumāhiehie, October 25, 1906, 4.

30. Poepoe, September 23, 1910, 4; parallel passage found in Hoʻoulumāhiehie, April 28, 1906, 4.

31. "Kakua ae la keia i kona wahi pa-u a pae i ka hope ʻoni o Mauna Loa kikala upehupehu,' huli ae la a honi i ka ihu o ke aikane, me ka helelei pu ana iho o kona mau waimaka, a pela nohoi me Hopoe iloko oia haawina like. Me na huaolelo panai aloha hope loa mawaena o Hii ame kana aikane, huli ae la keia a hoi aku la me ke kaikunane no ka home lua o Kilauea. Ua olelo ia no nae ma keia moolelo, pupuu no a hoolei loa noho ana laua i ka lua." Poepoe, June 12, 1908, 1.

32. Bush and Paʻaluhi, "Ka Moolelo o Hiiakaikapoliopele," *Ka Leo o ka Lahui*, January 18, 1893, 1.

33. Hoʻoulumāhiehie, July 9, 1906, 3.

34. Poepoe, June 26, 1908, 1.

35. Poepoe, September 23, 1910, 4.

36. Papanuiolaka abandons the hui in Bush and Paʻaluhi, January 24, 1893. And Pāʻūopalaʻā departs the group of travelers to move to Kohala with Pakiu in Bush and Paʻaluhi, March 2, 1893.

37. Hoʻoulumāhiehie, January 20, 1906, 4.

38. Hoʻoulumāhiehie, 4.

39. Hoʻoulumāhiehie, February 23, 1906, 4.

40. Poepoe, July 24, 1908, 1.

41. Mākaia: "nvi. Revenge, vengeance, treachery, betrayal, traitor, betrayer, turncoat; treacherous. (*Laie* 513.) Kū hoʻi kāu hana i ka mākaia, you've behaved treacherously." Pukui and Elbert, *Hawaiian Dictionary*, 225. Naʻauʻauā: "nvi. Intense grief; anguish so great that it may lead to suicide; to mourn, grieve. Naʻauʻauā hele, to wander about in grief." Pukui and Elbert, *Hawaiian Dictionary*, 257.

42. "No ka pau ole o kona manao aloha i ke aikane ia Hopoe, no ka hooko ole o ke kaikuaana i ka ia nei kauoha, nolaila, e malama hoi keia i kana kauoha a hiki i kona alo, alaila, hooko keia i ko ia nei manao, a pela io no, no ka mea, o ka ia nei mea hoi i papa aku ai i ke kaikuaana, aole hoi ia i malama pono, nolaila, hoomau hoi keia i ko ia nei manao huhu malaila." Kapihenui, April 10, 1862, 4.

"me ka manao no nae o Hiiakaikapoliopele aia a hiki i Hawaii ike mai na maka o Pele, alaila, lilo mua no ia ia nei ka hoomaa o ke kane, pela ko ia nei manao iloko iho." Bush and Paʻaluhi, April 26, 1893, 4.

43. "Uwe ae ana keia me ka hemo pu o ka malo, alaila, olelo o Kahuakaiapaoa ma ka inoa o ka mea nana i hana ka lani, a me ka honua, ke hoohiki nei au, aole au e hume i ka malo kapu kuu mea a omuo i ka lihilihi o Pele, a hia i na maka o Pele, o kuu wahi hakina kalo hoi a i na maka o Pele, o ka walewale ae nei o na onohi o Pele, o ka ono o kuu wahi kalo, maʻu ola no ka hiki malihini ana i Hawaii." Bush and Paʻaluhi, June 30, 1893, 4.

44. Hoʻoulumāhiehie, October 18, 1906, 4.

45. Bush and Paʻaluhi, June 30, 1893, 4. A similar passage appears in Kapihenui, July 10, 1862, 4: "Oia wale no ke holo i Hawaii, e uwe ai i ka makena o ke aikane, i make aku no ia ua pono no, no ka mea, o ko Kauakaiapaoa [sic] manao no ia, e naauauwa ana no, a make pu me ke aikane, no ka mea, ua pili aloha laua."

46. Kōkoʻolua: "n. Companion, partner, associate, fellow worker, mate, partnership, second (in a dual), union (always of two). Kona kōkoʻolua, his companion." Pukui and Elbert Hawaiian Dictionary, 162.

4. ʻĀINA, THE AHO OF OUR ʻUPENA

1. Trask, From a Native Daughter, 17.

2. Kameʻeleihiwa, Native Land and Foreign Desires, 20.

3. Kapihenui, "He Moolelo no Hiiakaikapoliopele," Ka Hoku o ka Pakipika, December 26, 1861, 1.

4. Bush and Paʻaluhi, "Ka Moolelo o Hiiakaikapoliopele," Ka Leo o ka Lahui, January 6, 1893, 1.

5. When mā follows a person's name, it denotes that the person is moving, traveling, or working with family, partners, or an entourage of sorts.

6. Bush and Paʻaluhi, January 6, 1893, 1.

7. Kameʻeleihiwa, Native Land and Foreign Desires, 19.

8. Poepoe, "Ka Moolelo Kaao o Hiiakaikapoliopele," Kuokoa Home Rula, January 10, 1908, 1.

9. "Ma ko Oahu nei mahele Hiiaka, ua oleloia, he waa e holo ana mai Keawaula mai no Kauai, o ia ka waa i kau ai o Hiiaka ame Wahineomao, a holo ai laua a pae i Kalihikai, i Kauai ka pae ana. O na mea no laua keia waa oia o Kawaikumuole (K) ame Kalehuapeekoa (W)." Poepoe, September 10, 1909, 2.

10. Poepoe, November 27, 1908, 1.

11. Poepoe, December 18, 1908, 3.

12. Silva, "Pele, Hiʻiaka, and Haumea," 173–76; hoʻomanawanui, "Mana Wahine, Education and Nation-Building," 209; hoʻomanawanui, "Pele's Appeal," 418–35.

13. Kapihenui, January 23, 1862, 1.

14. Kapihenui, February 28, 1862, 1; Bush and Paʻaluhi, January 12, 1893, 1.

15. Bush and Paʻaluhi, January 12, 1893, 1.

16. Poepoe, April 22, 1910, 4; parallel passage in Hoʻoulumāhiehie, "Ka Moolelo o Hiiakaikapoliopele," Ka Naʻi Aupuni, April 3, 1906, 4.

17. Hoʻoulumāhiehie, June 2, 1906, 3. *Ka aoao oolea,* the strong group (sex), is a common phrase in nineteenth- and twentieth-century writing used to describe kāne, while the phrase *ka aoao palupalu,* the soft (or weak) group (sex), is usually offered as the female counterpart. Although beyond the scope of this book, this phrase in our ʻōlelo makuahine brings up important questions about the way haole ideas about male supremacy were imported into our own language. Therefore, it will take more than simply addressing the issues of translation and presentation of our moʻolelo in English to sufficiently address male supremacy in our communities and moʻolelo.

18. Hoʻoulumāhiehie, July 27, 1906, 3.

19. Hoʻoulumāhiehie, June 7, 1906, 3.

20. "He mea oiaio, ua hookuu pau iho la ua Moiwahine nei o ka hikina a ka La ma Haʻehaʻe i kona nani apau maluna iho ona. A ua oleloia, ua like ka lamalama o na helehelena o ua Pele nei i keia wa me ka mahina piha i ka po o Mahealani. He ui hoi tau!" Hoʻoulumāhiehie, June 8, 1906, 3.

21. Kapihenui, January 2, 1862, 1.

22. "E kokoke mai ana i kou wahi, kahi aʻu i kau aloha aku ai ia aikane a kaua, oia nohoi o Hopoe. No ia wahine kaʻu i ula leo ae nei. A i maliu mai ke kaikuaana o kakou pono, a i maliu ole mai, aohe mea kaumaha a koe wale aku o nei huakai a kakou e hele nei." Poepoe, February 5, 1909, 4.

23. Bush and Paʻaluhi, March 29, 1893, 4.

24. Hoʻoulumāhiehie, May 29, 1906, 4; Kapihenui, February 20, 1862, 1; Bush and Paʻaluhi, April 26, 1893, 4.

25. Hoʻoulumāhiehie, June 13, 1906, 3.

26. Hoʻoulumāhiehie, June 14, 1906, 3.

27. Hoʻoulumāhiehie, August 18, 1906, 4.

28. Hoʻoulumāhiehie, January 18, 1906, 4, January 19, 1906, 4.

29. Hoʻoulumāhiehie, October 25, 1906, 4.

30. Bush and Paʻaluhi, January 10, 1893, 1.

31. "Ike e aku la o Pele ia Hopoe laua o Haena e hula mai ana iloko o ke kai o Puna." Bush and Paʻaluhi, 1.

32. Arista, "Navigating Uncharted Oceans of Meaning," 666.

33. McDougall, *Finding Meaning,* 5.

34. O ka manu mukiki,
    Ale lehua aka [*sic*] manu;
    O ka Awa iwi lena,
    I ka uka o ka Liu;
    O ka manu,
    Hahai lau awa o Puna;
    Aia [*sic*] ika laau,
    Ka Awa o Puna;
    O Puna hoi—e. (Bush and Paʻaluhi, February 7, 1893, 4)

35. "Kauoha mai hoi o Hiiakaikapoiliopele i ke kaikuaana. Ke kii nei au i ke kane, a kaua, ke noho nei hoi oe, a i ai hoi oe i kahi nei o kaua, e ai no oe ma na wahi o kaua a pau, a o kuu moku lehua nei la, mai ai oe malaila, ae mai la o Pele. Olelo hou aku la no o Hiiakaikapoliopele, i noho oe a, kuia e ko la inaina, i ai oe i uka nei, a i iho oe i kai o Puna e ai ai, ai no oe ma na wahi a pau o Puna, o kuu aikane, mai ai oe, ae mai la o Pele i na kauoha a pau o ke kaikaina. No ka mea ua maikai ia mau mea i ko Pele manao, e like hoi me ka Pele kauoha iaia nei." Kapihenui, January 2, 1862.

36. 'Ai is eat and rule, and ai is sex. In the texts themselves there is no visible difference except that 'ai would be ka 'ai and ai would be ke ai, but the difference in meaning is/was still apparent to the reader.

37. Bush and Pa'aluhi, April 26, 1893, 4.

38. These kau can be found in the following sources: Ho'oulumāhiehie, April 21–23, 1906, 4, September 26–27, 1906, 4; Poepoe, July 23, 1909, 4, April 23, 1910, 4.

39. These kau can be found in the following sources: Kapihenui, March 6, 1862, March 20, 1862, April 3, 1862; Bush and Pa'aluhi, April 28, 1893, May 1, 1893, May 9, 1893, June 20, 1893, June 23, 1893.

40. Bush and Pa'aluhi, June 21, 1893, 4, June 22, 1893, 4.

41. "Ke ano o keia olelo a Wahineomao, e hooweliweli nei i ka hewa no Pele, he olelo naauauwa no, i ke aloha i ke kane a me ke aikane me Hiiakaikapoli-opele, e manao ana o Wahineomao e hoowili ana keia i kela olelo i mea no Pele e huhu ai ia iaia, hookahi la hoi ka make pu ana me ke kane, a me ke aikane no ko ia nei manao aole e ola ana ke aikane e make ana no." Bush and Pa'aluhi, June 22, 1893, 4.

42. Bush and Pa'aluhi, 4.

43. Kapihenui, July 3, 1862, 4.

44. "Hooalohaloha aku no oe, ma kahi no a olua i hele ai la, i pili ai olua la, malaila, no oe, e hooalohaloha aku ai, malia o o [sic] aloha mai, hoi mai hoi." Kapihenui, July 3, 1862, 4; parallel passage in Bush and Pa'aluhi, June 23, 1893, 4.

45. "Ka! owau ka mea loaa ole o ke mele o ka maua hele ana, a hoi wale mai no makou, a Oahu, i ka hale hula kilu o Peleula, o ia nei no o ke kane a maua ka mea mele o makou, owau, aole au wahi mele, na ke kane mai a maua ka'u wahi mele i ao mai ia'u, ole loa aku hoi paha keia, I mai o Keowahimakaakaua. Noonoo ae no oe ma kahi no a olua i hele ai la, malia o loaa ae kahi mele, alaila, kulou keia noonoo, oia kulou no o ia nei a liuliu, i aku keia, ka!" Kapihenui, July 3, 1862, 4.

46. "A pau ia mele a ia nei, nonoi ae no o Hiiakaikapoliopele i ka ihu o ke aikane, a hookuu aku ia ia e naauauwa no i ke aloha o ke kane, o ka luhi no o laua i hele ai i na wahi pilikia, ka makamaka i ike ia'i kela aina o Kauai, pela mai no ke aikane." Kapihenui, July 10, 1862, 4.

47. "I aku la o Wahineomao i kona hoa, o na wahi iho la no ia a maua i hele pu ai la, i pili ai, aole aku wahi i koe." Bush and Pa'aluhi, June 27, 1893, 4.

48. Bush and Paʻaluhi, 4; parallel passage in Kapihenui, July 10, 1862, 4 (damaged and partially illegible).

49. Kapihenui, July 10, 1862, 4; parallel passage in Bush and Paʻaluhi, June 27, 1893, 4. These episodes are also included in the Hoʻoulumāhiehie mana, although not identically with how they appear here.

50. Trask, *From a Native Daughter*; Trask, "Writing in Captivity"; Trask, "Decolonizing Hawaiian Literature"; Silva, *Aloha Betrayed*; Silva, *Power of the Steel-Tipped Pen*; hoʻomanawanui, *Voices of Fire*; hoʻomanawanui, "Pele's Appeal"; hoʻomanawanui, "Mana Wahine, Education and Nation-Building"; hoʻomanawanui, "Mana Wahine: Feminism"; McDougall, "ʻO ka Lipo o ka Lā, ʻO Ka Lipo o ka Pō"; McDougall, *Finding Meaning*; Iaukea, *The Queen and I*.

51. Tuck and Yang, "Decolonization Is Not a Metaphor," 1.

52. Finley, "Decolonizing the Queer Native Body," 38.

5. KAMAʻĀINA

1. State of Hawaiʻi, "Visitor Statistics."

2. Vizenor, *Survivance.*

3. Pukui and Elbert, *Hawaiian Dictionary,* 179.

4. Pukui and Elbert, *Hawaiian Dictionary,* 179.

5. Nākoa, *Lei Momi o ʻEwa,* 21.

6. In her interview with Larry Kimura on the show *Ka Leo Hawaiʻi,* Nākoa uses the words *kuaʻāina* and *kamaʻāina* to describe her family's pilina to ʻEwa. Kimura, *Kaniʻāina,* 24:12. One translation of ʻāina is "that which feeds."

7. Kapihenui, "He Moolelo no Hiiakaikapoliopele," *Ka Hoku o ka Pakipika,* July 3, 1862, 4.

8. Hoʻoulumāhiehie, "Ka Moolelo o Hiiakaikapoliopele," *Ka Naʻi Aupuni,* September 28, 1906, 4.

9. Hoʻoulumāhiehie, September 12, 1906, 3.

10. Hoʻoulumāhiehie, September 13, 1906, 3.

11. "Ma kou wahi e hele ai, malaila au e hele ai, ma kou wahi e moe ai, malaila au e moe ai: o kou poe kanaka, noʻu ia poe kanaka, o kou Akua, noʻu ia Akua." Ruta 1:16.

12. Hoʻoulumāhiehie, September 15, 1906, 3; Bush and Paʻaluhi, "Ka Moolelo o Hiiakaikapoliopele," *Ka Leo o ka Lahui,* January 24, 1893, 4.

13. "The concept of positionality is used by cultural studies writers to indicate that knowledge and 'voice' are always located within the vectors of time, space and social power. Thus, the notion of positionality expresses epistemological concerns regarding the who, where, when and why of speaking, judgement and comprehension. That is, specific acculturated persons make truth-claims at an exact and distinct time and place with particular reasons in mind. Consequently, knowledge is not to be understood as a neutral or objective phenomenon but as

a social and cultural production since the 'position' from which knowledge is enunciated will shape the very character of that knowledge." C. Barker, *SAGE Dictionary of Cultural Studies*, 154.

14. Trask, *From a Native Daughter*, 88.

15. Trask, 88.

16. Pukui and Elbert, *Hawaiian Dictionary*, 233.

17. Andrews, *Dictionary of the Hawaiian Language*, 378.

18. Parker, *Dictionary of the Hawaiian Language*, 411.

19. Pukui and Elbert, *Hawaiian Dictionary*, 124.

20. Andrews, *Dictionary of the Hawaiian Language*, 254.

21. Parker, *Dictionary of the Hawaiian Language*, 255.

22. Arvin, Tuck, and Morrill, "Decolonizing Feminism," 12.

23. Trask, "Decolonizing Hawaiian Literature," 168.

24. Hoʻoulumāhiehie, June 16, 1906, 3.

25. Hoʻoulumāhiehie, June 13, 1906, 3.

26. Nakuina, *Moolelo Hawaii o Pakaa a me Ku-a-Pakaa.*

27. Hoʻoulumāhiehie, April 26, 1906, 4.

28. Hoʻoulumāhiehie, April 27, 1906, 4.

29. "I keia wahi, akahi no o Lohiau a pane mai ia Hiiaka me keia mau olelo: 'He keu io no kʻou [sic] kamaaina i nei oKauai [sic] nei; a kamaaina pu nohoi oe i na makani. Kuhi au o kela wahine wale no ke kamaaina ia Kauai nei, eia ka hoi o oe kekahi kamaaina. O makou ka poe i hanau ia Kauai nei, aohe paanaau ia makou keia mau wahi, a he oki loa aku hoi na makani. E ia nae, ia oe keia, ua hele a wale waha.'" Poepoe, "Ka Moolelo Kaao o Hiiakaikapoliopele," *Kuokoa Home Rula*, August 19, 1910, 4.

30. Poepoe, January 10, 1908, 1.

31. Hoʻoulumāhiehie, September 29, 1906, 3.

32. When Hiʻiaka mā arrive at Peleula's home in Kou (Honolulu), Peleula suggests that all engage in a game of kilu. Hiʻiaka responds to this invitation by saying, "Mamua aku paha kamaaina, a honua, alaila, mahope aku ka malihini," First perhaps all the kamaʻāina should partake, and then the malihini after. Peleula agrees and they engage in an exciting game of kilu. Kapihenui, April 3, 1862, 1.

33. Young, *Rethinking the Native Hawaiian Past*, 19.

34. Trask, "Decolonizing Hawaiian Literature," 169.

35. Pukui, *ʻŌlelo Noʻeau*, 115.

36. Wolfe, "Settler Colonialism and the Elimination of the Native."

37. Goodyear-Kaʻōpua, Hussey, and Wright, *Nation Rising.*

38. Kameʻeleihiwa, "Waikīkī."

RISE LIKE A MIGHTY WAVE

1. Those arrested were William K. Freitas, Gene Burke, John Keone Turalde, Richard Daleon, Michelle Noe Noe Wong-Wilson, Kaliko Kanaele, Dr. Pua

Kanakaʻole Kanahele, Luana Busby-Neff, Mililani Trask, Damian Onaona Trask, Walter Ritte, Loretta Ritte, Flora Hookano, Maxine Kahaulelio, James Naniʻole, Alika Desha, Desmond Haumea, Keliʻi Skippy Ioane, Daniel Li, Tomas Belsky, James Albertini, Donna Keala Leong, Renee Price, Momi Patricia Green, Ana Kahoʻopiʻi, Raynette Robinson, Edleen Peleiholani, Haloley Reese, Deena Oana-Hurwitz, Mahea Kalima, Sharol Kuʻualoha Awai, Linda Leilani Lindsey-Kaʻapuni, Deborah Lee, Carmen Hulu Lindsey, Marie Alohalani Brown, Daycia-Dee Chun, Abel Lui, and Martin Liko-o-Kalani.

2. Those blocking delivery were Walter Ritte, Kaleikoa Kaʻeo, Noelani Goodyear-Kaʻōpua, ʻĪmaikalani Winchester, Mahiʻai Dochin, Jamaica Heolimeleikalani Osorio, Malia Hulleman, and Kamuela Park.

3. In 1897 the Hui Aloha ʻĀina (Hawaiian Patriotic League) established a petition drive against the proposed annexation of Hawaiʻi to the United States. At that time, our population was estimated at thirty-nine thousand, and twenty-two thousand kingdom subjects signed the petitions. Duarte et al., *Kūʻē Petitions.*

4. These agencies included DOCARE, Honolulu PD, Maui PD, Hilo PD, Hawaiʻi Island Serifs, and the National Guard.

5. The weapons included riot gear, sound cannons, mace, tear gas, and wooden batons.

6. The closing oli, composed by Kumu Pua Case, at every Puʻuhuluhulu protocol ends with the recognition of our people rising like a mighty wave, "E Hū E." Rise like a mighty wave has become somewhat of a rallying call at the puʻuhonua.

7. On March 25, 2020, after more than nine months of continued occupation, the kiaʻi of the Puʻuhonua o Puʻuhuluhulu made the difficult decision to pack up and return home because of the growing COVID-19 pandemic. With the understanding that there were no immediate plans for construction on the mountain, the puʻuhonua leadership and the Royal Order of Kamehameha have made it clear that the kiaʻi will be reactivated if there is any movement on the side of the state or the TMT corporation to resume construction. In their official statement, they announced, "Kapu ke ola iā Kāne. All life is sacred to Kāne. There is no imminent threat posed by the TMT and there is an imminent threat posed by COVID-19. Therefore, we've made the decision to pack up and come off of the mauna. We will return if and when the TMT or anything else attempts to desecrate Maunakea." Puʻuhonua o Puʻuhuluhulu, "For the Safety of Our Kupuna and Camp Kiaʻi."

6. KŪ KIAʻI MAUNA

1. "Ceded lands" is the common name for the combined kingdom and Crown lands seized (and never returned) by the United States during the faux annexation of the Hawaiian Kingdom.

2. "Timeline of Mauna Kea Legal Actions since 2011," Kahea: The Hawaiian-Environmental Alliance, accessed January 21, 2020, http://kahea.org/issues/sacred-summits/timeline-of-events.

3. "From a cumulative perspective, the impact of past and present actions on cultural, archaeological, and historic resources is substantial, significant, and adverse; these impacts would continue to be substantial, significant, and adverse with the consideration of the Project and other reasonably foreseeable future actions." Hawai'i Department of Health, "Final Environmental Impact Statement."

4. "Sacred Summits," Kahea: The Hawaiian-Environmental Alliance, accessed January 21, 2020, http://kahea.org/issues/sacred-summits.

5. For additional details of the court hearings, see "Timeline of Mauna Kea Legal Actions since 2011."

6. Dayton and Cocke, "TMT Law Enforcement Costs."

7. Sai, "'Ceded' Lands"; Preza, "What Was the 1848 Mahele?"

8. Beneficiaries are Hawaiians of more than 50 percent blood quantum who qualify for DHHL lands and resources. This situation is complicated further with the knowledge that the DHHL was created and is maintained by the occupying State of Hawai'i. Like the Office of Hawaiian Affairs (OHA), the DHHL exists as a contradiction in the occupying state. The DHHL and the OHA are completely unable to serve their constituency because their existence requires the maintenance of the occupying force, the State of Hawai'i.

9. Richland, "Jurisdiction," 209. Mahalo to Jonathan Goldberg-Hiller for directing me to this particular analysis of jurisdiction.

10. Richland, 209.

11. Beamer, *No Mākou ka Mana*.

12. For more insight on the role of translation and the law, see Bryan Kamaoli Kuwada's brilliant dissertation, "Ka Mana Unuhi."

13. For example, the first Hawaiian constitution was called Ke Kumu Kānāwai (The source of kānāwai). For more on nineteenth-century kānāwai, see Osorio, *Dismembering Lāhui*; and Beamer, *No Mākou ka Mana*.

14. Andrews, *Dictionary of the Hawaiian Language*; Parker, *Dictionary of the Hawaiian Language*.

15. For more insight on the 'Ai Kapu, see Kame'eleihiwa, *Native Land and Foreign Desires*; T. Baker, "'Au'a' Ia"; and Johnson, "Mauna Kea Series."

16. Johnson, "Mauna Kea Series."

17. Kame'eleihiwa, *Native Land and Foreign Desires*.

18. The 'Ai Kapu did not fall without resistance. In fact, there was an uprising led by Kekuaokalani (Liholiho's kaikua'ana) and Manono. These ali'i and their koa believed that to break the 'Ai Kapu would be an offense against the gods, and they gave their lives to protect the kapu. This rebellion is one of the earliest documented acts of collective resistance to the "state" in Hawai'i.

19. The name Ka Wahinekapu appears in all four mana of Hiʻiaka studied for this book.

20. One of the most-cited kānāwai in moʻolelo o Hiʻiaka is the kānāwai kaiʻokia, which prohibits Lohiʻau from engaging in any sexual acts before being returned to Pele. This kānāwai fits within the larger schema of power that enables Pele to dominate and exercise control of Puna, Kīlauea, and even Hāʻena. As I discussed in chapter 4 about the way pleasure, desire, and sex can also demonstrate mana to rule or invade certain ʻāina, Peleʻs kānāwai kaiʻokia that she places on their kāne helps maintain and exercise Peleʻs mana to rule Kīlauea and Hāʻena through her union with Lohiʻau. In many mana of the moʻolelo, the kānāwai is also placed upon Hiʻiaka. She is commanded to follow this kānāwai during her journey. As someone whose sexual excursions are written through the offering of Puna, it seems that her exercising that right would very much threaten Peleʻs assumed supreme mana to rule their home.

21. Kanahele, *Ka Honua Ola,* 70.

22. Kanahele, 72.

23. Kanahele, 73.

24. Kanahele, 73.

25. Perez, "Public Testimony."

26. Williams et al., *ʻO Kamehameha Nui,* 87.

27. Bush and Paʻaluhi, "Ka Moolelo o Hiiakaikapoliopele," *Ka Leo o ka Lahui,* January 5, 1893, 1.

28. Bush and Paʻaluhi, January 6, 1893, 1.

29. "Ua holo mai o Pele me kona mau kaikaina a me na kaikunane ma ka lakou huakai nai aina." Bush and Paʻaluhi, 1.

30. Throughout the moʻolelo, there is an obsession with categorizing Kānaka as kanaka maikaʻi versus kanaka ʻino. Kānaka maikaʻi are physically strong and beautiful in appearance; however, their beauty also comes with a particular ʻano and virtue. Kānaka ʻino are of little virtue, and their ugliness is derived from their vices and lack of morality.

31. Kapihenui, "He Moolelo no Hiiakaikapoliopele," *Ka Hoku o ka Pakipika,* January 2, 1862, 1; parallel passage (with minor differences) in Bush and Paʻaluhi, February 7, 1893, 1.

32. Hoʻoulumāhiehie, "Ka Moolelo o Hiiakaikapoliopele," *Ka Naʻi Aupuni,* August 20, 1906, 4.

33. Hoʻoulumāhiehie, August 21, 1906, 4.

34. "*Mō ka piko la* ('severed are the umbilical cords') was a clear pronouncement that a family tie was broken." Pukui, Haertig, and Lee, *Nānā I Ke Kumu,* 185.

35. Hoʻomanawanui, *Voices of Fire,* xl.

36. These movements to protect ʻāina are ongoing and growing out of our beautiful and resilient communities throughout Hawaiʻi. To follow along and learn

more about these movements and communities, please consult the following resources: https://www.puuhuluhulu.com/ (Mauna a Wākea), http://facebook.com/ groups/2283005395101115 (Kū Kia'i Kahuku), https://saveoursherwoods.com/ (Hūnānāniho), https://www.huionawaieha.org/nawaiehainformation (Nā Wai 'Ehā), "Protect Pa'akai in Hanapēpē," http://www.change.org (Hānāpepe), https://protectpohakuloa.org/ (Pōhakuloa), http://www.protectkahoolaweohana.org/ (Kaho'olawe).

Bibliography

Act of War: The Overthrow of the Hawaiian Nation. Honolulu: Na Maka O Ka 'Āina, 1993.

Aiu, Pua'ala'okalani D. "Ne'e Papa I Ke Ō Mau: Language as an Indicator of Hawaiian Resistance and Power." In *Translation, Resistance, Activism*, edited by Maria Tymoczko, 89–107. Amherst: University of Massachusetts Press, 2010.

Akaka, Moanike'ala, Maxine Kahaulelio, Terrilee Keko'olani-Raymond, and Loretta Ritte. *Nā Wāhine Koa: Hawaiian Women for Sovereignty and Demilitarization*, edited by Noelani Goodyear-Ka'ōpua. Honolulu: University of Hawai'i Press, 2018.

Allen, Paula Gunn. *The Sacred Hoop: Recovering the Feminine in American Indian Traditions*. Boston: Beacon, 1986.

Andrews, Lorrin. *A Dictionary of the Hawaiian Language*. Printed by Henry M. Whitney, 1865.

Arista, Noelani. "Davida Malo, A Hawaiian Life." *The Mo'olelo Hawai'i of Davida Malo: Hawaiian Text and Translation*, edited and translated by Charles Langlas and Jeffrey Lyon. Honolulu: University of Hawai'i and Bishop Museum Press, 2020.

Arista, Noelani. *The Kingdom and the Republic: Sovereign Hawai'i and the Early United States*. Philadelphia: University of Pennsylvania Press, 2019.

Arista, Noelani. "Navigating Uncharted Oceans of Meaning: Kaona as Historical and Interpretive Method." *PMLA: Journal of the Modern Language Association of America* 125, no. 3 (2010): 663–69.

Arvin, Maile, Eve Tuck, and Angie Morrill. "Decolonizing Feminism: Challenging Connections between Settler Colonialism and Heteropatriarchy." *Feminist Formations* 25, no. 1 (2013): 8–34.

Bacchilega, Cristina. *Legendary Hawai'i and the Politics of Place: Tradition, Translation, and Tourism*. Philadelphia: University of Pennsylvania Press, 2007.

Baker, C. M. Kaliko. "A-Class Genitive Subject Effect: A Pragmatic and Discourse Grammar Approach to A- and O-Class Genitive Subject Selection in Hawaiian." PhD diss., University of Hawaiʻi at Mānoa, 2012.

Baker, Tammy Hailiʻōpua. "Auʻa ʻIa: Holding On." Unpublished manuscript, 2019, in author's possession.

Barker, Chris. *The SAGE Dictionary of Cultural Studies*. London: SAGE, 2004.

Bassnett, Susan. *Translation Studies*. New York: Routledge, 1980.

Beamer, Kamanamaikalani. *No Mākou ka Mana: Liberating the Nation*. Honolulu: Kamehameha Publishing, 2015.

Brisset, Anne. "The Search for a Native Language: Translation and Cultural Identity." In *Translation Studies Reader*, 3rd ed., edited by Lawrence Venuti, 281–311. New York: Routledge, 2012.

Bush, John E., and Simeon Paʻaluhi. "Ka Moolelo o Hiiakaikapoliopele." *Ka Leo o ka Lahui*, January 5, 1893–July 12, 1893.

Chapin, Helen Geracimos. *Guide to Newspapers of Hawaiʻi, 1834–2000*. Honolulu: Hawaiian Historical Society, 2000.

Charlot, John. "Pele and Hiʻiaka: The Hawaiian-Language Newspaper Series." *Anthropos* 93 (1998): 55–75.

Da Silva, Denise, Maile Arvin, Brian Chung, Chris Finley, Ma Vang, Lee Ann Wang, and Kit Myers. "Decolonial Love and Loving in the Academic Industrial Complex as a Radical Form of Resistance." Roundtable, Critical Ethnic Studies Association Conference, York University, Toronto, Ont., May 2, 2015.

Davis, Angela. "Freedom Is a Constant Struggle." Speech, Kennedy Theater, Honolulu, Hawaiʻi, April 8, 2016.

Dayton, Kevin, and Sophie Cocke. "TMT Law Enforcement Costs Jump to $11M, Almost Half Spent by Hawaii County." *Star Advertiser* (Honolulu), November 5, 2019.

Desha, Stephen L., Sr. *Kamehameha and His Warrior Kekūhaupiʻo*. Translated by Frances N. Frazier. Honolulu: Kamehameha Schools Press, 2000. Originally published as *He Moolelo Kaao no Kuhaupio: Ke Koa Kaulana o ke au o Kamehameha ka Nui, Ka Hoku o Hawaii*, December 16, 1920–September 11, 1924.

Driskill, Qwo-Li, Chris Finley, Brian Joseph Gilley, and Scott Lauria Morgensen, eds. *Queer Indigenous Studies: Critical Interventions in Theory, Politics, and Literature*. Tucson: University of Arizona Press, 2011.

Duarte, Nicole, Ahukini Fuertes, J. Hauʻoli Ikaika Poʻokela Lorenzo-Elarco, Matt Mattice, Maile Meyer, Teri Skillman-Kashyap, Nālani Minton, Jamaica Heolimeleikalani Osorio, Jon Kamakawiwoʻole Osorio, and Noenoe K. Silva. *Kūʻē Petitions: A Mau Loa Aku Nō*. Honolulu: Kaiao Press with Friends of the Judiciary History Center, 2021.

Dudoit, D. Māhealani. "Against Extinction: A Legacy of Native Hawaiian Resistance Literature." 1999. http://www2.hawaii.edu/~aoude/ES350/SPIH_vol39/17Dudoit.pdf.

Elbert, Samuel H. *Spoken Hawaiian*. Honolulu: University of Hawai'i Press, 1970.

Finley, Chris. "Decolonizing the Queer Native Body (and Recovering the Native Bull-Dyke): Bringing 'Sexy Back' and out of Native Studies' Closet." In *Queer Indigenous Studies: Critical Interventions in Theory, Politics, and Literature*, edited by Qwo-Li Driskill, Chris Finley, Brian Joseph Gilley, and Scott Lauria Morgensen, 31–42. Tucson: University of Arizona Press, 2011.

Goeman, Mishuana. *Mark My Words: Native Women Mapping Our Nations*. First Peoples. Minneapolis: University of Minnesota Press, 2013.

Goodyear-Ka'ōpua, Noelani. "Domesticating Hawaiians: Kamehameha Schools and the Tender Violence of Marriage." In *Indian Subjects: New Directions in the History of Indigenous Education*, edited by Brian Klopotek and Brenda Child, 16–47. Santa Fe, N.M.: School for Advanced Research Press, 2011.

Goodyear-Ka'ōpua, Noelani, Ikaika Hussey, and Erin Kahunawaika'ala Wright, eds. *A Nation Rising: Hawaiian Movements for Life, Land, and Sovereignty*. Durham, N.C.: Duke University Press, 2014.

Goodyear-Ka'ōpua, Noelani, and Bryan Kamaoli Kuwada. "Remaking the 'Aha: Braiding Strands of Hawaiian Self-Rule, Genealogy and Ritual." Conference presentation, Native America Indigenous Studies Association Conference, University of Hawai'i, Mānoa, May 21, 2016.

Grimshaw, Patricia. *Paths of Duty: American Missionary Wives in Nineteenth-Century Hawaii*. Honolulu: University of Hawai'i Press, 1989.

Hale'ole, S. N. *Laieikawai*. Rev. ed. Edited by Dennis Kawaharada, Richard Hamasaki, and Esther Mo'okini. Translated by Martha Warren Beckwith. Honolulu: Kalamakū Press, 2006. Originally published as *Laieikawai, ke kaikamahine kaulana o Kahauokapaka me Malaekahana, Ka Nupepa Kuokoa*, November 29, 1862–April 4, 1863.

Hale'ole, S. N. *Laieikawai*. Translated by Martha Warren Beckwith. Honolulu: First People's Productions, 1997.

Hall, Lisa Kahaleole. "Navigating Our Own 'Sea of Islands': Remapping a Theoretical Space for Hawaiian Women and Indigenous Feminism." *Wicazo Sa Review* 24, no. 2 (2009): 15–38.

Hawai'i Department of Health. "Final Environmental Impact Statement: Thirty Meter Telescope Project." University of Hawai'i at Hilo, 2010.

ho'omanawanui, ku'ualoha. "Mana Wahine, Education and Nation-Building: Lessons from the Epic of Pele and Hi'iaka for Kanaka Maoli Today." *Multicultural Perspectives* 12, no. 4 (2010): 206–12.

ho'omanawanui, ku'ualoha. "Mana Wahine: Feminism and Nationalism in Hawaiian Literature." *Anglistica* 17, no. 1 (2013): 27–43.

ho'omanawanui, ku'ualoha. "Pele's Appeal: Mo'olelo, Kaona, and Hulihia in 'Pele and Hi'iaka' Literature (1860–1928)." PhD diss., University of Hawai'i at Mānoa, 2007.

hoʻomanawanui, kuʻualoha. *Voices of Fire: Reweaving the Literary Lei of Pele and Hiʻiaka.* Minneapolis: University of Minnesota Press, 2014.

Hoʻoulumāhiehie. "Hiʻiakaikapoliopele." Translated by Mary Kawena Pukui. Bishop Museum, HEN II, 1161–1224 (December 1, 1905—January 16, 1906).

Hoʻoulumāhiehie. "Hiʻiakaikapoliopele." Translated by Mary Kawena Pukui. Bishop Museum, HEN V.3 (September 18, 1924–July 17, 1928).

Hoʻoulumāhiehie. "Kamehameha I: Ka Nai Aupuni o Hawaii." *Ka Naʻi Aupuni,* November 27, 1905–November 16, 1906.

Hoʻoulumāhiehie. "Ka Moolelo o Hiiaka-i-ka-poli-o-Pele." *Ka Naʻi Aupuni,* December 1, 1905–November 30, 1906.

Hoʻoulumāhiehie. *Ka Moʻolelo o Hiʻiakaikapoliopele / The Epic Tale of Hiʻiakaikapoliopele.* 2 vols. Edited and translated by Puakea Nogelmeier. Honolulu: Awaiaulu Press, 2007.

Iaukea, Sydney L. *The Queen and I: A Story of Dispossessions and Reconnections in Hawaiʻi.* Berkeley: University of California Press, 2012.

Jaimes, M. Annette. "'Patriarchal Colonialism' and Indigenism: Implications for Native Feminist Spirituality and Native Womanism." *Hypatia* 18, no. 2 (2003): 58–69.

Johnson, Kahala. "Mauna Kea Series: Kahala Johnson on Hale Mana Māhū." *Native Stories,* October 20, 2020. https://nativestories.org/podcast/mauna -kea-series-kahala-johnson-on-hale-mana-mahu/.

Kalahele, Imaikalani. "Make Rope." In *Kalahele: Poetry and Art,* 29–31. Honolulu: Kalamakū Press, 2002.

Kamakau, Samuel Mānaiakalani. *Ke Aupuni Mōʻī: Ka Moʻolelo Hawaiʻi No Kauikeaouli, Keiki Hoʻoilina a Kamehameha a Me Ke Aupuni Āna I Noho Mōʻī Ai.* Honolulu: Kamehameha Schools Press, 2001.

Kamakau, Samuel Mānaiakalani. *Ke Kumu Aupuni: Ka Moʻolelo Hawaiʻi No Kamehameha Ka Naʻi Aupuni a Me Kāna Aupuni i Hoʻokumu Ai.* Edited by Puakea Nogelmeier. Honolulu: ʻAhahui ʻŌlelo Hawaiʻi, 1996.

Kamakau, Samuel Mānaiakalani. *Ruling Chiefs of Hawaii.* Honolulu: Kamehameha Schools Press, 1992.

Kameʻeleihiwa, Lilikalā. *Native Land and Foreign Desires: Pehea Lā E Pono Ai?* Honolulu: Bishop Museum Press, 1992.

Kameʻeleihiwa, Lilikalā. *Nā Wāhine Kapu: Divine Hawaiian Women.* Honolulu: ʻAi Pōhaku Press, 1999.

Kameʻeleihiwa, Lilikalā. "Waikīkī." Keynote address, NASPA Western Regional Conference, Waikīkī, Hawaiʻi, June 6, 2017.

Kanahele, Pualani Kanakaʻole. *Ka Honua Ola: ʻEliʻeli Kau Mai / The Living Earth: Descend, Deepen the Revelation.* Honolulu: Kamehameha Publishing, 2011.

Kapihenui, M. J. "He Moolelo no Hiiakaikapoliopele." *Ka Hoku o ka Pakipika,* December 26, 1861–July 27, 1862.

Kauanui, J. Kēhaulani. *Hawaiian Blood: Colonialism and the Politics of Sovereignty and Indigeneity.* Durham, N.C.: Duke University Press, 2008.

Kauanui, J. Kēhaulani. *Paradoxes of Hawaiian Sovereignty: Land, Sex, and the Colonial Politics of State Nationalism.* Durham, N.C.: Duke University Press, 2018.

Kimura, Larry Lindsey Kauanoe, producer. *Kaniʻāina,* http://www.ulukau.org. Digital repository of Ka Haka ʻUla O Keʻelikōlani College of Hawaiian Language, University of Hawaiʻi at Hilo, October 25, 1972, "Ka Leo Hawaiʻi 012." Larry Lindsey Kauanoe Kimura (presenter); Sarah Nākoa (guest).

Kuwada, Bryan Kamaoli. "Ka Mana Unuhi: An Examination of Hawaiian Translation." PhD diss., University of Hawaiʻi at Mānoa, 2018.

Kuwada, Bryan Kamaoli. "To Translate or Not to Translate: Revising the Translating of Hawaiian Language Texts." *Biography: An Interdisciplinary Quarterly* 32, no. 1 (2009): 54–65.

Liliʻuokalani, trans. *The Kumulipo: An Hawaiian Creation Myth.* Edited by James Kimo Campbell. Kentfield, Calif.: Pueo Press, 1978. Adapted and translated from *He pule hoolaa alii: He kumulipo no Ka-I-imamao, a ia Alapai Wahine* (Honolulu, 1889).

Malo, Davida. *Hawaiian Antiquities (Moolelo Hawaii).* Translated by N. B. Emerson. Honolulu: Hawaiian Gazette Co., 1903.

Malo, Davida. *Ka Moolelo Hawaii: Hawaiian Traditions.* Edited and translated by Malcolm Naea Chun. Honolulu: First People's Press, 1996.

McDougall, Brandy Nālani. *Finding Meaning: Kaona and Contemporary Hawaiian Literature.* Tucson: University of Arizona Press, 2016.

McDougall, Brandy Nālani. "'O ka Lipo o ka Lā, ʻO ka Lipo o ka Pō: Cosmogenic Kaona in Contemporary Kanaka Maoli Literature." PhD diss., University of Hawaiʻi at Mānoa, 2011.

Million, Dian. *Therapeutic Nations: Healing in an Age of Indigenous Human Rights.* Tucson: University of Arizona Press, 2013.

Mookini, Esther K. *The Hawaiian Newspapers.* Honolulu: Topgallant, 1974.

Morgensen, Scott Lauria. *Spaces between Us: Queer Settler Colonialism and Indigenous Decolonization.* Minneapolis: University of Minnesota Press, 2011.

Nākoa, Sarah. *Lei Momi o ʻEwa.* Honolulu: ʻAhahui ʻŌlelo Hawaiʻi, 1979.

Nakuina, Moses K. *Moolelo Hawaii o Pakaa a me Ku-a-Pakaa, Na Kahu Iwikuamoo o Keawenuiaumi ke Alii o Hawaii, a o na Moopuna hoi a Laamaomao! Ke Kamaeu nana i Hoolakalaka na Makani a pau o na Mokupuni o Hawaii nei, a uhao iloko o kana Ipu Kaulana i Kapaia o ka Ipumakani a Laamaomao.* Honolulu: published by the author, 1902.

Niranjana, Tejaswini. "Introduction: History in Translation." In *Siting Translation: History, Post-structuralism, and the Colonial Context,* 1–46. Berkeley: University of California Press, 1992.

Nogelmeier, Puakea. *Mai Paʻa i Ka Leo: Historical Voice in Hawaiian Primary Materials; Looking Forward and Listening Back.* Honolulu: Bishop Museum Press, 2010.

Osorio, Jonathan Kay Kamakawiwoʻole. *Dismembering Lāhui: A History of the Hawaiian Nation to 1887.* Honolulu: University of Hawaiʻi Press, 2002.

Parker, Henry, ed. *A Dictionary of the Hawaiian Language by Larrin Andrews.* Honolulu: Board of Commissioners of Public Archives, 1922.

Perez, Andre. "Public Testimony." Office of Hawaiian Affairs Board of Trustees Meeting, June 29, 2017.

Piʻilani. *The True Story of Kaluaikoʻolau.* Translated by Frances N. Frazier. Honolulu: University of Hawaiʻi Press, 2001. Translated and reduced from J. G. M. Sheldon and Piʻilani, *Kaluaikoolau, ke kaeaea o na Pali Kalalau a me na Kahei o Ahi o Kamaile: Piilani, ka wahine i molia i ke ola, ke kiu alo ehu poka: Kaleimanu, ka hua o ko laua puhaka, ka opio haokila iloko o na inea: he moolelo oiaio i piha me na haawina o ke aloha walohia* (Honolulu, 1906).

Poepoe, Joseph Mokuʻōhai. "Ka Moolelo Kaao o HiiakaikaPoliopele." *Kuokoa Home Rula,* January 10, 1908–January 20, 1911.

Preza, Donovan. "What Was the 1848 Mahele and Was It Great?" YouTube, December 6, 2019. http://www.youtube.com.

Pukui, Mary Kawena. *ʻŌlelo Noʻeau: Hawaiian Proverbs & Poetical Sayings.* Honolulu: Bishop Museum Press, 1983.

Pukui, Mary Kawena, and Samuel H. Elbert. *Hawaiian Grammar.* Honolulu: University of Hawaiʻi Press, 1979.

Pukui, Mary Kawena, and Samuel H. Elbert. *Hawaiian Dictionary: Hawaiian-English, English-Hawaiian.* Honolulu: University of Hawaiʻi Press, 1986.

Pukui, Mary Kawena, Samuel H. Elbert, and Esther T. Mookini. *Place Names of Hawaii.* Rev. and enl. ed. Honolulu: University Press of Hawaiʻi, 1974.

Pukui, Mary Kawena, and E. S. Craighill Handy. *The Polynesian Family System in Ka-ʻu, Hawaiʻi.* Wellington, N.Z.: Polynesian Society, 1950.

Pukui, Mary Kawena, E. W. Haertig, and Catherine A. Lee. *Nānā I Ke Kumu: Look to the Source.* 2 vols. Honolulu: Hui Hānai, 1979.

Puuhonua o Puuhuluhulu. "For the Safety of Our Kupuna and Camp Kiaʻi." March 14, 2020. http://www.puuhuluhulu.com/.

Rice, William Hyde. "He Moolelo no Pele a me kona Kaikaina Hiʻiaka i ka Poli o Pele." *Ka Hoku o Hawaii,* May 21, 1908–September 10, 1908.

Richland, Justin. "Jurisdiction: Grounding Law in Language." *Annual Review of Anthropology* 42, no. 1 (2013): 209–26.

Rifkin, Mark. *When Did Indians Become Straight? Kinship, the History of Sexuality, and Native Sovereignty.* New York: Oxford University Press, 2011.

Sai, Keanu. "'Ceded' Lands, TMT, Denationalization, Occupation and Annexation." YouTube, August 11, 2019. http://www.youtube.com.

Shankar, Subramanian. "The 'Problem' of Translation." In *Flesh and Fish Blood: Post-colonialism, Translation, and the Vernacular,* 103–42. Berkeley: University of California Press, 2012.

Silva, Noenoe K. *Aloha Betrayed: Native Hawaiian Resistance to Annexation.* Durham, N.C.: Duke University Press, 2004.

Silva, Noenoe K. "Hawaiian Literature in Hawaiian." In *The Oxford Handbook of Indigenous American Literature,* edited by James H. Cox and Daniel Heath Justice, 102–17. New York: Oxford University Press, 2014.

Silva, Noenoe K. "Pele, Hi'iaka, and Haumea: Women and Power in Two Hawaiian Mo'olelo." *Pacific Studies* 30, nos. 1–2 (2007): 159–81.

Silva, Noenoe K. *The Power of the Steel-Tipped Pen: Reconstructing Native Hawaiian Intellectual History.* Durham, N.C.: Duke University Press, 2017.

Simpson, Leanne. *As We Have Always Done: Indigenous Freedom through Radical Resistance.* Minneapolis: University of Minnesota Press, 2017.

Smith, Andrea. "Heteropatriarchy and the Three Pillars of White Supremacy: Rethinking Women of Color Organizing." In *Color of Violence: The INCITE! Anthology,* 66–73. Cambridge, Mass.: South End, 2006.

Spivak, Gayatri. "The Politics of Translation." In *The Translation Studies Reader,* 3rd ed., edited by Lawrence Venuti, 312–30. New York: Routledge, 2012.

State of Hawai'i. "Visitor Statistics." Department of Business, Economic Development & Tourism. Accessed November 29, 2019. http://dbedt.hawaii.gov/visitor/.

TallBear, Kimberly. *Native American DNA: Tribal Belonging and the False Promise of Genetic Science.* Minneapolis: University of Minnesota Press, 2013.

Teaiwa, Teresia. "Bikinis and Other S/pacific N/oceans." In *Militarized Currents: Toward a Decolonized Future in Asia and the Pacific,* edited by Setsu Shigematsu and Keith L. Camacho, 15–32. Minneapolis: University of Minnesota Press, 2010.

Teves, Stephanie Nohelani. *Defiant Indigeneity: The Politics of Hawaiian Performance.* Chapel Hill: University of North Carolina Press, 2018.

Trask, Haunani-Kay. "Decolonizing Hawaiian Literature." In *Inside Out: Literature, Cultural Politics, and Identity in the New Pacific,* edited by Vilsoni Hereniko and Rob Wilson, 167–82. Lanham, Md.: Rowman & Littlefield, 1999.

Trask, Haunani-Kay. *From a Native Daughter: Colonialism and Sovereignty in Hawai'i.* Honolulu: University of Hawai'i Press, 1999.

Trask, Haunani-Kay. *Light in the Crevice Never Seen.* Corvallis, Ore.: Calyx Books, 1994.

Trask, Haunani-Kay. *Night Is a Sharkskin Drum.* Honolulu: University of Hawai'i Press, 2002.

Trask, Haunani-Kay. "Writing in Captivity: Poetry in a Time of Decolonization." In *Inside Out: Literature, Cultural Politics, and Identity in the New Pacific,* edited by Vilsoni Hereniko and Rob Wilson, 51–55. Lanham, Md.: Rowman & Littlefield, 1999.

Tuck, Eve, and K. Wayne Yang. "Decolonization Is Not a Metaphor." *Decolonization: Indigeneity, Education & Society* 1, no. 1 (2012): 1–40.

Tymoczko, Maria. "Translation, Resistance, Activism: An Overview." In *Translation, Resistance, Activism*, 1–22. Amherst: University of Massachusetts Press, 2010.

Venuti, Lawrence. *The Scandals of Translation: Towards an Ethics of Difference.* New York: Routledge, 1998.

Vizenor, Gerald. *Survivance: Narratives of Native Presence.* Lincoln: University of Nebraska Press, 2008.

Wendt, Albert. "Towards a New Oceania." *Seaweeds and Constructions* 5 (1997): 71–85.

Williams, Julie Stewart, et al. *'O Kamehameha Nui.* Hawaiian-language ed. Honolulu: Hale Pa'i o nā Kula 'o Kamehameha, 1996.

Wolfe, Patrick. "Settler Colonialism and the Elimination of the Native." *Journal of Genocide Research* 8, no. 4 (December 1, 2006): 387–409.

Wong, Laiana. "Authenticity and the Revitalization of Hawaiian." *Anthropology & Education Quarterly* 30, no. 1 (1999): 94–115.

Young, Kanalu G. Terry. *Rethinking the Native Hawaiian Past.* New York: Routledge, 2012.

Index

(continued from page ii)

Indigenous Americas

Robert Warrior, Series Editor

Firsting and Lasting: Writing Indians out of Existence in New England
Jean M. O'Brien

Remembering Our Intimacies: Moʻolelo, Aloha ʻĀina, and Ea
Jamaica Heolimeleikalani Osorio

Inter/Nationalism: Decolonizing Native America and Palestine
Steven Salaita

As We Have Always Done: Indigenous Freedom through Radical Resistance
Leanne Betasamosake Simpson

Noopiming: The Cure for White Ladies
Leanne Betasamosake Simpson

Everything You Know about Indians Is Wrong
Paul Chaat Smith

Queering Native American Literatures
Lisa Tatonetti

Written by the Body: Gender Expansiveness and Indigenous Non-Cis Masculinities
Lisa Tatonetti

Bear Island: The War at Sugar Point
Gerald Vizenor

The People and the Word: Reading Native Nonfiction
Robert Warrior

Like a Loaded Weapon: The Rehnquist Court, Indian Rights, and the Legal History of Racism in America
Robert A. Williams, Jr.

JAMAICA HEOLIMELEIKALANI OSORIO is a Kanaka Maoli wahine artist, activist, scholar, and educator. Heoli is assistant professor of Indigenous and Native Hawaiian politics at the University of Hawaiʻi at Mānoa.

Made in the USA
Las Vegas, NV
18 June 2022

50410076R00134